To Helsinki

Duke Press Policy Studies

New Edition

To Helsinki
The Conference on Security and
Cooperation in Europe 1973–1975

John J. Maresca

Foreword by William E. Griffith

Duke University Press   Durham and London

The opinions expressed in this book are the personal
views of the author. They do not necessarily
represent policies of the U.S. Department of State.

© 1985, 1987 Duke University Press
All rights reserved
Printed in the United States of America
on acid-free paper ∞

Library of Congress Cataloging-in-Publication Data
Maresca, John J., 1937–
To Helsinki—the Conference on Security and
Cooperation in Europe, 1973–1975.
(Duke Press policy studies)
Includes index.
1. Conference on Security and Cooperation in Europe.
I. Conference on Security and Cooperation in Europe.
II. Conference on Security and Cooperation in Europe
(1973–1975: Helsinki, Finland) III. Title.
IV. Title: To Helsinki. V. Series.
JX1393.C65M37   1987   327.1'7'094   87-22261
ISBN 0-8223-0791-X (pbk.)

Contents

Foreword

The Conference on Security and Cooperation in Europe (CSCE) is an important, extremely complex, institutionalized, continuing, intermittent, and in the United States too little known group of meetings. It has certainly not "solved" any of the major problems of Europe or the world. But it is as close as we have come, or are likely to soon, to a peace treaty in Europe after World War II. It is something like a very partial, imperfect, indeed minimal Concert of Europe and North America — cacophonous, an institutionalization more of conflict than of concert, and yet the only ersatz peace treaty we have.

Mr. Maresca is uniquely qualified to write its history, for he was one of its key participants, "present at the creation," so to speak, and he has somehow found the time and energy, while pursuing his career as a senior foreign service officer, to write the history of the first, most important phase of the conference. Because its proceedings were secret, because there were no agreed minutes, because so much was done informally, and, finally, because the crucial items of difference were almost always secretly compromised between Moscow and Washington, only a Russian or an American could write a full, inside history. Since no Russian is likely to be either able or willing to, and because Mr. Maresca was the only senior American diplomat involved in the whole process through the final signature in Helsinki of the Final Act in 1975, he was the ideal candidate for the job. We can all be very thankful that he has undertaken it so successfully.

Mr. Maresca chronicles substantively the delicate, ambiguous compromise reached between East and West: a limited acceptance of the European status quo, as the Soviets wanted, and a limited acceptance of peaceful change thereof, as the Federal Republic insisted on, and of emphasis on human rights, which the Soviet Union most reluctantly accepted, "with a forked tongue," so to speak. He also sets forth with clinical precision how the initial lack of enthusiasm for the whole conference shown by Dr. Kissinger helped working-level diplomats to compromise and unconsciously helped the Soviets to believe that the results would cause them no problems. But Kissinger was later forced to take a harder line at the conference, and thereby upgrade it from the U.S. perspective, because of the decline of pro-detente sentiment in the United States, and Carter went even further in advocacy of human rights. Had the Soviets realized how much detente would decline, and how much their final, reluctant agreement to the human rights provisions in Basket III of CSCE would come home to haunt them, they would hardly ever have agreed to the Final Act at all. Such are the ironies of history.

Dr. Kissinger was too pessimistic, and the Soviets too optimistic, about the unsuccessful impact of the East on the West and the successful Western impact on the East. But neither foresaw, nor probably could have foreseen, how Europe and the world would look a decade after the signature of the Final Act. Despite peace movements, ecologists, and other hindrances, Western European governments held firm in favor of deployment of intermediate nuclear forces in reply to Soviet SS-20 deployment. Their firmness was strengthened by the general decline in Western Europe of the image of the Soviet Union, which has become, perhaps first among *rive gauche* French leftist intellectuals, no longer a future to be hoped for or a model to be imitated, but only a military power to be feared. Moreover, as much as one may be of two minds—and I am—about its domestic costs, Reagan has rebuilt U.S. military power and revived U.S. political will. Finally, the U.S. economic recovery, and above all its increasing lead, along with Japan's, in high technology, *the* revolution of our times, have made the Soviet Union look like an increasingly tyrannical, self-encircled, and technologically backward empire. Nor has the German question, which CSCE was designed in large part to contain, become virulent again, nor is it likely to, all false prophets of *furor teutonicus* to the contrary. Finally, the CSCE successor conferences continue. The CSCE process has thus contributed to keeping Europe an island of detente during the recent period of renewed Soviet-American cold war and indeed may be revitalized by renewed Soviet-American arms control negotiations.

William E. Griffith

Introduction to the New Edition

The Conference on Security and Cooperation in Europe (CSCE) opened as detente was beginning to bloom. In 1972–73 the prospects for success seemed excellent. But by the time the Helsinki Final Act was signed in August of 1975, detente had already begun to sour; by the end of the decade, it was dead—at least for the moment. The Helsinki Summit was the high-water mark of the detente era of the 1970s; it was the very symbol of detente, and its most ambitious manifestation.

As it evolved over two and a half years, the CSCE reflected the many political pressures and changes that were taking place in and among the countries represented. During the negotiations, Richard Nixon was replaced by Gerald Ford in the U.S. presidency; Willy Brandt by Helmut Schmidt as chancellor of the Federal Republic of Germany (FRG); Georges Pompidou by Valery Giscard d'Estaing as president of France; and Edward Heath by Harold Wilson as prime minister of Great Britain. The period was rich in events that cast their shadows in the CSCE.

Putting together a document that 35 heads of state or government would be willing to sign, at the same time and in the same place, was a more difficult task than anyone had anticipated. National objectives clashed and the complexities of the subject matter defied easy solutions. In addition, the historical moment during which such a monumental event was politically acceptable to the major players proved extremely brief. Had the Summit not taken place in the summer of 1975, chances are that it would not have taken place at all. A singular diplomatic drama was played out as the final pieces were fitted together in order to meet the Summit timetable.

The CSCE was controversial from its inception, and it has been subject to widely differing analyses. U.S. Secretary of State Henry Kissinger saw it basically as a Western concession in a global chess game against the USSR. He became frustrated when Western attachment to "minor" negotiating points resisted his efforts to bring about an early conclusion. Kissinger's attitude produced a unique and widely criticized U.S. negotiating posture in the early stages of the Conference—the low profile—under which the American delegation did not exert aggressive leadership and the Europeans were left to work out problems among themselves.

But events crept up on this attitude. By the time the Conference was rushing inexorably toward its conclusion, American policies had begun to change and the United States took a tough negotiating stance. Despite his initially negative view of the CSCE and his periodic efforts to wind it up, Kissinger affected the

Conference at two key negotiating junctures. It was Kissinger who successfully managed the negotiation—conducted secretly between the United States and the USSR—of the clause on possible future peaceful changes in frontiers, which made it possible for the West German government to accept the Final Act. And it was Kissinger who, in the closing weeks of the Conference, made it crystal clear to Gromyko that the USSR would have to grant further human rights concessions if the West was to accept the final Conference results and go to Helsinki.

This may be seen as one of the ironies of Kissinger's career, since he did not seek either of these roles. Or it may be seen as the most natural of developments; the key issues in multilateral negotiations are always destined to be negotiated by the great powers, and any resulting agreements are destined to be hammered out between them.

Kissinger's view of the Conference was one of the principal elements that colored the attitudes of the press when it learned that the Helsinki Summit at last was on. Without having read the document that the Conference had produced, many Western journalists condemned it. Several American newspapers, and some prominent political figures, appealed to the U.S. president not to go to Helsinki. Later, human rights activists discovered the Final Act, and the popular image of the CSCE became distorted in another direction. It was oversimplified as providing a "charter of human rights" for the peoples of the Soviet Union and Eastern Europe. In both these negative and positive views of the CSCE, all its nuances, complexities, and ambiguities have been lost.

The two most important aspects of the CSCE have generally been overlooked. The first is its historic role as a surrogate World War II peace treaty. A peace treaty of classic form is not possible in the present circumstances, since it would have to be signed with Germany, as one of the principal belligerents. Yet Germany is now divided into two countries, which could not by themselves sign a peace treaty underlining the fact that they really form one nation. By including the two Germanies in a much larger conference, it became possible to address the issues left from the war and to reach a conclusion that, accepted by all the belligerents, formally consigned the war to history.

The second point is the CSCE's role as a continuing European institution, now ten years old and still a dynamic enterprise. This institution is broad in scope and membership, flexible, and resistant to the moods of international relations. It has become a forum for debate and discussion between East and West, neutral and engaged, large countries and small, and has proven itself capable of positive contributions, even during periods of East-West tension. It has not been subverted to Soviet objectives—on the contrary, it has been used to advance many Western views—and its possibilities are far from exhausted. It seems clear that the CSCE has become a permanent part of the European landscape.

Despite its central place in the period of detente, the CSCE remains almost totally unknown to those not directly involved in it, and is fully understood by very few. Almost no official records were kept during the negotiations, and individual national documents are by their nature incomplete.

After three review sessions, a number of subsidiary experts' meetings, and the prospect of more gatherings in the years ahead, the CSCE has its own past, present, and future. The Helsinki "process" has evolved into one of the major elements of the relationship between East and West in Europe and has come to resemble an embryonic European security system. It is important that its history, rules of behavior, prospects, and limitations be understood, at least by those with an active interest in this significant aspect of our foreign policy. Moreover, the Helsinki experience brings out some of the basic lessons of the detente era, which should not be forgotten.

This book attempts to make a contribution to the knowledge and understanding of the CSCE and its place in the detente period. It is not a book for everyone; it is not an overview of detente. Others have written about the detente relationship as a whole; this book offers a different perspective: that of a working diplomat deeply involved in one set of negotiations.

Washington, D.C., May 1987

Acknowledgments

It would not have been possible for me to complete this book without the encouragement and help of Professor William E. Griffith of MIT, John D. Panitza of the *Reader's Digest*, Ambassador Albert W. Sherer, Jr., John E. Kornblum, Warren Zimmerman, Rebecca Waters, and Sandra Odor.

J.M.

Thirty years have passed since the end of the Second World War, but the nations of the world still long for peace.

Josip Broz Tito   Helsinki   July 31, 1975

Part I

1972   Agreement on Negotiations

1 The Inevitability of Compromise
The Origins of the CSCE

*These twin gulfs had to be bridged by compromise and to
a later generation these compromises seem hypocritical
and deceptive. Yet were they not inevitable?*

Harold Nicolson *Peacemaking, 1919*

History is formed by the interaction of people, ideas, and events, and no one is master of it. Over the centuries mankind has produced leaders, groups, and even whole nations who believed they could alter the world but whose achievements crumbled or were swept away. Humbler men, homelier ideas have at times grown to influence the course of history beyond all expectations. Everything depends on what actually happens, and while this may sometimes be predictable, it is never fully controllable. Nothing is permanent; time forces all circumstances to change; sooner or later, even the most intractable problems are resolved or rendered irrelevant by the evolution of events. The challenge to statesmen and diplomats is to channel these currents so that changes are positive and essential values preserved.

Europe's central problem since the end of the Second World War has been its division, which has affected every phase of life on the continent. Despite recurring efforts to improve the situation, solutions have remained elusive. The early 1970s saw the beginning of an optimistic phase of intensified search for these solutions. It was called detente, and its underlying thesis was that closer, more open relations between East and West could over time lead to a more normal situation.

The Conference on Security and Cooperation in Europe (CSCE) was an important part of that search. Its Final Act, signed at the Helsinki Summit of 1975, was an attempt to bury the past and to establish a new set of guidelines for the detente era.

The Helsinki Conference—the CSCE—buried the past by serving as a substitute for a peace conference bringing the Second World War to a formal conclusion. The Helsinki Final Act is probably as close to a World War II peace treaty as we shall ever see—for, as Grotius pointed out more than 300 years ago, peace treaties can be tacit as well as explicit. The CSCE was also an attempt to bring the cold war to a formal close, more as a reflection of changing realities than as a decisive factor in itself. The early 1970s marked the end of the cold war in Europe.

At the same time, the CSCE attempted to put on paper some points of reference for intergovernmental relations in a period of detente. The basic concept of the Final Act is that, while national sovereignty must be respected, there should also be a gradual lowering of the barriers that have separated East and West since the end of World War II.

In broad terms, the USSR sought multilateral confirmation in the CSCE of the geopolitical realities that resulted from the war, while the West tried to obtain more normal relations between East and West—freer movement of persons, information, and ideas, and broader contacts between people. The East wished to confirm the status quo as the foundation of European security. The West wanted to ensure that the status quo would be an acceptable one allowing for peaceful evolution, in the belief that security is built not on re-cognition of spheres of influence, but rather on mutual understanding and confidence.

These conflicting ambitions made the CSCE a deeply ambiguous conference. The Final Act's three "baskets"—and its 30,000 words—will be subject to varying interpretations for many years to come. The signing of the Final Act thus resolved very little in any specific sense; rather, it preserved more or less intact the various territorial and ideological disagreements, contradictions, and inconsistencies that have made up the postwar equilibrium in Europe.

But the Final Act also recognized the human element in international rela-tions and accepted that change is possible. It evoked a fragile spirit of mutual concession and restraint between East and West, and offered the prospect of movement toward greater openness in relations among people, as well as gov-ernments. The Final Act could not have done more than this, since it was by definition subject to the agreement of all the nations concerned.

Exactly when the Soviet concept of a European security conference emerged is somewhat obscure. The Soviets themselves state that they were already thinking about a pan-European security system of some kind before the Second World War. Postwar considerations of proposals relating to such a scheme parallel the history of East-West detente, and are generally considered to date from a proposal in 1954 by Soviet Foreign Minister Vyacheslav M. Molotov for a European security conference that would work out a collective security agreement. Molotov suggested that the United States might have observer status at the conference.

This initiative was followed by a number of ideas brought forward by statesmen and scholars in both East and West and based on the concept of pan-European security. For example, Polish Foreign Minister Adam Rapacki circulated in 1958 a detailed proposal for establishment of a denuclearized zone in Central Europe, with "control machinery" to ensure that commit-ments were carried out. Under the Rapacki Plan the control machinery would have included representatives of East, West, and neutral European states, with the four powers, France, Great Britain, the USSR, and the United States, undertaking to implement the denuclearization. Rapacki followed up this initiative in 1964 by proposing that a European security conference be held, and that the United States be included. This proposal was subsequently endorsed by the Warsaw Pact as a whole.

By 1966 the idea of a European conference had become a recurring theme in Soviet and Eastern European pronouncements, with statements by Andrei Gromyko and Leonid Brezhnev, and a further and more detailed Warsaw Pact endorsement in the Budapest Declaration of July 1966. A dialogue of sorts between East and West was established by the so-called Group of Nine (later Ten), which included representatives of smaller states belonging to the North Atlantic Treaty Organization (NATO) and the Warsaw Pact, and which met during the period 1965–68 to discuss possibilities for collective security. These beginnings were temporarily halted by the Soviet occupation of Czechoslovakia in August of 1968, which put a damper on most Western efforts toward detente.

In March of 1969 the Warsaw Pact countries issued an Appeal to All European Countries, renewing their efforts to assemble a "general European conference to consider questions of European security and peaceful cooperation." This document listed three basic preconditions for security in Europe, presumably intended to form the conference agenda: inviolability of existing frontiers, recognition of the existence of two German states, and West German renunciation of possession of nuclear arms in any form. As a first step toward convening a conference and thereafter setting up a "durable system of European security," this "Budapest Appeal" proposed a preparatory meeting including representatives of all European states, to establish an agenda and procedures for convening the conference.

The Budapest Appeal was published at a time when Western countries for their own reasons wished to pick up again the process toward detente, which had been hesitantly begun in the early and mid-1960s. It thus evoked a response from the NATO countries in the communique of the meeting of foreign ministers of the North Atlantic alliance in Washington in April 1969, on the twentieth anniversary of the North Atlantic treaty. This communique, noting that U.S. and Canadian participation would be necessary in any eventual conference, stated that the Western countries were prepared to explore with the East "which concrete issues best lend themselves to fruitful negotiation and an early resolution," and indicated that, within the alliance, study was being undertaken on potential issues for negotiation and "how a useful process of negotiation could best be initiated."

The subsequent period saw an acceleration of consideration and exchanges of views between East and West on an eventual security conference. The Finnish government, interpreting the attitude of the NATO countries as indicating that the West was now prepared in principle to join in a security conference, delivered diplomatic notes to all European states, the United States, and Canada, on April 5, 1969, offering to act as host for preparatory talks, and for the conference itself, thus giving the idea of a conference its first fixed element: the site.

In October of the same year a Warsaw Pact communique proposed a two-item agenda for the conference: security, and expansion of economic, scientific, and technological relations. NATO countered with a declaration, issued at its meeting of foreign ministers in December, specifying the areas it considered ripe for East-West negotiations: Mutual and Balanced Force Reductions (MBFR) in Central Europe, and possible accompanying measures such as prior notification of military maneuvers and exchanges of observers at such maneuvers; easing of the practical situation of the city of Berlin; an interim modus vivendi settlement of the German situation; economic, technical, and cultural exchanges, especially the freer movement of people, ideas, and information; and the environment. The tone of the NATO declaration was generally receptive to the idea of a security conference, but only if it were carefully prepared and offered prospects of concrete results. It also warned that "any such meeting should not serve to ratify the present division of Europe."

The complex of initiatives mentioned in the NATO declaration, as well as the U.S.-Soviet Strategic Arms Limitation Talks (SALT), which had been initiated previously, moved forward more rapidly in the following months, a period that served to clarify the agenda of a security conference. Four-power talks were opened on Berlin, and the Federal Republic of Germany initiated contacts with Poland and the USSR, with a view to settling the frontier questions arising out of the results of World War II and concluding renunciation-of-force treaties. Further NATO consideration of prospects for MBFR made it clear that this would have to be treated in a forum separate from—and more limited than—a Europe-wide security conference. The other subjects mentioned in the NATO declaration, including certain aspects of military security, were considered suitable for a security conference, and the communique of the NATO ministerial meeting of May 1970 suggested a two-point agenda for the conference: "(a) The principles which should govern relations between States, including the renunciation of force; (b) The development of international relations with a view to contributing to the freer movement of people, ideas and information and to developing cooperation in the cultural, economic, technical and scientific fields as well as in the field of human environment." The communique suggested, however, that progress in the East-West negotiations that had already been undertaken—particularly on Germany and Berlin—would be necessary before multilateral preparatory talks leading to a conference could begin.

The Warsaw Pact communique of June 1970 took this dialogue one step further by confirming that the United States and Canada could participate fully in the conference, and by accepting the Western idea for an agenda item on freer movement. For their part, the Eastern countries proposed that the setting up of "an appropriate body" on questions of security and cooperation should also be discussed at the conference.

With the signing of the FRG-Soviet and FRG-Polish treaties on renunciation of force in August and December 1970, the principal remaining Western condition for entering preparatory talks for a conference became conclusion of an agreement on Berlin. Settlement of this issue was specified by NATO in its December 1970 communique as the sole precondition for joining in preparatory talks for the conference. A four-power agreement on Berlin was reached in 1971, but the USSR refused to sign it until the West German Bundestag had ratified Bonn's treaties with the Soviet Union and Poland. This was accomplished in the spring of 1972, thus opening the way for the convening of multilateral preparatory talks for the Conference. It was generally accepted by this time that the Conference agenda would include the following subjects: (1) Security, including principles of interstate relations and certain military subjects; (2) cooperation in the fields of economics, science and technology, and the environment; (3) cultural relations, including the freer movement of people, information, and ideas; (4) the possibility of establishing a permanent body on European security and cooperation.

Informal contacts took place in Helsinki during the months of September–November 1972, under the guise of an ambassadorial "tea party." Multilateral preparatory talks were convened on November 22, 1972, in the modern assembly hall of a technical institute on the outskirts of Helsinki. (The name of the site, Dipoli, became an informal way of referring to the talks themselves.) These preparatory talks were in many ways the key to the entire subsequent negotiation, since they set the agenda and the procedures that guided the Conference throughout its existence. The issues dealt with at the preparatory talks ranged from fundamental questions of substance, such as the titles of the ten principles whose texts were to be negotiated, to minor but important points of detail, such as the seating arrangements. This latter point was difficult because the FRG wanted to follow the French alphabetical order, which would make it possible for them to be seated next to the German Democratic Republic (GDR), while Austria objected to this arrangement since it would put Austria next to the two Germanies (Allemagne in French) in a sort of Germanic bloc. To resolve the impasse, the United States volunteered to be seated under the title, Amerique, Etats-Unis de, thus separating Austria from the two German states.

Six months of preparatory talks consolidated agreement on the issues to be negotiated at the Conference itself, and made it possible to convene the opening stage of the CSCE in Helsinki in July of 1973. The results of the preparatory session, the Final Recommendations of the Helsinki Consultations (Appendix I), became the sole guidebook for the subsequent negotiations.

2 Rising Hopes
The Nixon Administration
Approaches the Conference

Everywhere new hopes are rising for a world no longer shadowed by fear and want and war.

Richard M. Nixon Address to joint session of Congress
on return from his visit to the USSR June 1, 1972

"One picture will always remain indelible in our memory," Richard Nixon told Congress after his historic visit to Moscow, "the flag of the United States of America flying high in the spring breeze above Moscow's ancient Kremlin fortress." And indeed, Nixon's visit to Moscow, May 22–30, 1972, was a landmark event — the first visit ever by a president of the United States to the Soviet Union. But it was only one of several major events during 1972 that formed the background for the CSCE and made its opening possible.

It was an election year in the United States, and for Nixon and National Security Adviser Henry Kissinger the principal immediate challenge was to bring the Vietnam War to an honorable conclusion. The Vietnam protest movement had grown in intensity, the war was costing many millions of dollars per day, and Congress was threatening to cut off funding. In July the Democratic party would nominate an antiwar candidate, George McGovern, to run on the promise that he would withdraw all American troops from Vietnam within 90 days.

Nixon had been steadily reducing U.S. troop strength (in May, when he went to Moscow, the number of U.S. troops in Vietnam was down to 69,000). But the end of the U.S. intervention had proved difficult to arrange, and Kissinger was devoting much of his time to personal efforts to find a solution. As the elections approached, this problem became a fixation for both men. It increasingly appeared politically necessary to show that the administration was capable of reaching an agreement that would permit complete, honorable U.S. withdrawal.

The development of more positive relations with the Soviet Union and China contributed to this effort. The two communist giants were hostile to each other, but both supported the North Vietnamese. By playing them off against one another, it was possible to bring pressure to bear on the North Vietnamese. Nixon used this tactic in the lead-up to his Moscow visit, gambling that the Soviets would not want to spoil that visit after Nixon's triumphal trip to China. The Soviets responded as he anticipated, despite the increase in bombing of North Vietnamese cities and the mining of Haiphong harbor just before he left for Moscow.

Alternating brutal bombing raids with peace talks, Nixon and Kissinger pressed hard, and Kissinger succeeded in reaching agreement with the North Vietnamese negotiator, Le Duc Tho, in Paris in October. Despite the reluctance of the Saigon government to go along with the deal, Kissinger made his startling announcement on October 26 that peace was "at hand"—just in time to influence the November elections.

More broadly, Nixon and Kissinger saw 1972 as a year of strategic opportunity to improve relations with both the USSR and China, which Kissinger had visited secretly the year before. The possibility of better relations with both communist powers offered an unprecedented range of opportunities. In his state of the nation speech on January 20, Nixon made it clear that he thought 1972 offered a special opportunity. "Peace," he said, "depends on the ability of great powers to live together on the same planet despite their differences. We would not be true to our obligation to generations yet unborn if we failed to seize this moment to do everything in our power to insure that we will be able to talk about these differences rather than to fight about them in the future."

Nixon and Kissinger had in mind a broad world structure in which balances of power among the United States, the USSR, and China could be used to assure stability and maintain peace. In a radio address on February 9, Nixon expressed this vision: "We must work with our friends and adversaries to build an international structure of peace which everyone will work to preserve because each nation will realize its stake in its preservation."

In February of 1972 Nixon visited China. He recognized that the trip was important, and even though neither side changed its position on the basic issues, the world understood the symbolism of the friendly gestures the United States and China extended to each other.

Two months later Nixon was in Moscow. U.S.-Soviet relations had improved steadily during the Nixon administration, and Nixon told a radio audience on November 4 that he saw the visit as a unique opportunity: "It is precisely the fact that the elements of balance now exist which gives us a rare opportunity to create a system of stability that can maintain the peace, not just for a decade, but for a generation and more." He took care to make use of this visit, and it was fruitful. Nixon's meetings with General Secretary Brezhnev produced a Declaration on Basic Principles of U.S.-Soviet Relations; a Treaty on Limitation of Antiballistic Missile Systems; an Interim Agreement on Certain Measures with Respect to the Limitation of Strategic Offensive Arms; agreements on prevention of incidents at sea and cooperation in science and technology, space, health, and the environment; and decisions to open the second round of SALT negotiations (which convened in Geneva in November of 1972) and to negotiate agreements on maritime matters, trade, and a lend-lease settlement.

Movement toward a CSCE was given a strong boost; the U.S.-Soviet communique foresaw the opening of multilateral consultations on a CSCE as soon as the final Quadripartite Protocol on Berlin was signed and said that the CSCE should be convened "at a time to be agreed by the countries concerned, but without undue delay."

On his return to the United States, Nixon in his address to Congress sounded a note of caution: "This does not mean that we bring back from Moscow the promise of instant peace, but we do bring the beginning of a process that can lead to lasting peace. . . . We must remember that Soviet ideology still proclaims hostility to some of America's most basic values. The Soviet leaders remain committed to that ideology."

U.S.-Soviet relations continued to prosper. A U.S.-Soviet grain purchasing agreement was signed on July 8, a maritime agreement on October 14, and the ill-fated trade agreement, along with a lend-lease settlement, was reached on October 18.

As U.S.-Soviet relations improved, Nixon and Kissinger could not avoid a positive response to Brezhnev's strong desire to hold a CSCE. They were skeptical that such a venture could produce much of significance, but nonetheless portrayed the proposed Conference in a positive light. On April 25, 1972, Assistant Secretary of State for European Affairs Martin Hillenbrand described the U.S. attitude in measured terms before the subcommittee on Europe of the House Foreign Affairs Committee. "We believe," said Hillenbrand, "that the Conference can constitute a modest step forward within a broader and long-range process of negotiation intended to lead toward more stable East-West relations—even though representatives of some thirty states of diverse interests and regimes cannot directly address the central problems of European security."

By agreeing with the Soviets in the communique signed in Moscow that the Conference should be convened "without undue delay," Nixon had given the Soviets the endorsement they sought. When Nixon reported to Congress that the United States and the USSR had agreed to proceed "later this year" with multilateral consultations leading to a CSCE, no one appeared to notice—the other aspects of the developing relationship between the two superpowers completely overshadowed this relatively minor announcement.

As the United States improved its relations with Moscow, the major West European nations felt an increasing political need to broaden their own channels of communication with the Soviets. They could not risk being put in the position where the United States and the Soviet Union appeared to be negotiating over their heads, especially on matters relating to European security. West German Chancellor Willy Brandt's ostpolitik and French efforts toward detente with Moscow were already moving well, but they were intensified in 1972 under the impetus of the need to clear away the preconditions for opening of the CSCE. The FRG treaties with the Soviet Union and Poland, which settled the territorial issues created by the war, were both ratified on May 23, 1972, and entered into force on June 3, along with the Quadripartite Agreement on Berlin. These were the last stated preconditions for the Conference. U.S. and West European interest in accepting a CSCE coincided, and when the NATO foreign ministers met in Bonn on May 30–31, they gave formal agreement to the opening of the multilateral preparatory talks in Helsinki. And on December 21, the two Germanies finally signed the basic treaty between them, thus formally recognizing the division of the German nation.

One problem related to this complex of issues remained unresolved: how to obtain Soviet agreement to opening of negotiations on Mutual and Balanced Force Reductions in Central Europe. The NATO allies wished to open these negotiations as soon as possible to ease U.S. congressional pressures for unilateral troop withdrawals from Europe. But the Soviets had refused to receive a NATO envoy (former NATO Secretary General Manlio Brosio), who had been designated by the alliance to explore the issue with Moscow. The Soviets had not responded to Brosio's application for a visa, but a Warsaw Pact communique indicated that the Eastern side would not negotiate with a representative of NATO as a bloc. To force a positive response from the Kremlin, Kissinger linked U.S. acceptance of the opening date of the CSCE to Soviet acceptance of the opening of MBFR during his visit to Moscow in September of 1972, and the Soviets finally accepted. The result was a carefully orchestrated set of invitations and responses. The allies planning to participate in MBFR sent invitations to the Warsaw Pact participants on November 15. On November 16 the United States accepted the Finnish invitation to open the CSCE talks on November 22. Preparatory MBFR discussions began in Vienna in January.

These rapidly moving events obscured a basic weakness in the U.S. approach to detente that later proved to be an important omission: the absence of human rights from the public agenda of U.S.-Soviet relations. In his address to Congress following his return from Moscow, Nixon highlighted the Declaration on Basic Principles of U.S.-Soviet Relations, which he and Brezhnev had signed on May 29. These principles, said Nixon, provided a "solid framework for the future development of better American-Soviet relations." But the principles did not mention human rights, which had been a major element in the American view of the USSR throughout the history of the relationship and had even colored the American view of czarist Russia. Assistant Secretary Hillenbrand's description of U.S. objectives in a CSCE also downplayed the human rights aspect of the proposed Conference. Though he referred to the concept of freer movement and increased contacts among European states, an implicit reference to expanded human rights, this was not stated explicitly or even positively, and the overall tone of Hillenbrand's statement of objectives delivered to the House subcommittee on Europe was defensive: to avoid confirmation by the Conference of the division of Europe: "We would be firmly opposed to any attempt to use the Conference to perpetuate the division of Europe. Instead, we see the Conference as one small step on the long road to a new situation in which the causes of tension are fewer, contacts greater, and Europe could again be thought of as one continent rather than two parts."

This omission, or rather this timid attitude toward what later became the central Western concern in the CSCE, was little noticed at the time because the Nixon-Kissinger approach was understood as a broad and well-reasoned strategy designed to obtain a more cooperative Soviet attitude on issues such as arms control, Vietnam, and regional conflicts, which were major dangers to peace.

Nixon told the Soviet people in an address on May 28 that his approach was to avoid questioning of internal matters such as the choice of social, economic, or governmental systems: "The only sound basis for a peaceful and progressive international order is sovereign equality and mutual respect. We believe in the right of each nation to chart its own course, to choose its own system, to go its own way, without interference from other nations."

The Declaration on Basic Principles of U.S.-Soviet Relations reflected this approach. The stress was on respect for the other country's system of government and noninterference in internal matters. The contrast with the document later produced by the CSCE is striking, and the political importance of this gap emerged in the course of the next few years.

Nixon's sweeping reelection on November 7, 1972, with 60.7 percent of the popular vote, against 37.5 percent for McGovern, confirmed public support for his policies and strengthened his hand in continuing the policy of detente that he and Kissinger had laid out. Two weeks later, multilateral preparatory talks for the CSCE opened as foreseen in Helsinki.

3 The Way It Was Organized
The Structure and Organization
of the Negotiations

*By the way it has been organized and has developed, our
Conference demonstrates the spirit of detente which
moves us.*

Valery Giscard d'Estaing Helsinki July 31, 1975

Participation

The Finns invited all European states, the United States, and Canada to the
preparatory talks. Albania, which intensely disliked the idea of the CSCE, did
not accept the invitation. Monaco did not participate in the preparatory discussions, but asked to join prior to the opening of the Conference itself.
Andorra was not invited, since France is responsible for its foreign affairs.
Thus, there were thirty-four participating states at the opening of the preparatory talks, and thirty-five (with Monaco) at the opening of the Conference
itself. Each of these participants was equal to the others. In other words, the
voice of San Marino or Liechtenstein was theoretically equal to that of the
United States or the USSR. While these ministates are perhaps poor examples
because their personnel and resources were not sufficient for them to play a role
equal to that of larger countries, it is a fact that middle-sized states, such as
Romania, Switzerland, or the Netherlands, were able to deal with the great
powers as equals in this negotiation, and did so. All proposals for observer
status, for interested non-European states or international organizations, were
rejected.

The Three-Stage Conference

The Soviets and their allies wanted the Conference to be a brief, high-level,
ceremonial meeting that would, simply by being convened and agreeing to a
short, generally worded document, accomplish much in terms of their objectives. The Western participants did not wish to go to a high-level conference

until there had been some movement toward their own aims, which required considerable negotiation. This issue was open when the Finns first invited the participating states to Helsinki. During the course of the Helsinki consultations, both sides argued their case. The result, as always in CSCE, was a compromise, in this case conceived by the French: a three-stage Conference. The Conference was to convene for Stage I in Helsinki at the level of foreign ministers, thereby giving the Soviets an early symbolic meeting at high level. Stage II was to meet in Geneva for the substantive negotiations of interest to the West. The final stage, or Stage III, was to be held in Helsinki on a date and at a level to be determined during the negotiations. As it turned out, the Final Act of the Conference was signed on August 1, 1975, by ten presidents, seventeen prime ministers, four first secretaries of Communist parties, two foreign ministers and two personal representatives of government leaders.

The Stage II negotiations were held in Geneva instead of Helsinki primarily for practical reasons. Helsinki had proven itself during the preparatory talks to be well isolated from most of Europe, and while this was an advantage because it forced diplomats to concentrate on their work, Geneva's central location was more convenient for a long-term negotiating effort, with a broader range of conference facilities, hotel space, and communications. (One West German diplomat said that his telephone calls from Helsinki to Bonn were often routed through Moscow and East Berlin, which did not exactly guarantee privacy.) The Finns were given the honor of being host for the two ceremonial stages of the Conference because of their untiring efforts in getting the CSCE off the ground.

The chronology of the Conference was as follows. Helsinki Consultations: November 22, 1972–June 8, 1973; Stage I, Helsinki: July 3–7, 1973; Coordinating Committee Meeting, Geneva: August 29–September 2, 1973; Stage II Negotiations, Geneva: September 18, 1973–July 21, 1975; Stage III, Helsinki: July 30–August 1, 1975.

Consensus Decision-making

Many of the Western countries at first favored establishment of decision-making rules requiring consensus on questions of substance and majority voting on procedural matters. Such arrangements would have made the Conference more efficient, but were not acceptable to all participating states. The Eastern bloc suspected that they would be outvoted on procedural matters by the larger group of fifteen NATO members plus a few sympathetic neutrals, and the neutrals and smaller participants generally saw in the simple rule of consensus the possibility of enlarging their own role and of participating on a truly equal basis with the larger powers. Consensus was the only possible solution, but its use was tempered by a widely felt understanding that, while there was no majority vote, there should be no veto, either. The one recognized instance of abuse of this understanding (by Malta during the closing days of the negotiations in Geneva) brought severe criticism from all sides, and a formal apology to the Conference by the Maltese representative at the final Summit session. It was virtually universally recognized that the consensus rule was properly intended as a defensive mechanism to protect essential national interests from being overridden, but that it should not be used as an offensive negotiating weapon to obtain, through a form of blackmail, acceptance of an otherwise unpopular idea. This rule of consensus, and the unwritten code of ethics surrounding it, was one of the most important and interesting features of the Conference. While perhaps inefficient and anachronistic, it worked reasonably well in the relatively civilized negotiating milieu of the CSCE.

Rotating Chairmanship

At the outset there were several ideas as to who should preside at CSCE meetings. This function could have been confided to the host country or to the executive secretary and his representatives. It could have been given to a recognized expert on the topic under discussion, or a neutral country, or allowed to rotate among the neutrals; it could have been shifted periodically among East, West, and neutrals. But the simple system of rotation among all participating states seemed to reflect best the idea of the equality of all participants and the underlying principle that the Conference was being held "outside the military blocs."

The system of rotation also became an important precedent during the Conference, and at the end of the Geneva negotiations this precedent was a major argument in favor of choosing as a site for the planned follow-up meeting a city that had not been a site for any stage of the Conference itself.

Committee Structure

The basic structure of the Conference was sketched out during the preparatory talks in Helsinki. The text of the Helsinki Recommendations mentions a Coordinating Committee, committees, and subcommittees, with the clear intention of establishing a three-level structure. Nevertheless, the committee structure of the CSCE was a difficult question to settle when the Conference got down to work in Geneva.

The Soviets and their allies wanted to reduce the number of negotiating groups in order to make the discussions as general as possible, to finish quickly, and to produce a generally worded text consisting mainly of intergovernmental principles. The West, on the other hand, preferred to establish specific groups concerned with each of the subjects to be covered by the Conference. Their aim was a text that would be as concrete and specific as possible, and specialized groups were essential to the drafting of such a document. The agreed structure consisted of a Coordinating Committee, whose functions were defined by the Helsinki Recommendations, and three committees, covering the three substantive baskets. ("Basket," as used in the CSCE, means "a group of related subjects." The term originated during the preparatory discussions in Helsinki when it was difficult to group together under broad headings several diverse subjects. In order not to prejudice the importance of any single subject, it was suggested that they be gathered into "baskets" for convenience. The name stuck.) Eleven subcommittees were set up, covering the various subjects on the agenda and responsible to the three committees. In addition, a "special working body" was established at the insistence of the Swiss and Romanian delegations, each of which had submitted a proposal relating to the list of interstate principles but sufficiently important for separate treatment. The Swiss proposal was for a system for the peaceful settlement of disputes in Europe. The Romanian proposal was designed to give effect to the principle of refraining from the threat or use of force. The special working body had the same status as the subcommittees.

During the course of the negotiations, several other bodies were created, including working groups on follow-up to the Conference, on the Mediterranean, and on the organization of Stage III of the Conference.

Basic Documents

The CSCE produced two basic documents, which will be referred to often in this book and which are included as appendixes.

The Final Recommendations of the Helsinki Consultations was produced by the preparatory talks in Helsinki and approved by acclamation by the foreign ministers of the participating states during Stage I of the Conference. This slim blue pamphlet, also known as the Helsinki Recommendations, or simply the Blue Book, contains the agreed organization of the three-stage Conference; a detailed agenda; agreed provisions on participation, contributions, and guests; rules of procedure for all three stages; and a breakdown of financial assessments. The Helsinki Recommendations are arranged according to numbered paragraphs, which are referred to in this book by the abbreviation HR followed by a paragraph number (i.e., HR 12 refers to Helsinki Recommendations, paragraph 12). The negotiations in the committees and subcommittees at the CSCE itself generally followed the order and breakdown of the agenda contained in the Helsinki Recommendations.

The Final Act of the Conference was produced during the two-year Stage II negotiations in Geneva and was signed by heads of state or government in Helsinki at Stage III. This voluminous document contains all the substantive provisions agreed to at the Conference. Although the Final Act as approved contains no paragraph numbering, the text included as an appendix to this book has been numbered for convenience. References to the text will be made using the abbreviation FA followed by a paragraph number (e.g., FA 12).

A verbatim record of Stages I and III was published, but there were no formal records of the preparatory talks or the Stage II negotiations. Delegations could, of course, keep their own records, but very few had the personnel or the inclination to do so in view of the very high number of meetings. For all formal meetings the secretariat produced a Journal, which recorded opening and closing times, chairmanship, topics discussed, decisions taken, and provided space for formal statements any delegation wished to enter into the record, such as formal reservations.

The only other officially recognized Conference documents (apart from administrative documents and decision sheets, which listed decisions entered in the Journal) were proposals introduced ("tabled") by national delegations, which were identified with the name of the sponsoring country, and provisionally agreed ("registered") texts, which were identified by the name of the Conference body approving them. These provisionally agreed texts were eventually assembled, edited, and pieced together to form the Final Act.

Delegations

National delegations varied widely in size, strength, and organization: The Soviet delegation included between sixty and one hundred people; the delegation of Monaco consisted of a single official who came to a meeting of the Coordinating Committee about once a month. Most delegations were headed by an ambassador. In the case of the USSR, this position was held by a deputy foreign minister. Some delegations were headed at a lower level, notably the U.S. and French delegations during part of the negotiations. Another variation was the head of delegation who was the ambassador of his country at another post. Several ambassadors who were the permanent representatives of their countries to UN organizations in Geneva doubled as heads of delegations at the CSCE. In other cases ambassadors resident in Helsinki (or elsewhere, as in the U.S. case, Prague) came to Geneva to head their delegations but retained their responsibilities at their bilateral posts.

Most delegations of reasonable size had three diplomats in charge of negotiations in the three baskets. Some basket chiefs had highly specialized backgrounds—in the economic or trade fields, disarmament, international law, or cultural exchanges—but many were simply career diplomats with broad general experience.

The larger delegations had between one and three specialists working within each basket, in order to cover all the specialized subcommittee meetings. The

Soviets were something of a special case, with an ambassador-level official in charge of each basket, at least one specialist for each subcommittee, and legal advisers for the principal subjects.

Some of the most impressive diplomats in the Conference, however, were those from the smaller countries, who were obliged by the small size of their delegations—sometimes no more than one or two officials—to keep up with the negotiations on all subjects. This was the case, for example, with the delegations of Malta, the Holy See, Liechtenstein, Luxembourg, and Iceland; the extraordinary efforts of these diplomats, who at times made key contributions to the work of the Conference, were a real tour de force.

Groups

The groupings of like-minded delegations played important roles but varied widely in terms of discipline, homogeneity, and purpose.

The Warsaw Pact

The traditional Soviet bloc, led by the USSR and including Poland, the GDR, Czechoslovakia, Hungary, Bulgaria, and Romania, was unquestionably the most disciplined group in the Conference, to the extent that it often appeared to function merely as a claque for Soviet positions and thus lost much of the impact and influence that a group of seven independent states might ordinarily exert. No one really expected different positions from any of the Warsaw Pact countries except Romania. Thus, the Soviet position was the number one question on any Conference issue, because five or six other delegations could be assumed to take the same line.

Romania was a clear exception to this rule. At times it seemed as though the Romanians were deliberately taking positions separate from those of the other Warsaw Pact countries, so different were their perceptions. This was especially true on certain questions: the principles guiding relations among states, where the Romanians laid great stress on the sovereign equality of each participating state, noninterference in internal affairs, and refraining from the threat or use of force, as levers for their independence from the Soviet bloc; the military area, in which the Romanians were interested in identifying a number of confidence-building measures as a means to enhance their own possibilities for defending themselves against invasion by their Warsaw Pact colleagues; certain economic questions, which the Romanians also wished to use to separate themselves from the Warsaw Pact; and the question of Conference follow-up, which for the Romanians represented a kind of insurance that would permit them to continue their independent foreign policy line. On the other hand, on most Basket III issues, especially freer movement questions, the Romanians were at times more Soviet than the Soviets themselves. It was the Romanians, not the Soviets, who were the last country to accept the agreed text on the "Improvement of Working Conditions for Journalists."

The EC-Nine

The member countries of the European Community ("the Nine") had two distinct roles in the Conference. The first related to economic questions and derived from the statutory responsibility under the Treaty of Rome for the Commission of the European Communities to conduct trade negotiations on behalf of all Common Market countries. As a result of this responsibility, the commission itself was represented in the Basket II negotiations relating to trade. Commission officials were included as members of the delegation holding the presidency of the Nine. (During the course of the Geneva negotiations, the presidency of the Nine was held in rotation on a six-month basis by Denmark, the FRG, France, Ireland, and Italy.) They were supported by an ad hoc group of EC-Nine representatives responsible for the economic portions of Basket II.

The innovation of using commission officials to represent all nine countries threatened to disrupt the negotiations at the opening of Stage II, when the Soviets refused to agree to the listing of the commission officials with a national delegation and challenged the representative of the commission when he first took the floor. Denmark held the presidency at that time, and the challenge was made on the grounds that the person asking to speak for Denmark was not Danish. The Danish delegation head, Ambassador Sjold Mellbin, rushed immediately to the meeting where this incident was taking place and responded firmly that he and no one else had the prerogative to decide who could speak at the Conference on behalf of Denmark. The challenge was abandoned, and the Nine succeeded in establishing an important precedent for being represented by the Commission of the European Communities in East-West trade negotiations.

The second role of the Nine in the CSCE was much less formal or disciplined, deriving as it did from the evolving pattern of consultations among the Nine on foreign policy. To coordinate their positions on political, as opposed to economic, questions in Geneva, the Nine established an internal subcommittee on CSCE, which was composed of CSCE delegation heads and was responsible to the political directors of the nine foreign ministries. The Nine were reasonably successful in their effort to follow joint policies on political issues in the CSCE, although not with the same discipline as resulted from the legal commitment to follow the same line on trade questions. Both the ad hoc group on Basket II and the CSCE subcommittee submitted periodic reports and recommendations to the Nine political directors, and the political directors gave them joint policy guidance on most major questions. The Nine regarded this coordination as a particularly successful example of foreign policy coordination, an area in which they are still attempting to build habits and traditions.

The North Atlantic Alliance

The NATO group of fifteen overlapped largely with the Nine, since eight of the Nine were also members of the alliance. NATO had served as the primary locus of Western policy coordination during the period leading up to the Conference, and it was the semiannual NATO communique that had been the vehicle for the Western half of the East-West dialogue on the possibility of a European security conference. Most Western ideas on substance or procedure had been aired in NATO before the Conference, and U.S. leadership in these preparations had been strong.

However, there were problems with a clear NATO role in CSCE. Primarily because of French objections to a "negotiation between the military blocs" (which in the French view could have resulted in American dominance of the Western position), it proved impossible to agree on any form of institutional link between NATO as such and the NATO group at the site of the negotiations. While obviously there was a certain amount of cross-fertilization through national channels among capitals, NATO headquarters in Brussels, and the Conference site, there was no formal channel or group responsibility, such as was the case within the EC-Nine. In addition, the French at first made it a point of principle not to attend NATO caucus meetings, which limited their value. (Later the French attended selectively and toward the end of the negotiations were regularly present.)

The Nine felt a need to coordinate among themselves prior to discussions within the NATO caucus. An informal two-tiered Western coordination process grew up, which allowed the Nine to consult before NATO caucus meetings. This tended to further downgrade the importance of the NATO caucus, especially since the non-Nine NATO members held a variety of political views and had idiosyncratic problems that at times distracted their interest from the primary Conference issues. Finally, the chosen U.S. role in the Conference permitted the Nine greater leeway to coordinate among themselves than would have been the case if the United States had chosen a militant posture.

The NATO caucus, nevertheless, had an important place in the negotiations because of its size (at fifteen members it was the largest bloc in the Conference), and because the United States, which alone could counter-balance a strong Soviet position, was a member.

Berlin Groups

The four wartime allies (United States, France, Great Britain, USSR) share rights and responsibilities for Berlin and Germany as a whole deriving from their victory in the Second World War. They held consultations on the language introduced into the Final Act to preserve these quadripartite rights and responsibilities and made a joint effort to obtain agreement on it. To coordinate this effort with their West German allies, the three Western powers also consulted in the traditional Bonn Group format (United States, Great Britain, France, FRG) on questions relating to Berlin and Germany.

The Neutral and Nonaligned

The group of neutral and nonaligned states did not begin to organize until late in the negotiating phase of the Conference. Since they held strongly to the principle that each state was participating in the Conference as an independent entity, they could not immediately enter into negotiation by bloc. However, beginning with certain procedural issues, such as the writing of the monthly meeting schedule, the neutrals became more cohesive. Their group formed around the important neutrals—Finland, Sweden, Switzerland, Austria, and Yugoslavia—and included Cyprus, Malta, Liechtenstein, and the Holy See. Spain considered itself neither neutral nor nonaligned and participated in no group.

The neutral group had similar views on several issues. Being left out of the negotiations on force reductions in Vienna, they were eager to enhance and broaden the military content of the CSCE. They were also generally favorable to an early, successful conclusion to the Conference and an elaborate follow-up mechanism that would provide them with a forum for multilateral consultations on European issues. Their cohesiveness on these issues was surprisingly strong.

The Mediterranean Group

This group never regularized its consultations, although a number of meetings were held to coordinate views on Mediterranean issues, which were the special interest of the group. However, the similarity of the views of the Mediterranean littoral states was evident on such problems as the degree of prominence that the Mediterranean should be given within the CSCE and the migrant labor issue. These and a number of other questions brought out the north-south aspect of the Conference: the common differences between the largely industrialized societies of northern Europe and North America and the less developed countries of the south.

The Nordic Caucus

This modest group stepped up its consultations and became in the end one of the more interesting minor phenomena of the Conference, since it consisted of three NATO members (Iceland, Norway, and Denmark), one member of the Nine (Denmark), and two neutrals (Sweden and Finland). The attraction felt by the NATO Nordics for the approach taken by their neutral colleagues was evident, and on certain questions Nordic solidarity was stronger than Nine or NATO solidarity (e.g., the question of fixing a date for the third stage of the Conference, which was vital to the Finns).

The Secretariat

Unlike the secretariats of some international organizations, the prerogatives of the CSCE secretariat were severely limited by the Helsinki Recommendations (HR 74–79) to strictly technical matters, and this fact prevented the executive secretary from exercising any substantive influence. The few attempts made in this direction (all well-meaning efforts to help things along) were quickly squelched by one or more delegations, who reminded the executive secretary of his purely technical role. The one successful effort by the executive secretary to take a positive initiative was made during the invited appearances of representatives of non-European Mediterranean states. Prior to each of these appearances, the executive secretary brought together the visiting representative and the chairman of the meeting at which he would appear. This helped to eliminate misunderstandings and avoid possibly embarrassing mistakes.

Six Languages

There were six official languages in the CSCE: English, French, Russian, German, Spanish, and Italian. The Conference could have been less complicated, and cheaper, if the number of official languages had been smaller, but this was not possible.

The question of languages was settled during the preparatory talks. English was probably the most widely spoken language among the delegations present, and if English alone could have been selected as the official Conference language, the Soviets might have accepted the omission of Russian. But the French argued that French was the traditional language of diplomacy and should have equal status. This meant that Russian also had to be included.

German was a special case; it was the only language spoken in both communist and capitalist Europe. This, coupled with the fact that so much of the Conference's work related to German issues, made German useful as an official language. It can even be argued that the German-language text of the Final Act is the most authoritative, since it is the only one on which native-speaking capitalist, communist, and neutral countries agreed. To achieve agreement on the German-language text, a five-nation group (FRG, GDR, Austria, Switzerland, and Liechtenstein) carried on a sporadic parallel negotiation among themselves as sections of the Final Act were agreed.

The number of official languages might have been limited to English, Russian, French, and German, but Italy argued that, since Italian is spoken by some 50 million people, it, too, should be included. The Italian argument logically meant that Spanish should also be an official language, since on a worldwide basis Spanish is spoken by more people than Italian. This raised the question of whether Portuguese and Dutch were eligible, and where indeed the list should stop. The Italian case was supported by Switzerland and Malta, however, and had the sympathy of other Mediterranean countries, and in the end both Spanish and Italian were included.

4 A Challenge, not a Conclusion
The Helsinki Final Act

We have learned from the experiences of the last 30 years
that peace is a process requiring mutual restraint and
practical arrangements. This Conference is part of that
process—a challenge, not a conclusion.

Gerald Ford Helsinki July 31, 1975

It was difficult in 1972–73 to see how the CSCE would turn out, and what its effect would be on the East-West equation in Europe. Because the Conference had been proposed by the USSR, the tendency in the West was to be cautious in entering it. The objectives of the Soviets grew clearer during the years preceding the CSCE. Moscow wanted (1) to legitimize the geopolitical changes resulting from the Second World War, the existence of communist regimes in Eastern Europe, and their frontiers; (2) to promote a general relaxation of West European attitudes toward the East; and (3) to advance toward creation of a pan-European system of security in which the USSR would dominate and ties with the United States would gradually wither.

Within these broad objectives, specific Soviet aims evolved considerably before and during the Conference, as some possibilities were denied them, others appeared more difficult to obtain in the short term, and still others were achieved independently. For example, when Molotov first advanced the idea of a European security conference, the Soviets were deeply concerned by the prospect of FRG entry into NATO. The Conference would have offered the possibility of establishing an alternative security system to the NATO-Warsaw Pact balance. It seems possible that the Soviets hoped this prospect would divert German interest in NATO, but this objective was overtaken by events. The original Soviet idea of excluding the United States and Canada from the European Conference, a part of their broad effort to loosen transatlantic ties, was also rejected.

The idea of setting up a permanent CSCE organ as the nucleus of a pan-European security system became less and less attractive to the Kremlin as Western interest in using CSCE to advance human rights emerged. The possibility of a pan-European security system, while perhaps not abandoned as a long-range Soviet aim, has certainly been recognized as unobtainable in the CSCE context in the foreseeable future.

On the other hand, certain Soviet objectives had been at least partially achieved by the time the preparatory talks opened in Helsinki. The communist regimes of Eastern Europe, with the single exception of the GDR, were universally accepted as the governments of their countries. The last postwar border changes to be formally legitimized (those between Poland and the USSR, Germany and Poland, and the FRG and the GDR) had been recognized in West Germany's series of Eastern treaties. (The USSR, nevertheless, had a continuing interest in achieving multilateral confirmation of the legitimacy of these border changes.) And, following conclusion of the Quadripartite Agreement on Berlin and the basic treaty between the FRG and the GDR, the GDR was in the process of being recognized diplomatically by virtually all Western countries. (The GDR and the FRG were admitted to the UN on September 18, 1973. The United States opened full diplomatic relations with the GDR on September 4, 1974.) In addition, bilateral movement toward detente, particularly by France, the FRG and the United States, had brought about a certain relaxation of the East-West tensions of the cold war era, to the point where the CSCE appeared more as a reflection of the new atmosphere than an initiator of it.

For the West, the period prior to the CSCE was also one of defining objectives. While rejection of the idea of a European security conference reflected the East-West equation during the cold war, the emergence of a detente relationship made it necessary to review what the West could obtain from a conference, and how such a meeting could contribute to the achievement of overall Western aims. In general terms, the Western countries sought (1) to maintain Western unity and to exclude a growth of Soviet influence in Western Europe; (2) to keep open the possibility of peaceful evolution, such as peaceful changes in frontiers, for the day when, for example, German reunification might be more possible; (3) to achieve some concrete improvements in relations between East and West, particularly some that would result in freer movement of people and ideas, greater openness, lowering of barriers, and enhanced military security; and (4) to use the Soviet desire first to convene the CSCE, and later to conclude it at the summit level, to obtain Moscow's agreement to a variety of Western desiderata.

Some of these objectives were achieved before or during the Conference. The United States participated in the CSCE and the West remained united. In fact, one of the most significant features of the CSCE, during the negotiations and since Helsinki, has been that its human rights content differentiates between the fundamental concepts of the Western democracies and those of the communist states, and tends to reinforce the sense of identity among the Western countries, based on their allegiance to a common set of ideals. The attitude of the communist countries toward individual liberties has underlined how profoundly antithetical the communist system is toward the ideas that form the basis of Western civilization.

The USSR's desire to open, then to conclude, the CSCE was fairly successfully used. By linking them to the opening of the CSCE, the West obtained, or at least accelerated, completion of the Quadripartite Agreement on Berlin, the opening of Mutual Balanced Force Reductions negotiations, and a number of other lesser items. By holding out the prospect of a summit-level conclusion, the West was able to negotiate a Final Act that was meaningful both in terms of basic Western principles, and also in terms of the specific concrete improvements the West was seeking. For example the important objective of keeping open the possibility of peaceful changes in frontiers was attained in the Final Act. Of course, offering the Summit in trade meant that, once their conditions had been met, Western leaders were obliged to go to Helsinki, but by the time the Final Act began to take definitive form, it appeared useful—even essential—to commit the USSR and the Eastern European countries at the highest level to actually carrying it out.

The West has clearly been unsuccessful in bringing about full implementation of the commitments in the Final Act, especially those relating to freer movement of people, information, and ideas. While the specific undertakings contained in the Final Act are worthwhile even though they are in many cases ambiguous, there is no way to enforce their implementation. This is an area requiring careful, continuing encouragement; progress will come only very slowly.

The CSCE was not simply a two-sided negotiation. The neutral participants also had objectives that they pursued in the Conference. These were similar to the Western objectives identified above, for the European neutrals generally share the principles and concepts of the other Western Europeans. In addition, however, the neutrals had some special objectives of their own: (1) to participate in the detente process, which was otherwise understood as an East-West development; (2) to express their own views on East-West issues; and (3) to ensure a successful Conference, which would make it possible for them to have a continuing voice in pan-European matters. It is probably fair to say that these objectives were achieved.

Because of the conflicting aims of the various parties, the complexity of the subject matter, and the individual views of the thirty-five participating states on each specific topic, it was impossible at the outset of the negotiations to foresee what the result would look like. It was generally assumed that whatever agreement could be reached would be recorded in a document or documents of some kind, but beyond this basic notion, there was very little definition. In addition, the differing substantive objectives of the various sides controlled their attitudes toward the form that the results of the Conference would take. The Soviets wished to enshrine the concept of immutability of frontiers as the basic law of relations among states in Europe and to relegate virtually everything else to a lesser (preferably very low) status. The West wanted to have a balance among all the concepts contained in the list of interstate principles, and also between the principles and the concrete measures that they hoped to introduce into the Conference texts.

The very nature of the detailed negotiations that characterized the CSCE from the beginning suggested that a voluminous document (or documents) would be the result. While the Soviets would have preferred a very simple negotiation about the basic principles of interstate security, "the CSCE," as President Gerald Ford described it in a report to the U.S. CSCE Commission in December 1976, "in fact became a negotiation about the manner and pace of breaking down the division of Europe and alleviating the human hardships engendered by it." The Soviets slowly realized that the results of the Conference would contain much about human rights and freer movement of people and ideas, and that it would not be desirable from their point of view to include these results in a treaty or other document with a legal status in international law.

This Soviet conclusion joined the Western view that the results of the Conference should contain moral, but not legal, commitments. It was difficult for many Western countries to negotiate treaties concerning the activities of private individuals, groups, or companies. The United States, for its part, wished to avoid difficulties with Congress either over the status of an ambiguous, treaty-like document, or in ratification proceedings over the complex text that was likely to emerge from the negotiations. The British delegation resolved this problem by proposing that the Conference adopt a "final act" as its concluding document, since this is an accepted format for recording the results of an international meeting without giving them a legally binding character. The nonlegal nature of the Final Act is made clear in the text (FA 67), which states that it is "not eligible for registration under Article 102 of the Charter of the United Nations," the article providing for registration of treaties and agreements. In addition, an agreed letter transmitting the Final Act to the secretary general of the UN (Appendix II, following the Final Act) specifically states that it is not a "treaty or international agreement."

The Final Act of the CSCE (full text at Appendix II) is a complex document, reflecting the results of the two years of negotiation, the opposing objectives of the participants, and the compromises necessary to achieve consensus. The Final Act begins with a preamble and ends with some final clauses. In between are five major documents, each of which appears to be self-contained but which are linked in concept and phraseology. Some of these documents are divided into numbered sections and subsections. The organization and textual character of the different parts vary considerably.

The first major document, called "Questions Relating to Security in Europe" (Basket I), contains a "Declaration on Principles Guiding Relations between Participating States," and a "Document on Confidence-building Measures and Certain Aspects of Security and Disarmament." The declaration lists the ten CSCE principles, and includes inter alia the concepts of nonuse of force, inviolability of frontiers, territorial integrity of states, peaceful settlement of disputes, nonintervention in internal affairs, and respect for human rights and fundamental freedoms. The declaration is followed by a subsection further developing the ideas of nonuse of force and peaceful settlement of disputes. The document on confidence-building measures sets out agreed provisions relating to military security.

The second major document, "Cooperation in the Field of Economics, of Science and Technology, and of the Environment" (Basket II), enumerates agreed provisions in these areas, and contains sections on commercial exchanges, industrial cooperation and projects of common interest, provisions concerning trade and industrial cooperation, science and technology, environment, and cooperation in other areas. Each of these sections is in turn broken down into subheadings such as tourism, transportation, arbitration, business contacts, and facilities.

The third major document is called "Questions Relating to Security and Cooperation in the Mediterranean," and attempts to define the relationship between what has been agreed among the European states and the nonparticipating states of the Mediterranean area.

The fourth major document, "Cooperation in Humanitarian and Other Fields," is the now-famous Basket III. It contains sections on human contacts, information, culture, and educational exchanges. The first two sections of this document are undoubtedly the most innovative contribution of the CSCE in that, by their inclusion in the Final Act, they establish as legitimate subjects for discussion and negotiation between states the specific human-rights-related subjects that they cover. Furthermore, the fact that these are included as sections of a final act dealing with the overall relationship among states creates a link between improvement in interstate relations and improvement in these human rights areas. The firm message of this linkage is that progress in detente depends in part on progress toward the freer movement of people, ideas, and information, which Basket III is about.

The last major document contained in the Final Act, "Follow-up to the Conference," describes the agreed arrangements for post-CSCE activity, particularly the 1977 Belgrade review meeting, which has now become a precedent for regular gatherings at which implementation of the Final Act's provisions will be examined and possible new proposals received.

Part II
1973   Opposing Strategies

5 Moral Dilemmas and Policy Choices

As the CSCE Begins, the Nixon Administration Faces Problems

It is clear that we face genuine moral dilemmas and important policy choices. But it is also clear that we need to define the framework of our dialogue more perceptively and understandingly.

Henry Kissinger Address to Third Pacem in Terris Conference
Washington, October 3, 1973

The ending of U.S. involvement in the Vietnam War, the runaway reelection of President Nixon, and the apparent success of the policy of detente toward the Soviet Union and China gave a deceptively optimistic aura to the beginning of 1973. Richard Nixon's second inaugural address on January 20 reflected this spirit and a justifiable pride in the accomplishments of his first term, especially 1972. It had been, he said, "the year of the greatest progress since the end of World War II toward a lasting peace in the world."

On January 23, Henry Kissinger initialed the Agreement on Ending the War and Restoring Peace in Vietnam, and Nixon announced on nationwide television that "peace with honor" had finally been attained; U.S. troops were to be withdrawn and prisoners of war returned within sixty days. The accomplishment was of historic proportions, and Kissinger would earn the Nobel Peace Prize for it.

The administration's mood in the early days of January was positive. With the problem of the Vietnam War essentially resolved, Nixon and Kissinger hoped to turn U.S. foreign policy toward further milestones: the consolidation of detente, the expansion of U.S.-Chinese relations, and the revitalization of the transatlantic relationship. These possibilities seemed within reach; in February, Kissinger visited Peking and agreed with the Chinese that the United States and China would open "liaison offices" in each other's capitals. The post in Peking was to be headed by the distinguished diplomat, David K. E. Bruce; the fact that Bruce was a Democrat gave this step a bipartisan aspect, which Nixon had been seeking in his foreign policy.

The enlargement of the European Community took effect on January 1, as

Great Britain, Denmark, and Ireland acceded to membership. Preliminary talks on Mutual Balanced Force Reductions (MBFR) negotiations opened January 31 in Vienna, and the CSCE preparatory negotiations were going well in Helsinki. The time looked right for greater U.S. attention to Europe.

Kissinger launched his transatlantic initiative in a speech to Associated Press editors in New York on April 23. He called for a "new Atlantic charter," to be worked out with the Europeans prior to a Nixon trip to Europe later in the year. "It is the president's purpose," said Kissinger, "to lay the basis for a new era of creativity in the West." This ambitious objective was justified, Kissinger argued, because "today the need is to make the Atlantic relationship as dynamic a force in building a new structure of peace [as it had been in providing for Western defense], less geared to crisis and more conscious of opportunities, drawing its inspirations from its goals rather than its fears."

The new Atlantic charter that Kissinger proposed was defined somewhat vaguely. It would be a document that "builds on the past without becoming its prisoner; deals with the problems our success has created; creates for the Atlantic nations a new relationship in whose progress Japan can share."

For many Europeans, however, the real meaning of the proposal was reflected in two key passages from his remarks to the editors: "The U.S. has global interests and responsibilities. Our European allies have regional interests. These are not necessarily in conflict, but in the new era neither are they automatically identical." And: "We cannot hold together if each country or region asserts its autonomy whenever it is to its benefit and invokes unity to curtail the independence of others. We must strike a new balance between self-interest and the common interest."

Led by Gaullist French Foreign Minister Michel Jobert, many Europeans interpreted these phrases as a way of subordinating European independence to U.S. global interests, as a way of saying the Europeans should blindly support the United States on a worldwide basis. Such a concept was unacceptable to the French, for whom independence of foreign and defense policy had become a basic credo, and was strongly resisted by many other Europeans.

Nixon's "state of the world" report to Congress on May 3 pursued the administration's optimistic view of what was possible. "During the next four years," wrote Nixon, "with the help of others, we shall continue building an international structure which could silence the sounds of war for the remainder of this century." The momentum of events sustained a positive look in foreign relations. The preparatory work for the CSCE was successfully completed on June 8, with agreement to convene the opening stage on July 3. The NATO foreign ministers, meeting in Copenhagen June 14–15, agreed with Kissinger that the time had come to examine alliance relationships in the light of changing circumstances. And the United States was preparing for a visit by Brezhnev, which, it was hoped, would produce as dramatic a success as Nixon's visit to Moscow.

But even as the president and his national security adviser were contemplating these new foreign policy advances, the seeds of future problems were sprouting in Washington. On January 30 the burglars who had broken into Democratic campaign headquarters in the Watergate complex were convicted in Judge John Sirica's courtroom. A Senate select committee was established under the chairmanship of Senator Sam Ervin to investigate implications of the Watergate affair. On March 21 White House Counsel John Dean advised Nixon that "a cancer" was developing within the presidency, and it was made known that "intensive new inquiries" had been undertaken in the White House to determine involvement in Watergate.

By April 30 Nixon was forced to admit at a press conference that there had been "an effort to conceal the facts both from the public, from you, and from me." In moves that shook the nation he accepted the resignations of two of his closest aides, H. R. Haldeman and John Ehrlichman, as well as those of Attorney General Richard Kleindienst and John Dean. Elliot Richardson took over as attorney general and Archibald Cox was named special prosecutor, with authority to investigate all aspects of the Watergate affair.

Events steadily closed in around the president. In May former Attorney General John Mitchell, a close associate of the president's, and former Secretary of Commerce Maurice Stans were indicted for mishandling a campaign contribution. On May 17 Senate Watergate hearings began on nationwide television, thus concentrating public attention on the unfolding drama. Kissinger was implicated in questionable wiretapping practices, which tarnished his otherwise unsullied reputation. And President Nixon himself, increasingly cornered, publicly denied any personal participation in or knowledge of the Watergate affair or its cover-up.

As the Brezhnev visit approached, the Watergate problem looked for the first time as though it could prove an embarrassment to the nation. On June 16, just two days before Brezhnev arrived, testimony before the Ervin committee revealed that senior White House officials might well have been implicated in the Watergate bugging. John Dean's testimony was actually postponed until after Brezhnev's departure to avoid undercutting the president during the summit.

The June 18–25 visit of Leonid Brezhnev, at the time general secretary of the Communist party of the Soviet Union, was a watershed in many ways. It took the U.S.-Soviet relationship one step further with the secretly negotiated Agreement on Prevention of Nuclear War, signed by the two national leaders on June 22, and it advanced a number of negotiations. It sketched out the shape of a SALT II agreement through signature of a document entitled Basic Principles of Negotiations on the Further Limitation of Strategic Offensive Arms, and, according to Kissinger, it pinned down the official opening date for the MBFR negotiations. "At this meeting," said Kissinger at a press conference on June 25, "it was decided that the MBFR conference would begin unconditionally on October 30." Kissinger candidly told the press that the holding of periodic summits "permits the quick resolution of particular issues which, if left to the expert level, could produce extended stalemate."

But the Brezhnev visit also produced the first strong reactions against the evolving relationship between the United States and the Soviet Union. Many allies were concerned over the implications of the Agreement on Prevention of Nuclear War, as well as the way it had been concluded with only cursory consultation. The agreement's language stating that Washington and Moscow "shall immediately enter into urgent consultations" whenever there was a danger of war seemed to echo the obligations of the North Atlantic Treaty. Some allies wondered which obligation would take precedence in such circumstances, and whether the United States would consult first with them or the USSR.

Moreover, this second Nixon-Brezhnev summit helped to jell growing American resistance to closer relations with the Soviet Union in the absence of significant progress in Soviet human rights practices. Debate on this issue focused on the proposed Trade Reform Act of 1973, which would have authorized the president to extend to the USSR Most Favored Nation (MFN) trading status. The trade agreement with Moscow had committed the United States to grant MFN status to the Soviet Union, and the Trade Reform Act was the vehicle for obtaining Congressional approval. But a growing number of congressmen and senators opposed granting such status to the Soviet Union unless it permitted unrestrained emigration by Soviet Jews who wished to leave. The idea of establishing a linkage between trade and emigration steadily gained support in Congress until it became a serious problem for the administration.

Nonetheless, Kissinger was optimistic at the end of the summit, predicting at his June 25 press conference that a new SALT agreement would be concluded the following year, and Nixon confidently accepted an invitation to visit the USSR in 1974. The two sides were also optimistic with regard to the CSCE and noted the possibility of concluding it at the highest level.

On July 3, Secretary of State William Rogers traveled to Helsinki to represent the United States at the opening of the CSCE. The Conference was at the crossroads of the gathering debate on relations with the Soviet Union. It was, of course, a product of the momentum of detente. But it was also a forum in which the United States would be forced to take a stand on human rights in the USSR. It would be necessary in the CSCE to measure the extent to which further progress in detente would depend on a revised Soviet attitude toward human rights, as well as how much human rights pressure the growing detente relationship could bear. The warning signals for Nixon and Kissinger were already there: a policy toward Moscow that appeared to overlook human rights would not retain public support for very long.

Rogers approached the issue gingerly in his July 5 speech at Helsinki: "For a quarter century," he said, "division has been the dominant feature of Europe.

We all recognize that this Conference must not confirm the barriers that still divide Europe. Rather . . . we have expressly undertaken to lower these barriers."

But Rogers's tenure expired shortly after his appearance in Helsinki; on August 16 he submitted his resignation. And on August 22 the president announced that Kissinger would succeed him, retaining his position as national security adviser. By the time Kissinger took office, the administration was besieged by a variety of foreign policy problems, which few could have foreseen. The Vietnam agreement was unraveling to the point that Nixon had accused the North Vietnamese of systematically violating it. American bombing continued in Cambodia, as the United States tried to shore up the Lon Nol regime. The Europeans were increasingly unhappy over U.S. pressures emanating from the "Year of Europe" initiative. The very basis for the detente relationship with the USSR was being criticized because of Soviet human rights practices, and the Jackson-Vanik amendment to the Trade Reform Act would soon bar the president from granting the USSR MFN status unless the Soviets removed limits on emigration. Congress was pressing a resolution to limit the warmaking powers of the president, and a new Mansfield amendment to require unilateral troop reductions in Europe was looming in Congress. Most importantly, Watergate-related difficulties were steadily mounting, reducing presidential authority and requiring the continuing attention of the White House.

Nixon nevertheless used his August 22 press conference to remind Americans, with some justification, that his first administration had been "one of the most successful eras of foreign policy in any administration in history," and Kissinger continued to exude optimism. His objective as secretary of State, he told reporters on August 23, would be "to conclude during the term of the president the building of a structure that we can pass on to succeeding administrations so that the world will be a safer place when they take over."

An already-challenging foreign policy picture was vastly complicated on October 6, when Egypt and Syria attacked Israeli positions on the Suez Canal and the Golan Heights. Realizing that such an attack could not have been launched without Soviet support, Kissinger used his Pacem in Terris Conference speech on October 8 to warn that "detente cannot survive irresponsibility in any area, including the Middle East." But the main message of this important speech was that relations with the USSR offer few alternatives to detente, or something very similar. Kissinger recognized "the profound moral antagonism between communism and freedom," but noted that the issue was really a matter of degree and asked rhetorically, "How hard can we press without provoking the Soviet leadership into returning to practices in its foreign policy that increase international tensions?" Responding to critics of detente, Kissinger was his most eloquent: "Foreign policy must begin with the understanding that it involves relationships between sovereign countries. Sovereignty has been defined as a will uncontrolled by others; that is what gives foreign policy its contingent and ever-incomplete character. . . . A nation's values define what is just; its strength determines what is possible; its domestic structure decides what policies can in fact be implemented and sustained." In an analysis that could easily be applied to the CSCE and that sheds light on his attitude toward the Conference, Kissinger said: "Until recently the goals of detente were not an issue. The necessity of shifting from confrontation toward negotiation seemed so overwhelming that goals beyond the settlement of international disputes were never raised. But now progress has been made—and already taken for granted. We are engaged in intense debate on whether we should make changes in Soviet society a precondition for further progress, or indeed for following through on commitments already made. . . . This is a genuine moral dilemma."

But there was little time in the autumn of 1973 for Nixon or Kissinger to reflect on this dilemma. While the CSCE convened in Geneva to discuss issues relating to Soviet human rights behavior, events elsewhere raced ahead. The initiative in the October War in the Middle East shifted from the Arabs to the Israelis. The Soviets, concerned that their Arab allies faced disaster, proposed a joint U.S.-Soviet intervention. When Nixon refused, Brezhnev evidently began planning a unilateral intervention, causing Nixon to put U.S. forces around the world on alert during the night of October 24–25. Though the alert was brief, and many suspected that the president had called it to garner public support in the face of his Watergate problems, it nevertheless reminded many of the realities of dealing with the USSR. For the allies, the alert without consultation underscored the growing divergence of U.S. and European interests in the Middle East, which had already been demonstrated by the fact that only one ally—Portugal—supported the U.S. airlift to Israel during the October War.

The Middle East crisis absorbed more and more of Kissinger's attention as he began his famous shuttle diplomacy in November, leading to a Middle East peace conference in Geneva on December 21, cochaired by the United States and the USSR.

With Kissinger personally handling the Middle East problem, the White House became almost totally absorbed in the Watergate issue. This was complicated on October 10 by the resignation under fire of Vice President Spiro Agnew, who was replaced by Gerald R. Ford. The Watergate stakes were raised even higher on October 20 with the so-called Saturday Night Massacre. The president fired Watergate Special Prosecutor Cox and accepted the resignations of the attorney general and his deputy. Nixon released some tapes to Judge Sirica and appointed a new special prosecutor, Leon Jaworski. In the House of Representatives impeachment proceedings were initiated, and a number of leading newspapers called for Nixon's resignation.

Problems had mounted, the foreign policy atmosphere had definitely soured, and the United States and the Europeans were trading criticisms about nonconsultation and noncooperation as the year drew to a close. As the allies tried to engage the Soviets in meaningful negotiations at the CSCE, Kissinger issued this warning in a December 12 speech to the Pilgrims of Great Britain in London: "Some Europeans have come to believe that their identity should be measured by its distance from the United States. . . . Europe's unity must not be at the expense of Atlantic community, or both sides of the Atlantic will suffer."

Despite the growing problems, Kissinger maintained his view of the desired relationship with the USSR, which he described at a December 27 press conference as "a conscious effort to set up rules of conduct and to establish a certain interconnection of interests and, above all, to establish communications between the top leaders and between officials at every level that make it possible in times of crisis to reduce the danger of accident or miscalculation."

Though Kissinger was surely not thinking of the obscure negotiations then beginning in Geneva when he said this, his definition might well have applied to the CSCE, as well.

6 Marking the Opening
The Foreign Ministers Meet in Helsinki, July 3–7, 1973

We are meeting to mark the opening of a conference for which it is difficult to find a historical parallel. Comparisons have been drawn with the Congress of Vienna and the Conference of Versailles. Those Conferences had a clear and urgent purpose: to bring peace and order to a continent ravaged by war. We have a different but no less important goal. It is not to make peace: it is to make a better peace.

Sir Alec Douglas-Home Helsinki July 5, 1973

The Conference opened in Finlandia Hall, Helsinki, at 11:30 A.M. on July 3, 1973, with welcoming speeches by the foreign minister and the president of Finland, and a speech of greeting by Secretary General Kurt Waldheim of the United Nations. Finnish President Urho Kekkonen tried to set the tone of the meeting by quoting a Finnish proverb: "Security is not gained by building fences; security is gained by opening gates," and urged the Conference to follow the course of "compromise and conciliation." But the gathering was immediately confronted with one of the issues that, though peripheral to the central significance of the CSCE, was to hound it until the very end: the Mediterranean.

The afternoon of the first day was scheduled as an open session of speeches by foreign ministers, but because of a proposal by Malta that the foreign ministers of Algeria and Tunisia should also address the Conference, the meeting began behind closed doors. Since it was clear that there would be no immediate consensus on the Maltese proposal, or a similar Spanish one, a working group was established to consider the matter, as well as the important practical questions of the dates for the opening of Stage II of the Conference and of the organizational meeting of the Coordinating Committee to precede it, and to draft a final communique for the Stage I gathering. The working group continued its work in parallel with the plenary sessions of the Conference throughout Stage I.

With the Mediterranean issue sidetracked for the moment into the working group, the Conference itself returned to its open session and the first speaker:

Andrei Gromyko, the foreign minister of the Soviet Union. Gromyko was the first speaker because of a curious Soviet effort. The Finns had announced that requests for places on the speakers' list would be accepted on a first-come-first-served basis from opening of business on a date several weeks earlier. The Soviets stationed a junior diplomat at the door of the Finnish foreign ministry the night before the appointed day. He remained there all night long (luckily for him, it was already late spring in Finland), and was the first to present a request the next morning.

In his hour-long speech Gromyko set a tone quite different from Kekkonen's. He singled out the principle of inviolability of frontiers as the point of departure for peace in Europe, and submitted a document on security in Europe, which became one of the basic drafts on which negotiations were later conducted. This draft was called a "General Declaration on the Foundations of European Security and the Principles of Relations among States in Europe." While he quoted Lenin as saying that a socialist state could have "unrestricted business relations" with capitalist countries, his comments on Basket III issues were highly guarded. "There should be no room," he said, for information relating to "hatred, aggression, militarism, the cult of violence, racial or national supremacy, or other objectives inconsistent with the goals of rapprochement and cooperation among nations, with the UN Charter, or in contradiction to generally recognized moral standards," a list that would allow the Soviets to exclude virtually any information with which they did not agree. Gromyko underlined that "cultural cooperation, development of contacts, and exchange of information should be effected with full observance of the principles . . . above all . . . of sovereignty and nonintervention," and insisted on "strict observance of the laws, customs, and traditions of each other." But Gromyko was optimistic: he stated that the Conference could be concluded at the highest level before the end of 1973.

Gromyko was followed by Danish Foreign Minister K. B. Andersen, who spoke as the representative of the presidency of the European Community. He announced the intention of the community to negotiate commercial questions in CSCE as the community, and not as individual states. As the first Western representative to speak, he emphasized the Western view of the Conference: interrelationship of all the principles; equality of all CSCE agenda items; importance of concrete progress under the Basket III headings of human contacts and information.

There followed a parade of speakers, which lasted from Tuesday until Friday evening. Secretary of State Rogers spoke twenty-first for reasons perhaps as symptomatic of the U.S. view of the Conference as were the Soviet efforts to speak first. Due to an oversight, both in the U.S. delegation to the preparatory talks and in Washington, the Secretary of State was not asked about his preferences for placement on the speakers' list, and the U.S. delegation sought no special place for him. All other states did ask for placement, and the United

States was therefore listed last. When Rogers discovered this situation upon his arrival in Helsinki, he strongly objected, and his subordinates desperately asked the Finns what could be done. The Finns, being good hosts, magnanimously offered to trade their own position on the list (twenty-first) with the United States.

While the speeches were being made upstairs in the beautiful and airy concert hall, the working group was struggling with its mandate in a narrow, windowless, and somewhat stuffy basement meeting room. Of the three questions before it, the date of the opening of Stage II was resolved relatively easily. But the Mediterranean issue posed by Malta was more difficult. It was not, in fact, a new problem. Soon after the opening of the preparatory talks, Algeria and Tunisia had informed the Conference by diplomatic note of their interest in participating in some fashion in the proceedings. There had been much discussion of the pros and cons of the idea.

It had been recognized that the Maghreb countries of North Africa had legitimate historical ties to Europe, and that they were manifesting something of a European "vocation," which was generally welcomed. Had the matter been that simple, the Maghreb states probably would have been accorded some relationship with the CSCE. However, it had also been recognized that any one of these countries could act as a spokesman for the Arab states, and that the acceptance of Algeria and Tunisia would immediately prompt an application for equal status by Israel, which would hardly wish to risk an Arab influence in a European conference treating questions of security without having the right of reply. While most participants in the Conference wished to keep discussion of the Middle East question out of CSCE, and had no particular desire to admit Israel, there had been a strong feeling, especially among certain Western states, that the Conference could not appear to be taking sides in the Middle East conflict, and that it was necessary to accord Israel, or any other nonparticipating Mediterranean state, equal treatment. A few countries definitely had wished to keep Israel out, and the Soviet Union had preferred strongly to avoid the possibly divisive, and certainly very difficult and time-consuming Middle East discussion that seemed certain to follow if Arab countries and Israel were admitted. With these different positions in play, a compromise had been found in the form of two procedural rules (HR 56 and 57), which permitted the Conference and its working bodies to "acquaint themselves, in such a manner as they may determine," with the views of the Mediterranean states.

As soon as the Conference itself opened, Malta and Spain submitted proposals for methods by which the Conference could acquaint itself with the views of Algeria and Tunisia. The Maltese proposal was a simple invitation to the foreign ministers of these two countries to address Stage I of the Conference. The Spanish proposed a provision under which Stage II of the Conference would receive, "both through documents and orally," the views of all Mediterranean states, while Algeria and Tunisia would be given a special place by having their foreign ministers address Stage I.

Once a working group had been established to deal with the proposals, a long week of debate and procedural maneuvering began, with Maltese Prime Minister Dom Mintoff fighting hard to give Algeria and Tunisia some special recognition and relationship with the Conference, while preserving the possibility of denying the same status to Israel. Spain, Yugoslavia, France, and others were sympathetic to the Maltese position. During the week the Conference received a message from Israel, requesting the same status as Algeria and Tunisia. Mintoff took the Catch-22 position that this letter could not be circulated because it was not related to the proposals under discussion, and that it was out of order to discuss its possible circulation because the Conference could not possibly know what was in a letter that had not been circulated. "I shall contend," said Mintoff, "that even to read the message would be out of order; it would be much less in order for us to consider a proposal when the contents had not been read."

On the opposite side were many Western states, led by Denmark, the Netherlands, and Canada, who insisted on equal treatment in the smallest detail for Israel. The Soviets and their allies were somewhat frantically looking for a solution that would permit the Conference to get off to a smooth start. Secretary Rogers took a hands-off attitude, saying to his subordinates, "Tell them anything they work out among themselves will be all right with us."

As the days of Stage I passed, it became apparent that it was no longer physically possible for the Algerian and Tunisian foreign ministers to appear before the ministerial gathering. The Maltese and Spanish abandoned their proposals for appearances at Stage I, with the clear intention of raising the issue again at the outset of Stage II.

By this time the working group had begun drafting the Stage I communique. The bulk of this document was bland and uncontroversial (see Appendix I), but the Maltese, Spanish, and others insisted on a paragraph covering the Mediterranean issue, with the same objective as before: to attribute a special status to Algeria and Tunisia. The Dutch, Danes, and Canadians again led a stiff resistance. In the last two days of the Stage I gathering, Mintoff, isolated on the issue, tried several rather hopeless parliamentary maneuvers and then withdrew, leaving a subordinate to maintain the Maltese position of principle.

In this situation it appeared that the simple solution was not to have a communique at all, but the Soviets were keenly interested in a communique that they could use to portray the Stage I meeting as a success. They were unwilling to see this objective blocked by the marginal problem of how to describe the consideration given to the Mediterranean participation issue during Stage I.

The final closed session of Stage I witnessed some sharp statements on this subject. Many ministers had already left, and the Stage I meeting was on the verge of expiring in frustration. When the Maltese representative stated that he would not join a consensus on a compromise version of the contested paragraph of the communique, an angry and exasperated Gromyko took the floor. He described the scene as nonsensical, which it clearly was. Recalling that it was the nations represented in the hall that had adopted the rule of consensus, he noted that these same nations could also change this rule. "Why," he asked, "can we not have a consensus minus one delegation, which does not want to cooperate with us in the interests of all?"

This intervention had the effect of converting the relatively minor issue under discussion into one of fundamental principle: whether the rule of consensus was to be overridden when it was put to a severe test. It is significant that the reaction of most delegations in the hall was that the rule of consensus was too important to abandon lightly, and that, as difficult as it seemed, a solution would have to be found to satisfy everyone, including the Maltese. The French representative, Ambassador Gerard Andre, expressed the feeling eloquently: "The principle of consensus," he said, "is an absolute one. . . . Whatever may be the desire to reach some sort of solution and spirit of conciliation, we cannot violate this rule." This scene, which had its echo two years later, brought home to everyone present the seriousness of the impasse the Conference had reached and what was at stake.

A recess was called to allow for private efforts to reach a solution. During the break the Soviets, who were deeply concerned about possible negative effects on the CSCE, dispatched one of their cleverest negotiators, Ambassador Lev Mendelevich, to arrange a compromise between the Maltese and those who insisted on preserving the principle of equal treatment. Mendelevich was physically impressive, with white hair and an enormous protruding belly. He had an intricate and devious negotiating style, which gave the appearance of great flexibility, coupled with personal wit and extraordinary ability to understand and master complex multilateral situations. His years of experience at the UN made him unquestionably the ablest man on the Soviet delegation. His personal effort was successful, a communique was agreed, and Stage I of the Conference adjourned on a positive note.

7 Their Own Vital Interests
Western Strategy and the U.S. Role

*It must be accepted as a fact that all our countries have
their own vital interests which have to be borne in mind.
This is only natural, the Conference not being a meeting
of victors of war nor a meeting of great powers.*

Urho Kekkonen Helsinki July 30, 1975

Many Western governments thought of the CSCE as a Soviet project and saw no reason to help it along; if the Soviets wanted to conclude the Conference successfully, they could pay for it. Moreover, it was well known among Western countries that the Soviets were in a hurry, and there was a widespread feeling that they were most likely to make concessions when they were really up against the wall and had to bring the Conference to an end. This attitude was tempered by the fact that each of the Western governments participating in the CSCE had its own political investment in the idea of detente, and none was willing to risk the total collapse of the Conference. Nevertheless, the Western strategy generally was to slow the negotiations down, to focus them on detailed, concrete Western proposals, and to engage the Soviets in negotiations on these specific ideas in the hope that, under time pressure to conclude the Conference, the Soviets would eventually make concessions on subjects of interest to the West and render the whole project worthwhile.

No Western government believed the CSCE could be used to fundamentally alter the nature of the Soviet state, or its hold on Eastern Europe. Even though the Soviets wanted a successful Conference very badly, there was a limit to the price they would pay for it, and it was the overall Western analysis that the most that could be hoped for would be acceptance of some principled language and a number of concrete improvements, especially in freer movement areas. Limited concessions of this type were the objectives of the Western strategy. At the same time, there was a generalized belief among the Western countries that the CSCE gave the East Europeans a useful measure of maneuvering room in their relations with the USSR. The CSCE provided an umbrella under which the East European governments could legitimately develop relations with other European countries. These were considered important benefits of the Conference, though they were difficult to measure.

Western strategy was reasonably successful. The first effort was designed to remove any illusions that a brief Conference producing a highly generalized document would be possible. To accomplish this, the Western delegations, much to the frustration of the Eastern side, imposed a phase of "general debate" on the beginning of the negotiations. This period produced a great many lofty speeches on the high ideals of democracy, and just as many on the high ideals of communism. No one was converted, and the speeches, unheard by press or public and unrecorded as well, disappeared into oblivion. But the first Soviet target date for conclusion of the Conference, the end of 1973, passed before any agreed language had been drafted.

The West insisted on creation of subcommittees on each topic to ensure that detailed consideration of specific proposals would take place. Once the general debate had concluded, numerous concrete drafts were tabled in these subcommittees. This had the desired effect, and although many drafts were rejected or greatly watered down, the result in each subcommittee was a detailed text. In the freer movement areas some of these "details" were important, and their acceptance was no doubt facilitated by the fact that they were obscured by the size and complexity of the Final Act.

The notion of holding out the possibility of a summit-level conclusion as an inducement to the Soviets to make concessions was much harder to use. Most Western leaders actually wanted to go to a summit to enhance their images and to draw domestic political benefits from the publicity. Though a few—principally French President Georges Pompidou—were hesitant, their attitudes were based less on the actual results of the CSCE negotiations themselves and more on the overall question of how participation in such a summit would be viewed by Western publics. This was, of course, only partially dependent on the content of the Final Act.

The United States generally supported the broad Western strategy, but the American role went through a number of phases reflecting evolving political attitudes in Washington. At the opening of the negotiations, the United States took up the "low profile" that later became the oversimplified caricature of United States activity in the CSCE. A lack of strong, specific instructions ensured that the United States could not assert its usual dominance of the Western camp.

In fact, the delegation had no written instructions whatsoever when it arrived in Geneva—not even the normal telegraphic statement of general objectives usually sent to a U.S. delegation at an international conference. While there was a vivid desire in the delegation and at the working level of the State Department to support the Western side, the officials concerned were afraid that if they attempted to put instructions in writing, Kissinger would not agree to a strong U.S. position. The central core of the delegation knew this and rarely asked for instructions. The delegation tried to give maximum support to Western positions, especially on human-rights-related matters, without going so far in confronting the Soviets that Kissinger would become personally involved and possibly rein in the U.S. position. Such a development would have been damaging to the Western effort, since it would have revealed that the U.S. delegation had only limited support from its own government.

The "low profile" was a reflection of Kissinger's desire to have a positive working relationship with the Soviet leadership, and to be able to negotiate with them on a broad range of issues. Kissinger did not wish to cause problems in this relationship over an issue—the CSCE—that was unimportant to him and clearly much more important to the Soviets.

Kissinger regarded the CSCE basically as a concession to the Soviets. While Western interests within the CSCE had to be protected, he saw Western participation in it as a trade-off, which had already been heavily used to obtain the Quadripartite Agreement on Berlin and the opening of the Mutual Balanced Force Reductions negotiations in Vienna. Kissinger saw nothing of major importance that the West could actually gain in the CSCE, an attitude that justified using it in trade against objectives outside the Conference. While this attitude arguably might have been correct in absolute terms, it did not take sufficient account of European views. The Europeans, with their more limited perspective, believed the CSCE was intrinsically more important. They thought the aims being pursued in the Conference were significant objectively and, in any case, politically. This mutual lack of understanding between Kissinger and the Europeans persisted, and manifested itself repeatedly during the negotiations.

Fortunately, the U.S. delegation leader during the Helsinki consultations, George S. Vest, was extremely clever at using a combination of personal prestige and Yankee common sense to exercise a major influence on events. His contribution to the elaboration of the Helsinki Recommendations was important, but not easily measurable, nor well known. Vest, who came from a deeply traditional, rural Virginia background, likened the Conference to a team of mules: it was always hard to get them pulling together. Asked by Secretary of State Rogers whether he should be given the title of ambassador, Vest declined with typical modesty, saying that being the senior American representative gave him sufficient prestige.

Vest and other career officials made the most of the "low profile." The officials backing up the delegation in the State Department trusted Vest's tactical judgment and gave him his head. Vest, in turn, stuck as close as possible to the strategy and decisions of the NATO caucus. NATO solidarity thus substituted for Washington instructions and was used by the U.S. delegation in its communications with Washington as justification for positions taken in the absence of instructions.

When Vest was withdrawn at the beginning of Stage II, his successor arrived with no prior experience of multilateral diplomacy and no expertise on the CSCE. The low profile sank even lower. A third delegation leader, Albert "Bud"

Sherer, arrived only a few months later. Though he, too, had no direct knowledge of the CSCE, he had prestige as the serving U.S. ambassador to Prague, and long experience dealing with the communist world. The low profile suited his personal style, but he nonetheless gradually developed a position of useful influence within the Conference by projecting the image of a "wise man," who was somewhat above the petty maneuvering of the negotiations. The pattern developed by Vest of using alliance solidarity as a substitute for Washington instructions was followed by the delegation throughout the low-profile phase.

But as bilateral U.S.–Soviet relations deteriorated in late 1974 and early 1975, Kissinger was more inclined to be firm with Moscow, and this attitude became increasingly visible in the CSCE toward the end of the negotiations. The overall slippage in American relations with the USSR coincided with a growing domestic political need. Kissinger wished to head off criticisms that the administration was too "soft" toward the Soviets. Also, as the Helsinki Summit approached, it looked more and more as though the results would be received negatively in the United States. In these circumstances it became essential to obtain the maximum Soviet concessions on the subjects still open to negotiation, in order to give the overall results of the Conference their best possible face. At the end of the negotiations, therefore, the U.S. delegation slowly raised its profile until it was tougher with the Soviets than any of the other participants. In the final months of the Geneva negotiations the United States held its normal leadership position in the Western group.

The evolution in the U.S. approach was not part of a U.S. strategy, which the U.S. side did not have, apart from the overall Western tactics described above. Rather, the U.S. role responded to changing political pressures and needs, which in fact often determine the U.S. attitude in negotiations.

In contrast to the tightly controlled approach pursued by the Soviets, the U.S. side, here as elsewhere, followed a more casual style that depended on openness, spontaneity, and common sense. This led to a number of mistakes (e.g., the speakers' list fiasco during Stage I), but it also gave the Western side a real strength in the face of the stolidly inflexible Soviet group. In a situation where original ideas for satisfactory resolution of complex problems were at a premium, the Western side was infinitely more likely to come up with a solution than any Soviet or East European diplomat.

In the circumstances, there was an obvious need for the Western side to stick together. The Western delegates all realized this, but the individual will to do so was not always very strong. The CSCE was not supposed to be a bloc-to-bloc negotiation, and it would not have been possible to achieve lockstep Western discipline. It can even be argued that there were some advantages to the fact that Western countries followed policies that were separate and independent. But the discipline of the Soviet bloc was such, and its interests so fundamentally opposed to those of the Western countries, that policy coordination was essential.

During the CSCE the Soviets capitalized on even minor differences among the Western allies to establish with a number of Western delegations "private" relationships, which were the cause of several potentially harmful splits in the Western side. Although the West developed a number of similar relationships with East European delegates, these were never as successful as the Soviet effort. A stronger U.S. leadership role would have contributed to the discipline of the Western side and would have reduced the opportunities for Soviet mischief.

The Western consultation process was the principal device for ensuring unity, and in spite of the U.S. low profile, it worked fairly well. The NATO caucus, in which the United States participated, was effective sporadically. Probably the EC-Nine caucus was even more useful. Ironically, the Nine were able to come to joint positions largely because of U.S. disinterest. The degree of U.S. interest in an issue appeared to have a direct, inversely proportional relationship to the Nine's ability to formulate and maintain a joint position. An informal two-tiered allied consultation process emerged, under which the Nine consulted first, then took their positions into the NATO caucus. Firm agreement among the Nine usually determined the attitude of the NATO caucus. These arrangements worked most of the time, although there were instances in which the difference in the U.S. and European appreciation of the importance of an issue complicated them.

Finally, it must be said that despite the effort to put forward a number of freer movement ideas on which it might be possible to achieve agreement, and in spite of the tactical effort to force the Soviets to deal with these specific proposals, the dynamics of the Conference depended almost entirely on the Soviet desire to bring the CSCE to a successful summit conclusion. This was the engine that powered the whole undertaking, and all Western strategy could do was to channel the Soviet effort by indicating what the Soviets would have to do to get what they wanted. In this sense, the Western role was secondary and passive, while the Soviets were the primary strategists and movers.

8 The Values of Others
General Debate, August–December 1973

*Foreign policy involves two partially conflicting
endeavors: defining the interests, purposes and values of a
society and relating them to the interests, purposes and
values of others.*

Henry Kissinger Address to Third Pacem in Terris Conference
October 8, 1973

The Swiss housed Stage II of the Conference in the newly completed International Conference Center, a squat, starkly modern building of stucco and glass, which was quickly dubbed the "blockhouse" by the curious journalists who gathered to observe the opening of this puzzling undertaking. For the first few days, television cameras focused on the self-conscious diplomats who entered the building: gesticulating Italians, ruddy-faced Irishmen, a phalanx of smiling, handshaking Russians, Vatican priests in round collars, oddly clothed East Germans, elegant Spaniards, and slouching, casual Americans. Considerable numbers of journalists of all nationalities mingled with delegates in the vast lobby, trying to understand what was taking place, if anything. The presence of the journalists caused an unusual phenomenon: during the "coffee breaks," which were called whenever an impasse was reached, diplomats gathered in amoeba-like clusters in the lobby, seeking procedural solutions to Conference problems. Often the journalists present not only joined these huddles, but also made contributions to the discussion. Since it was difficult at first to know the faces of all the delegates, suggestions by journalists were sometimes considered along with national proposals and may even, in a few cases, have helped things along.

It is difficult to convey the atmosphere of the Conference in those early days. It was so big and amorphous that it was impossible to come to grips with as a whole, much less steer it toward a rational path. Very little was really fixed, since even the Helsinki Recommendations were subject to interpretation, and everything was open to negotiation. An air of frantic negotiation filled the rooms and corridors of the Conference building, despite the fact that nothing of substance had yet been broached. A scrambling confusion of private contacts, rumors, proposals, tactical ploys, and inexplicable reversals prevailed. It is not surprising that the contingent of journalists present on the first day dwindled rapidly and within a week had all but disappeared. Making sense out of what was happening was not easy.

The committee structure of the Conference was agreed upon following considerable horse trading. The Soviets realized that it would not be possible to avoid committees and subcommittees and accepted this structure, as they accepted many disadvantageous procedures, in order to create a sense of momentum and to move the Conference on to more serious work.

Two specific problems prolonged the discussions of the committee structure. The first was the question of the body in which proposals submitted under HR 21 should be considered. Paragraph 21 (called the Blue Zone by Conference delegates after the limited parking areas of European cities) was a catchall agenda item for consideration of proposals designed to give expression to the principles of interstate relations. Two principles were specifically mentioned in HR 21: nonuse of force and peaceful settlement of disputes. Already a disputed point during the Helsinki consultations, this paragraph was attached to the agenda item on interstate principles as a second, related subparagraph, and many delegations in Geneva did not feel it deserved consideration in an independent subcommittee. However, the Swiss, who had written an elaborate and detailed proposal for establishing a system for the peaceful settlement of disputes in Europe, and the Romanians, who had drafted an equally ambitious proposal to give expression to the principle of refraining from the threat or use of force, badly wanted serious consideration of their ideas. The solution was to create a "special working body," with the same status as the subcommittees.

A second problem was how to consider the question of Conference follow-up. The Helsinki Recommendations made this question the special province of the Coordinating Committee, but it seemed unlikely that the Coordinating Committee itself would be capable of carrying out the detailed negotiations required. At the same time, most Western delegations took the position that the question of follow-up should not be considered until the Conference had made concrete progress on the substantive subjects on its agenda. To support their arguments, these Western delegations cited the language of HR 53: "The Coordinating Committee shall consider, on the basis of the progress made at the Conference. . . ." In the end this viewpoint prevailed, and it was agreed that the Coordinating Committee, assisted as might be required by a working group, would consider the question of follow-up when Conference progress justified this.

The solution laboriously found for receiving contributions from the non-participating Mediterranean states recognized the principle of equality between Israel and the Arab countries. It was agreed that any Mediterranean littoral state whose application was sponsored by a participating country prior to a specified date would be permitted to address the CSCE and to submit written contributions. The comments of these states were to be restricted to two agenda items: questions relating to security or to cooperation in economics, science and technology, and the environment (Baskets I and II). (During the multilateral preparatory talks, the relevance of Mediterranean considerations to these two subject headings had been recognized, but relating the Mediterranean to Basket III would have opened the door to a discussion of the emigration of Soviet Jews to Israel, which the Soviets could not accept.) Several participating states, including Yugoslavia, Malta, and the USSR, were unhappy about the decision to admit Israel, but accepted it either because it was the only way to bring the Arab countries into the Conference, or because it was the only way to conclude the discussion of this difficult side issue and get on to more central matters. The latter was probably the only reason the Soviets accepted the arrangement.

Following this invitation, six nonparticipating Mediterranean littoral states asked to present their views to the Conference: Algeria, Tunisia (these two had applied previously), Israel (whose letter of application was refused consideration at Stage I), Syria, Egypt, and Morocco. Only two littoral states, Libya and Lebanon, did not apply. While it was widely recognized that a late application by Libya or Lebanon would probably have been approved by the Conference, the term "nonparticipating Mediterranean States" as used during the CSCE and in the Final Act, referred specifically to the six states presenting their views to the Conference and thus establishing a relationship with it.

With the formal opening of Stage II on September 18, the procedural wrangling continued, provoked to a considerable extent by the Western delegations, who pressed for adoption of "work programs" or "agendas" for the work of each subcommittee and for a "general debate" on the subjects within each subcommittee mandate as a means of clarifying positions before drafting. The Eastern side and many of the neutrals reacted with exasperation and anger to these ideas. They argued, quite rightly, that the agendas for work in each of the bodies of the Conference were contained in the Helsinki Recommendations and that the principal purpose of the multilateral preparatory talks had been to draft these agendas. The communist delegations also warned of the practical problems of trying to agree on new agendas, which could in some cases have been as difficult to negotiate as substantive texts. They accused the Western delegations of bad faith and of trying to renegotiate the Helsinki mandates. Eventually, the proposal for agendas was withdrawn.

As for the idea of a "general debate," the reaction of the Soviets and their allies was one of great frustration. The Soviets were obviously under pressure to complete the negotiations in the shortest possible time, and feared Western filibuster tactics. To speed the Conference along, the Soviets had accepted expedient solutions on several procedural issues, but a general debate promised not only long delays before drafting could begin, but also the kind of polemical exchanges that could serve only to sharpen differences between East and West and make it more difficult to arrive at solutions in a short period of time. The

Soviets, with a delegation more than twice as large as any other, continued to press for the highest possible number of meetings for each of the working bodies in the hope that the debate would run its course and leave no alternative but to actually get down to work. As a result the first weeks of the negotiations saw a frenetic work schedule, under which eight to ten meetings per day were common. This pace posed problems for smaller (and even middle-sized) delegations, and was later slowed somewhat. It was also soon discovered that, despite the frequent meetings, or perhaps because of them, meetings at which no one had anything to say were not unusual.

The idea of a general debate also raised Soviet concerns that the Western countries would broaden the discussion to include subjects not specifically mentioned in the Helsinki Blue Book and extremely sensitive for them, such as Jewish emigration. Considerable publicity had been given to Basket III issues in the Western press, and Soviet dissidents had also picked up on Basket III as a potential lever for applying pressure within the Soviet system. The Soviets and their allies tried to focus discussion immediately on their own draft papers, which had been tabled either in Helsinki at Stage I or in the early days of Stage II. These papers were generally worded and contained a minimum of specifics, but they were draft documents, something the Western side had not yet put together.

Despite the procedural disputes, the early weeks of the Conference saw certain events that were important to the development of the Conference as a whole. Virtually all delegations agreed in general that the CSCE principles should not be legally binding or create new European international law, although the Soviet delegation leader, Deputy Foreign Minister Anatoly G. Kovalev, argued that what the Soviets wished to call the "general declaration" should contain "certain obligations" and be "as binding as possible." The Eastern countries tried unsuccessfully to challenge the right to speak of the representative of the Commission of the European Communities. The French delegation entered into the record a disclaimer stating that four-power rights in Berlin and Germany as a whole were not affected by the CSCE. The other two Western powers with rights and responsibilities in Germany, the United States and Great Britain, concurred in this statement.

Regular caucus meetings began among the NATO and EC-Nine groups in all the specialized subject areas, and negotiating patterns began to emerge. In the military area it became clear that the neutrals (plus Romania) were the most ambitious, while the Soviets gave the Helsinki Recommendations the narrowest possible interpretation and the NATO countries wished to concentrate on the three confidence-building measures specifically mentioned in the Helsinki Blue Book. In Basket III the Soviets revealed their defensive tactics, calling attention to the recent ratification by the Supreme Soviet of the UN Covenants on Social and Political Rights and laying great stress on the principle of nonintervention in internal affairs as it applied to Basket III.

With these cautious beginnings, the Conference moved gingerly into its work, and after about one month the basic procedural questions had been largely settled. But all of this activity was shadowboxing, and brought no substantive results. Speeches were often highly intelligent, but they had very little effect, since they did not engage the other side in a joint effort to agree on something concrete.

This was especially true in Basket III, a classic dialogue of the deaf. Here the problem for the West was to find a way to broach a meaningful discussion with the Soviets. It became apparent very quickly that the general debate idea was not the way to do this, but in spite of this widespread realization, general debate was pursued throughout the autumn.

Western tactics aroused concern among neutral delegations, whose governments were interested in a successful CSCE for reasons of their own, and who suspected that some of the NATO countries were determined to block an early conclusion of the Conference simply because it was a Soviet objective. While such a theory was exaggerated, it was true that the Western countries, to a greater or lesser degree, wished to put the Soviets in the *demandeur* position and that they saw no advantage in assisting the Soviets in pressing ahead.

By mid-October the Western countries were aware that their general debate tactic was having only limited success. It was, most agreed, increasing the time pressure on the Soviets, but it was also turning the neutrals, who wished to make progress, against the West. The lack of concrete Western documents for drafting gave the initiative to the Eastern bloc, even in the Western-objective areas of Basket III. The Soviets and their allies took advantage of this situation to launch a verbal attack on Radio Liberty and Radio Free Europe, two American-owned and operated stations broadcasting to the Soviet Union and Eastern Europe. The Soviets urged the Conference to adopt language banning these stations and the "misinformation" they spread. The Soviet attack was designed to put pressure on the West European countries from whose territory the stations transmit, and who are periodically embarrassed by their presence. The Soviets were in effect urging these countries to control the transmissions emanating from their soil, on the grounds that they constituted interference in the internal affairs of the communist states. The U.S. representative in the subcommittee on information, with support from the FRG and Great Britain, responded to these arguments, and referred to a Western proposal calling for free access to all radio broadcasts.

The Basket III situation was further complicated by a Soviet bloc proposal for a preamble to the Basket III document making any agreements that might be reached in Basket III subject to the "laws and customs of the participating states." The Soviets took the position that agreement should be reached on the general principles to be contained in this preamble before drafting began on the specific provisions to follow. The Western side assumed that any principles the Soviets managed to introduce into a Basket III preamble would be caveats. The notion that national laws and customs should prevail over Basket III provisions was anathema to the Western countries. The West insisted that, on the contrary, no preamble at all was necessary for Basket III and that specific provisions should be agreed upon before the possibility of a preambular *chapeau* was considered. The resulting impasse lasted for many weeks and brought home the need for concrete Western proposals and for turning soon to actual drafting.

It was in these circumstances that the U.S. delegation lost its chief. On October 13, George S. Vest, the amiable and gifted multilateral negotiator who had led the delegation since the beginning of the preparatory talks in Helsinki, was withdrawn on one day's notice by newly appointed Secretary of State Henry Kissinger to become the press spokesman for the State Department. He was replaced by another Foreign Service officer, Davis E. Boster, who had most recently been assigned as deputy chief of mission in Warsaw.

The October War in the Middle East also occurred at this time, causing many delegates to wonder if the CSCE could continue at all. Not only did the prospect of a U.S.-Soviet confrontation recall the fragility of the detente relationship between the superpowers, but the Conference itself was at that moment receiving the contributions of the nonparticipating Mediterranean countries, Israel and the Arab states. The link between East-West relations in Europe and Arab-Israeli relations in the Middle East was underlined by the relationship of these countries to the CSCE. It is a measure of the common desire to keep the Middle East conflict out of the CSCE that the Conference continued its business as usual throughout this delicate period. It was as though the CSCE had been insulated from outside events; hardly a reference was made to the hostilities raging in the Sinai and the Golan Heights. Without breaking step the CSCE continued its debate.

The Basket III preamble issue had by this time grown into a major Conference problem. The Soviets and their allies maintained that there would have to be a preamble to Basket III, including the caveat on national laws and customs, and refused to enter a meaningful discussion of specifics until such a preamble had been agreed. The Western and neutral countries were equally adamant that no preamble at all was required, that a caveat like the one the Soviets wanted would rob Basket III of its meaning, and that the specific provisions should be negotiated first.

Another fundamental issue was posed early in this period in the subcommittee on military aspects of security: the question of what link, if any, should exist between the CSCE and the negotiations on force reductions in Central Europe (MBFR) being conducted in Vienna. The neutrals, led by Yugoslavia, Sweden, Austria, Switzerland, and Finland, sought recognition that European states not participating in arms control negotiations on Europe had the "right" to be informed of developments in such negotiations and to have their views taken into consideration.

The Soviets, who for propaganda purposes had earlier suggested inclusion of the neutrals in the MBFR talks, played up to this neutral desire, but the NATO allies participating in MBFR were opposed to any such notion. Before MBFR began, the allies had agreed that the neutrals should be excluded, since the MBFR negotiations were complex enough without them. To keep the neutrals from becoming involved, or from seeking to have their views reflected in Western MBFR positions, the allies agreed privately that information on the progress of the MBFR talks could be given to neutral European states bilaterally by national delegations in Vienna, in response to requests from individual neutrals. Several of the NATO/MBFR participants, including the United States, were adamant that no linkage be created with CSCE that would undercut the intent of this arrangement by giving the CSCE, or states participating in it, some form of oversight of the MBFR negotiations. This question remained unresolved until shortly before the conclusion of Stage II.

Two other events of note occurred during this first autumn session of Stage II: the executive secretary of the UN Economic Commission for Europe (ECE), Janez Stanovnik, addressed Committee II, the overall Committee responsible for Economic issues (Basket II), on the section of the CSCE agenda corresponding to the ECE's sphere of activity and established that organization's interest in following up the CSCE in these fields, and the Coordinating Committee held its first desultory debate on the follow-up to the Conference.

The Conference adjourned on December 14 for four weeks. When asked what he would be reporting home, a Soviet delegate said, "Hard going so far, with limited results; reasonably good prospects ahead, but Moscow should not count on completion too soon." This was the appraisal of virtually all the delegations, and it proved to be correct.

9 Those Who Are Not
Soviet Strategy and Negotiating Techniques

He who wishes to be thoroughly nice toward those who
are not at all, cannot avoid perishing sooner or later.

Machiavelli *The Prince*

Strategy

For the Soviets, the CSCE was a key step in a broad strategy to consolidate their hold on Eastern Europe and to win an additional measure of influence over Western Europe. The so-called "peace program," enunciated at the Twenty-fourth Congress of the Communist Party of the Soviet Union, was the public reflection of this strategy; it sought to convey the impression that the Soviet Union is a legitimate, peace-loving neighbor to the rest of Europe. The clear intention was to lull the West into relaxing its defense efforts while the USSR continued its massive military buildup, and to create a situation where Soviet military dominance could be used to pressure Western Europe. The CSCE was the most far-reaching, concrete initiative undertaken by the Soviets in carrying out this "peace program."

By the time the Conference was convened, however, the Soviets were feeling the pressure of time. The Communist party was obliged by its own policies to convene its Twenty-fifth Congress before the spring of 1976, and a successful CSCE was all but essential to demonstrate that the Soviet government had correctly carried out the party's "peace program." Linked to this was a plan to use the thirtieth anniversary of the end of World War II to portray that war as a colossal Soviet victory and to reestablish Soviet leadership of the European (and later worldwide) communist movement by convening a conference of European communist parties. No doubt the ill health of the general secretary of the party, Leonid Brezhnev, added to the pressures for bringing this foreign policy program to a climax at a party congress that would credit him personally with its achievement. The CSCE had long been a subject of intense personal interest and commitment for Brezhnev.

These elements meant that the Soviets were in a hurry to conclude the CSCE. When they arrived at the site of the negotiations in late August and early September of 1973, they and their allies spoke uncompromisingly of finishing the Conference before Christmas. (This line evidently convinced the Swiss hosts that the building they had set aside to house the Conference would be free at the beginning of 1974, because they reserved it for other conferences starting about that time, and the CSCE had to be shifted about to various other meeting sites in Geneva for the remainder of the negotiations.)

The Soviets wanted the Conference to produce a very brief final document, consisting almost solely of a list of principles guiding relations among states, with a central place to be given to the all-important idea of inviolability of frontiers. They also hoped to squeeze out any undesirable proposals under the other subject headings of the agenda.

To accomplish these objectives, their strategy was evidently to overwhelm the other delegations, to create an irresistible momentum to finish the negotiations, to rush through the work in a general way, and to avoid being tied down in terms of time or language to any very specific discussions or agreements. By using political pressures at the top levels of government, they hoped to obtain early commitments from Western leaders to a date for Stage III of the Conference, and thus to generate internal pressures from Western governments on their own negotiators to finish the work in time to meet the agreed schedule.

Soviet actions were aimed at carrying out this strategy. The Soviets resisted specific discussions or precise language and urged the greatest possible number of meetings. They exhorted the Conference to move ahead more rapidly with its work and belittled all efforts to evoke specifics as attempts to sidetrack the historic significance of the Conference into meaningless details. These tactics found a certain sympathy on the part of many delegates, who felt the negotiations bogging down. More importantly, the Soviets complained of what many Western leaders and politicians already suspected: that the CSCE was "haggling over words" and getting nowhere.

Techniques

The CSCE offered some interesting examples of Soviet negotiating techniques, especially those relevant to multilateral situations. The intensity of the schedule, the number and informality of negotiating contacts, the variety of perceptions among the many delegations present, and the availability of the information circulating at the Conference all made it possible to observe closely the methods of the Soviet delegates. While many of these techniques were not uniquely Soviet, taken together they provide an interesting picture of how the Soviets approach their negotiating problems; they also provide some useful lessons for future negotiators who find themselves in similar situations.

Information Gathering
An essential element of the Soviet apparat was the intelligence-gathering force. In parallel with the operational structure of the delegation, the Soviets had a division of information-collecting officials whose chain of command

gave them direct access, through the "secretary general" of the delegation, to the delegation head and his principal subordinates. These information gatherers were junior-to-middle-grade officials with a variety of linguistic abilities and specialized backgrounds, who concentrated on "corridor work." They arrived at the conference center early, engaged other delegates in casual conversations, and gradually developed personal ties with them. Senior Soviet delegation members indicated to the information-gathering force what subjects were of current interest. The information gathered was funneled back to the senior delegates during the course of the day.

Immediate availability of fresh information was the objective, and while the Soviet effort was somewhat primitive at the outset, it became highly sophisticated and efficient by the end of the CSCE. To what extent this overt effort was supplemented by covert means is difficult to know, but there were many Western delegates who believed covert techniques were also being used.

Lengthy Probing

In general, the Soviets were extremely cautious negotiators. Before entering negotiations as such, they probed Western positions carefully and over a long period of time. They did this through the wide variety of means at their disposal: formally, in committee and subcommittee meetings; more informally, in private bilateral contacts with individual Western delegates, through the information-gathering technique in casual contacts and on social occasions, and through normal diplomatic contacts in Western capitals. Only when they were satisfied that they had identified the underlying basis and had thoroughly evaluated the strength of a Western position would they enter discussion.

In addition, the Soviets on occasion probed progressively higher in the chain of command to determine the levels at which there was knowledge of—and consequently backing for—a position taken by a negotiator. Following probing of the negotiator's position, the Soviets would sound out his delegation head on the matter. Subsequently, they would raise the same issue with the responsible working-level official in the delegation's foreign ministry; then a policy-level official in the ministry; and finally, if the question were sufficiently important, with the relevant foreign minister. If the Soviets found a lack of resolve at any of these levels, or if they found that the issue was simply unknown, they would conclude that the position of the Western representative was negotiable.

Avoiding the Demandeur Role

As a correlative of this technique, the Soviets also preferred to know the Western position before exposing their own view of an issue. Wherever possible they tried to place the Western side in a *demandeur* role and to stress that as far as they were concerned, nothing at all was necessary on that particular subject. Even in cases where some agreed solution was clearly needed, as on the structure and form of the final document of the Conference, the Soviets sought to make the Western side ask and to use Western desiderata as points of leverage. Only after the Western proposal had been carefully studied would the Soviets reveal their counterposition. This would usually be in the form of a formal counterproposal, presented either by themselves or by a trusted Warsaw Pact ally, or in the form of criticisms of the Western proposal.

Dealing with My Problems First

Despite the order of presentation of proposals, the Soviets invariably insisted on dealing with their own points first. While not always successful in this effort, their position was usually that unless their problem points were resolved, negotiations could not proceed. In such a situation they would try to take no obligation whatsoever regarding what would happen to the Western points if a satisfactory agreement were reached on their own. Instead, they might hint at some undefined measure of flexibility, which they would bring forward after their own problems were solved. In the instances where for various reasons hints of this kind were accepted (e.g., when because of other considerations the Western side also wished to settle a dispute quickly), the Western side was invariably disappointed afterwards.

"What Do You Really Want?"

This favorite Soviet question, asked in a dozen different ways, was a common ploy. The Soviets would ridicule a Western proposal, explaining in detail why it would be impossible for them to accept it in any form, and then, in a seemingly forthcoming and cooperative mode, ask a Western delegate (usually privately) to tell them what was really the essence of the Western proposal, its essential point. The objective here was not to determine what was essential, but what could be dropped. If the Western delegate took the bait and said the really essential point was the one contained, for example, in paragraph four of the proposal, the Soviets would conclude that the Western delegation concerned would be willing to drop all the other points. They might get different replies from different delegations, but by adding up all the replies they might still be able to identify two or three points the Western countries would be willing to drop. They would also use any inconsistencies they found to further ridicule the Western side, which "could not even agree among themselves on what they wanted."

Finding the Most Forthcoming Westerner

The Soviets were adept at identifying through their probing efforts which Western delegations were most willing to compromise on a given subject. Once they had found the most forthcoming delegation they would seek to work with it in trying to develop "compromise" formulations that suited their positions. They succeeded in achieving this on only a few occasions, but each of them was a key point, and inevitably led to divisive recriminations among the Western delegates. Even when they did not find a real Western partner on an issue, however, the Soviets used this technique to sow dissension among the Western delegations by making the most of the differences among the Western countries' national positions.

Developing "Special Relationships"
A variation on the preceding technique was the "special relationship" gimmick. Use of this device usually followed bilateral summits or high-level visits noted for their warm and cooperative atmosphere. Referring to this atmosphere, the Soviets would approach a Western delegation and seek to develop private cooperative arrangements and strategy. As bait they would tell the Western delegation of some minor new concessions they were willing to make if they and the Western delegation, "working together," were able to bring about a "compromise" favorable to the Soviets. The Soviets would stress that the whole affair should be conducted in the utmost secrecy, on the basis of the special relationship newly established between the two countries by their leaders. The Soviets pursued this technique effectively on several occasions, sometimes using to their advantage the fact that Western delegates were not always privy to what had taken place between their own political leaders and the Soviets.

"We Great Powers"
A nuance of the special relationship theme was the "great powers" line, intended especially for the U.S. delegation. Here, the Soviets would complain to the U.S. delegation head about the pettiness of the negotiating positions of other Western allies (specific details were indeed sometimes petty, but the sum total of the petty details would be a document of either Western or communist orientation). "We great powers," the Soviets would say in effect, "should not be concerned with such minor details; we can understand the broad strategic picture, which the smaller countries involved in the CSCE are incapable of understanding." The Soviets used this line to argue for yielding to them, for example, on minor linguistic points. Despite their apparently lofty attitude, they themselves were almost never willing to yield on "minor details."

The Equally Disagreeable Counterproposal
The Soviets clearly believed offense was the best defense. When presented with a Western proposal that was extremely difficult for them to accept, they would draw up a proposal on the same subject deliberately designed to be equally discomfiting for the West. Such proposals would put forward Marxist phraseology that the Soviets knew could not be accepted by the West; in fact, they did not care whether it was accepted. Their only aim was to have on the table a proposal balancing the Western one in terms of its unacceptability,

which they could then use for debate and trading purposes to neutralize the Western proposal.

Timing of Concessions

The Soviets timed their concessions carefully, with a view not only to the negotiating situation in Geneva, but also to the view held by Western leaders of the overall development of the Conference. On a few occasions they granted concessions in one part of the CSCE as sweeteners to obtain a responsive Western attitude toward a more important Soviet objective under negotiation in another part of the CSCE. The Soviets virtually always released one or two concessions immediately prior to high-level East-West visits or Western meetings, such as NATO foreign ministers' meetings, where progress in the CSCE would be appraised. The objective was to ensure that whenever the political levels of Western governments focused on the CSCE (which they did only rarely), the latest reports would be of Soviet concessions and forward progress, thus helping to convince Western statesmen that the Summit conclusion was just around the corner.

Another common Soviet practice was to save up concessions while building on the pressures that result from a stalemate. By withholding any concessions for an inordinately long time, the Soviets led some Western delegates to conclude that any Soviet concessions at all on the subject under negotiation would be difficult, if not impossible. This creeping suspicion would add to the natural Western impatience to get on with it, so that when, after a long period of stalemate, a minimal Soviet concession was offered, the West would jump at it and be tempted to drop further demands.

Use of Procedures

The Soviets knew their rules of procedure very well and used them to maximum advantage. Minor technical points, such as the nonavailability of a text in all six language versions, were used to block discussions. The Soviets also had no qualms about using rules in opposite ways when this was advantageous to them.

No Brackets

The Soviets resisted use of the widely accepted technique of bracketing in the drafting of documents. Their position on this point was one of the curiosities of the Conference. In essence, they argued that negotiable points could be placed in brackets in joint Conference documents, but that "unacceptable" points could not be included, even in brackets, since this would be misleading and unfair to delegations opposing their inclusion. There were long theological discussions of bracketing periodically throughout the CSCE, but Soviet application of their own rule of thumb indicated that their interpretation was more a device for advancing their own positions than a fair-minded general principle.

Since points opposed by the Soviets were almost always "unacceptable," they could never, according to the Soviet view, be included.

Silence

Occasionally, the Soviets simply would not respond to a proposal they did not like. The aim of this technique was to leave the unwanted proposal pending until the CSCE was almost over, when pressures to finish the Conference could be used to squeeze out the proposal or so water it down as to render it innocuous. This technique backfired when the Soviets applied it to the Maltese position on the Mediterranean, despite the fact that virtually all the other Conference participants were also using it.

Citing Western Documents

The Soviets used their vast delegation to perform the kind of research for which no other delegation was equipped. As a result, they often had available a stock of quotations from speeches and communiques by Western leaders, which they used to respond to Western arguments. There is nothing more embarrassing than to make a point in negotiation and to have your Soviet opponent quote from a speech by your foreign minister that seems to take the opposite line.

Hinting at Hard-liners Back in Moscow

Occasionally, the Soviets would attempt to persuade Western delegates to accept a position because doing so would strengthen the hands of those in the Kremlin who favored detente in their dealings with Moscow hawks. This reasoning was, of course, advanced only in private contacts and on a "personal" basis, but it was nevertheless effective at times, especially with Western delegates who fancied themselves Sovietologists or who liked to think they were having an effect on the internal Soviet power struggle.

"Approved at the Highest Level"

A similar device was the argument that a favored phraseology could not be changed because it had already been approved at the highest level in Moscow. All diplomats know how hard it is to go back on something agreed to by a head of government, and the message conveyed was therefore a strong one. Despite the fact that the Soviets used this line fairly often, it is possible, given Brezhnev's personal interest in the CSCE, that he did approve certain key phrases.

Translation Difficulties

The Soviets at times accepted certain points in English or French while stating unequivocally that it would be impossible to translate them precisely into Russian. The sense of the Russian version they offered would invariably be quite different, usually significantly weaker. In fact, the Soviets gave the impression at times that the Russian language was an extremely limited one and that there were a large number of rather common ideas that simply could not be expressed in it. In such circumstances there is no substitute for the very best linguistic expertise. Several Western delegates spoke Russian, but it was only when the U.S. and FRG delegations brought in native-speaking Russian-language experts that arguments on this basis could be satisfactorily settled.

Intimidation

The Soviets also used a variety of personal pressures to advance their own ideas. They commonly sought to intimidate individual Western delegates who took vigorous positions the Soviets disliked. Intimidation was carried out through public ridicule, heaping abuse on a delegate or his position in an open meeting, or, usually in more private circumstances, by a sometimes unnerving display of anger, complete with threats to ruin the delegate's career. In some instances, the Soviets actually did complain about individual Western delegates to their sponsoring governments, something to which most career diplomats are extremely sensitive, even though complaints from the Soviets should in most cases be regarded as compliments.

Embarrassment

The Soviets also occasionally sought to embarrass Western delegates by criticizing their positions to their superiors. In some instances they complained to a Western delegation head before the expert had fully explained the situation to his own boss. In a few cases, they berated expert negotiators in front of their delegation leaders, using the relative seniority of the Soviet negotiators to convey the feeling that the Western experts were being petty and obstructionist.

The Steamroller

This favorite Soviet device used a combination of many of the above techniques—public ridicule, procedural rules, friendly Western delegations, and maximum pressure—to force through a specific measure. The reason this technique was occasionally successful was that the Western delegations hesitated to confront the Soviets unless the issue was clear and the Western position easily defensible. They knew that their political leaders did not want to appear to be obstructing the progress of detente.

Pressing for Early Conclusion, While Withholding Concessions

This overall Soviet strategy may seem self-contradictory; in fact, it was fully consistent. The Soviets wanted an early conclusion on their own terms, and they therefore used all the techniques available to them to bring maximum pressure for commitments to conclude the Conference, while yielding the minimum number of concessions necessary to influence the Western view.

Lessons for U.S. Negotiators

The CSCE experience showed once again that the Soviets are deeply prudent negotiators. Their overriding priorities are defensive—not to lose anything they already have, whether it be territory, military superiority, or tactical advantage. To protect their initiatives, they prepare very carefully and keep the maximum number of options open as long as possible. They are sharp traders and never give away something for nothing. Their bureaucracy permits no idle whims, personal idiosyncrasies, independent actions, or informal probes. Faced with such an adversary, our negotiators must be at least as organized, as disciplined, and as patient as the Russians. We should never offer a concession without extracting the maximum in return, delivered at the same time. Promises don't count. We should never allow ourselves to be put in a position where we must negotiate under the pressure of time. Details are important; we should treat them accordingly. And our positions should be consistent up and down the chain of command; the Soviets should not be able to get the positions of U.S. negotiators overruled simply by going to someone at a higher level. If we are as firm at summit meetings as our negotiators are when they are bound by specific instructions, the Soviets will have to deal with our positions; if we are not, the Soviets will understand that our negotiating positions are meaningless.

10   What We Mean

Differences between the U.S.
and West European Views

*The people of all Europe and, I assure you, the people of
North America, are thoroughly tired of having their hopes
raised and then shattered by empty words and unfulfilled
pledges. We had better say what we mean and mean what
we say, or we will have the anger of our citizens to answer.*

Gerald Ford Helsinki August 1, 1975

There was a difference between the American and European perceptions of the
CSCE from the beginning. The United States, deeply involved in bilateral negotiations with the USSR, relegated the CSCE to the second rank. Despite the fact
that U.S. representatives in Brussels had played a leading role in the allied
consultations that prepared the Western negotiating positions and tactics for
the Conference, as soon as the preparatory talks began in Helsinki, U.S.
prominence diminished. This was the result of several factors: first, the apparently unimportant proposals under discussion; second, the small likelihood, in
U.S. eyes, of success; third, a desire to deliberately downgrade the significance
of the CSCE for fear of raising public expectations that could not be fulfilled;
and fourth, the evident desire of the Europeans, especially the EC-Nine, to
avoid American dominance of the Western side in a negotiation which was by
definition and title a European affair.

For the Europeans, on the other hand, the CSCE presented a key and, in some
cases, unique opportunity to negotiate with the Soviets and to participate in
the movement toward detente. For a variety of reasons, each West European
government wished to demonstrate an ability to deal successfully with the
Soviets. In some countries, such as France and Italy, this was essential for
political success, while in others, such as the Scandinavian countries, Great
Britain, and the FRG, it represented an important element of a more "balanced" foreign policy. Thus, the Western Europeans, as well as the Canadians,
took the Conference more seriously than did the United States, and attributed
to it much greater significance than did the U.S. government under Presidents
Nixon and Ford.

The result was a divergence of view which grew wider during the first year of the negotiations, as the Nixon administration, anxious for new foreign policy successes, became annoyed with the slow movement of the Geneva talks. The feeling in Europe from the start of the Geneva phase was that the United States had agreed with the USSR that the Conference should be ended quickly. As evidence, the Europeans cited the language of the communique of the Nixon-Brezhnev summit in the United States, June 18–25, 1973, shortly before Stage I of the CSCE was convened: "Reflecting their continued positive attitude toward the Conference, both sides will make efforts to bring the Conference to a successful conclusion at the earliest possible time. Both sides proceed from the assumption that progress in the work of the Conference will produce possibilities for completing it at the highest level."

This reference to the possibility that the Conference would end at the Summit, coming as it did before negotiations on substance had even opened, annoyed many Europeans and made them suspicious of the U.S. attitude. These suspicions grew, and the belief lingered on that, if the United States was not pressing for an early conclusion to the Conference, it was at least not actively opposing the Soviet desire for such a conclusion, and had adopted a rather passive stance in the negotiations to accommodate the USSR. The low profile of the U.S. delegation at the Conference throughout the first year of negotiations, and the fact that the U.S. delegation had three different leaders during the first six months, seemed to support this notion.

When Kissinger and Gromyko met in Geneva on April 28–29, 1974, the communique stated only that "they reviewed the work of the CSCE. The two sides reaffirmed their positions in favor of its successful conclusion as soon as possible." This formula was sufficiently ambiguous to cover most countries' attitudes toward the Conference. However, on May 17, a report in the *New York Times* indicated that after the meeting with Gromyko, Kissinger wrote to his British and FRG colleagues to support the idea of a summit-level conclusion. A "high-ranking European" was quoted as saying, "Kissinger wanted to know how much trouble he would have with the Europeans if he comes out formally for the Summit. We are trying to explain to him that there will only be trouble."

In the spring of 1974 the United States undertook a series of actions reinforcing the impression that the Nixon administration was more interested in an early conclusion than it was in meaningful substantive results, either to provide the Watergate-weakened president with a new foreign policy spectacular or as a bargaining counter to obtain concessions from the Soviets in other fields, such as SALT or the Middle East.

Kissinger had evidently concluded that he could not openly advocate an early Summit without risking a serious split with America's West European allies. He understood from their reactions that they wanted substantive results before agreeing to the Summit. But what substantive results would be judged satisfactory was an open question. The U.S. delegation in Geneva was instructed to begin sounding out other allied delegations on acceptable results and to urge the allies to take a more "reasonable" approach to the negotiations.

The NATO foreign ministers' meeting in Ottawa on June 18–19, 1974, appeared to have resolved these differences in the conservative language of the communique:

> [The Ministers] noted that in the second stage of the Conference, which should make a thorough examination of all aspects of the Conference Agenda, the work has advanced unevenly. Some progress has been made on certain issues, but much work remains to be done, as for example on such key questions as the improvement of human contacts and the freer flow of information, as well as confidence building measures and essential aspects of the principles guiding relations between states. Ministers expressed their governments' determination to pursue the negotiations patiently and constructively in a continuing search for balanced and substantial results acceptable to all participating states. They considered that, to bring the second stage to its conclusion, these results need to be achieved in the various fields of the programme of work established by the Foreign Ministers at the first stage of the Conference in Helsinki.

However, Nixon's trip to Moscow from June 26 to July 3, 1974, produced another communique, whose terms seemed fundamentally at variance with NATO's appreciation of the CSCE just one week earlier:

> Both [the U.S. and Soviet] sides expressed their conviction that successful completion of the Conference on Security and Cooperation in Europe would be an outstanding event in the interests of establishing a lasting peace. Proceeding from this assumption the USA and the USSR expressed themselves in favor of the final stage of the conference taking place at an early date. Both sides also proceed from the assumption that the results of the negotiations will permit the conference to be concluded at the highest level, which would correspond to the historic significance of the conference for the future of Europe and lend greater authority to the importance of the conference's decisions.

This language was particularly annoying to the West Europeans because it picked up phraseology that the Soviets had used for years to describe the Conference in their propaganda. On a swing through Europe following the Nixon-Brezhnev summit, Kissinger made clear his growing impatience with the progress of the CSCE and fueled speculation that he was catering to Soviet views. In Rome, for example, he was reported by the *International Herald Tribune*, July 6–7, as having called for an end to the "theological debate" in Geneva. This same report described Kissinger as saying there was no way to move ahead with twenty-five papers on various contested points "kicking around." Since by far the largest percentage of proposals at the CSCE was Western, it was clear that this statement was critical of the NATO allies themselves.

This point of view, conflicting as it did with the most basic Western aims in the Conference and the strategy being followed by the Western countries, was deeply worrisome to many West Europeans, and Kissinger went out of his way to deny that there was a U.S.-Soviet deal to wrap up the negotiations.

At the same time, the American Secretary of State continued to urge, both privately and in public, that the Western allies determine whether any results would warrant a Summit, and what those results would be. In a March 28 press conference in London, Kissinger had said, "There hasn't been a full discussion of what results would justify a Summit, and we think that this is a discussion that now should take place among the Western nations." And as he indicated in a press conference on June 19, he again pressed for urgent allied consultations on this question during the NATO meeting in Ottawa. The West Europeans concluded that the idea of consulting on what results would justify a Summit was a device to reduce the Western negotiating position to something more "reasonable" and to confirm agreement on a summit-level meeting. They were reluctant to enter such consultations because they feared the results would put them in the position of negotiating downward from reduced demands.

Kissinger nevertheless pressed ahead during the final days before the CSCE's summer recess in July of 1974, instructing the U.S. delegation in Geneva to ask the Western allies to identify the points they considered "essential," and to suggest to the allies more "reasonable" proposals in the sensitive Basket III area. In a press conference in Moscow on July 3, Kissinger even indicated publicly that "discussions [of essential Western demands] have begun in Brussels, and we hope to be able to have at least a Western answer to this in the relatively near future." A United Press International story in September asserted: "The United States, in a split with its European allies, is backing the Soviet wish for a quick finish to the European security conference." This was quickly denied by the State Department.

The reluctance of the Western Europeans to be drawn into a process of identifying what they considered essential in the negotiations sidetracked this exercise and slowed it down until it eventually fizzled out in the NATO consultation process during the autumn of 1974. By the time more "reasonable" Basket III proposals had been agreed among the allies, the negotiations had moved forward enough to make them timely.

The communique of the Brezhnev-Ford summit in Vladivostok on November 23–24 echoed the Nixon-Brezhnev language, stating: "Both sides concluded that there is a possibility for its [the CSCE's] early successful conclusion. They proceed from the assumption that the results achieved in the course of the conference will permit its conclusion at the highest level. . . ."

Once again, this language contrasted with appraisals of the CSCE among allied leaders. The language of the communique of the ministerial meeting of the North Atlantic Council on December 12-13 was typical; it noted that "important questions remain to be resolved." This guarded approach was also evident in communiques at the presidential level. At the conclusion of West German Chancellor Helmut Schmidt's visit to Washington December 5-6, the joint communique stated: "Both sides expressed the hope that the CSCE would soon complete its initial consideration of texts dealing with all items on the agenda. It would then be possible to enter the final stage of the negotiations. They agreed that certain progress had recently been made. . . . They noted, however, that important texts still remain to be agreed. . . ."

The effect of the divergence of view between Washington and its European friends was significant both for the West Europeans, who had to redraw their estimates of what might be possible in the CSCE, and for the Soviets, who, aware of the consultations being conducted among the NATO allies, waited for the new Western positions to be tabled before making any further concessions of their own. In addition, the press took its cue from Kissinger's public remarks, which appeared to ridicule the number of Western proposals, especially in Basket III, as well as the detailed negotiations required to obtain phraseology which would meet Western standards.

This public view of the CSCE as a somewhat silly haggle among diplomats dominated much of the American press throughout the Conference and was a principal cause of the negative public reaction in the United States when it was later announced that the president would attend an unprecedented thirty-five-nation Summit to sign the Final Act. The press then asked why, if the whole affair had amounted to little more than genteel arguments over the placement of commas, was it necessary to send the president of the United States to approve the outcome. In short, belittling the Conference was inconsistent with the continued acceptance by the president of the possibility of a Summit conclusion. The West Europeans saw basic similarities between the views of the United States and the USSR, while they themselves were working hard to introduce as much substance as possible into the documents under negotiation.

The difference in appreciation of the importance of the CSCE, of the need for a meaningful final document, and of the desirability of an early Summit conclusion faded gradually during the autumn and winter of 1974-75. Nixon's resignation and the need for President Ford to work into his new responsibilities removed considerable pressure for an early conclusion. It was unlikely that the new president would want to risk tarnishing his image by making his first official trip abroad to attend a Conference that was a favorite communist project. In addition, the reactions of the West European allies to U.S. pressure for winding up the Conference had been sharp, and evidently convinced Kissinger that a continuation in this direction risked deeply alienating our traditional allies.

Moreover, at the beginning of 1975, new factors combined with these to bring the U.S. attitude toward the csce back into harmony with that of the other Western participants. There was a growing skepticism among the American public of the whole concept of detente. While this skepticism did not change the majority view that it was necessary to work out a modus vivendi with the Soviets, it did produce a strong current of thought that the United States should deal more toughly with the Soviets in all areas of negotiation. This growing tendency was reflected in the White House and rubbed off on csce, along with many other East-West projects.

Later in the spring, the debacle of the final defeat of South Vietnam produced a clear toughening of the U.S. attitude in the csce, both as one of several signals to the Soviets and in order to assure the best possible results for what was by that time definitely shaping up as a Summit conclusion.

In a press conference on May 24, 1975, Kissinger demonstrated how far his own views had evolved: "The date for the European Security Conference does not depend on the United States. [It] will be determined by the negotiations that are now going on in Geneva in which there are a number of issues still outstanding on confidence building measures, on human contacts and on post-conference machinery. In each of these the West has put forward certain initiatives and is either awaiting the responses or analyzing responses that it has just received. The date of the security conference cannot be settled independent of the progress of the negotiations, and the best way to speed that conference would be if the Soviet Union considered carefully some of these considerations that we had put forward."

In the final months of the negotiations, the U.S. position remained generally very close to that of its allies and contributed measurably to the tough, unified Western front that made it possible to reach acceptable compromises with the Soviets on the remaining Conference issues.

Part III
1974   Frontiers

11   A Tale of Aspirations
Detente Slows as Presidents Change

History is a tale of efforts that failed, of aspirations that weren't realized, of wishes that were fulfilled and then turned out to be different from what one expected.

Henry Kissinger Interview with James Reston
The New York Times October 13, 1974

The unraveling of the Nixon presidency, as the Watergate investigation advanced, affected all aspects of American foreign policy in 1974, but it had a particular effect on U.S. relations with the Soviet Union, which suffered their most important setback since the beginning of detente.

The year began with a U.S. foreign policy success: on January 18, Egypt and Israel signed a disengagement agreement at Kilometer 101 on the Cairo-Suez road, largely as a result of Henry Kissinger's shuttle diplomacy. This accord was followed later in the spring by a disengagement agreement between Israel and Syria, signed in Geneva May 31, which permitted President Nixon to make a triumphal visit to the Middle East in June.

The Middle East crisis and its impact on oil supplies put energy at the top of the U.S. agenda and prompted the president on January 9 to invite the major industrial countries to a conference on energy in Washington February 11–13. Despite differences in view between the United States and France, the negotiations set in motion by this conference eventually produced the Agreement on an International Energy Program and the International Energy Agency.

These actions reflected a more general shifting of priorities toward a preoccupation with the state of Western economies, as the first effects of the post-1973 economic downturn began to be felt. Virtually all Western statesmen reflected this concern in their public statements, calling attention to the problem and the urgent need to find solutions.

But solutions were elusive, especially at a time when many political changes were taking place in the Western nations. In addition to Nixon's gathering Watergate difficulties in the United States, President Pompidou of France died on April 2, and West German Chancellor Brandt resigned on May 6, opening transitional periods in two other major Western powers. Pompidou was succeeded by Valery Giscard d'Estaing, who was elected on May 19, and Brandt by Helmut Schmidt on May 16. In Britain, the Conservative government of Edward Heath was replaced in March by a Labor government led by Harold Wilson. Portugal entered a period of turmoil on April 25, with the beginning of a revolution that would eventually lead to democratic government. And in Greece the regime of the colonels was replaced in July, when Constantin Caramanlis returned to Athens to become prime minister.

Changes of government in Portugal and Greece permitted NATO, in its twenty-fifth anniversary year, to affirm more strongly than ever that it stands for democratic, representative government, and this point was made in the Declaration on Atlantic Relations (also called the Ottawa Declaration), which was approved at the NATO foreign ministers' meeting in Ottawa, June 18–19.

This landmark document was the final result of the "Year of Europe" initiative of 1973, and helped to put into perspective many aspects of the evolving transatlantic relationship. The declaration asserted that the North Atlantic treaty provided to its members the security that had made possible the pursuit of detente with the USSR. "In Europe," the declaration stated, the objective of the allies "continues to be the pursuit of understanding and co-operation with every European country."

The Ottawa Declaration helped to smooth over residual U.S.–West European bitterness about failures in consultation and mutual support. Following approval of the declaration at the NATO twenty-fifth anniversary summit in Brussels on June 26, presidential spokesman Ron Ziegler described it as "a recognition that no member of the Alliance should consider taking any actions or action affecting the Alliance without seeking the support and understanding of its members."

The Ottawa Declaration also gave approval to efforts by many Western governments to advance detente, including through the CSCE. The declaration welcomed "the progress that has been achieved on the road towards detente and harmony among nations, and that a Conference of 35 countries of Europe and North America is now seeking to lay down guidelines designed to increase security and cooperation in Europe."

Relations among the European states—even among the NATO allies—were not consistently harmonious, however. One of the more politically sensitive and time-consuming foreign policy problems of 1974 was centered on Cyprus, and began on July 15 with a coup d'etat against President Makarios by the Greek-controlled Cypriot National Guard. This coup provoked an invasion on July 20 by 30,000 Turkish troops, who in August expanded the area under their control to include the northern third of the island. The Cyprus issue was especially complex for the United States because of the significant program of American military assistance to Turkey, and that country's key position on NATO's extreme southeastern flank. The Turkish actions stirred a domestic debate that absorbed much of the administration's attention in the summer and fall of 1974.

But the most significant development of 1974 was not in the area of foreign policy, though it affected virtually all foreign policy issues. It was the mounting Watergate scandal and its eventual impact on President Nixon.

At the opening of the year, Nixon pressed ahead with his now-familiar objective of building a "new structure of peace." This, he said in his state of the union speech on January 30, "has been and will remain my first priority and the chief legacy I hope to leave from the eight years of my Presidency." He argued that the nation might never again have the same opportunity to create such a structure. Juxtaposed with this image was Nixon's evident determination to ride out the Watergate storm: "And I want you to know," he said in a postscript to his state of the union address to the two houses of Congress, "that I have no intention whatever of ever walking away from the job that the people elected me to do."

Events, however, were taking their course and would make it impossible for Nixon to stick to this pledge. On April 28, former Attorney General Mitchell, former senior White House staff members Haldeman and Ehrlichman, and others with close White House links were indicted for their role in the cover-up of the Watergate burglary. In May several other former White House staffers were convicted on Watergate-related charges.

As more information became available from the court cases involving his subordinates, the likelihood of the president's involvement was also more apparent. President Nixon himself came squarely into jeopardy on July 24, when the House Judiciary Committee began a nationally televised debate on the impeachment of the president. On the same day the Supreme Court unanimously upheld Judge Sirica's ruling that sixty-four tapes of White House conversations should be provided to Special Prosecutor Jaworski. From July 27 to 30 three articles of impeachment were approved by the Judiciary Committee, and debate in the full House was scheduled to begin by August 19.

At the beginning of August, President Nixon released the transcripts of three conversations with Haldeman on June 23, 1972, just six days after the Watergate break-in; these transcripts suggested that the president's knowledge of the matter was greater than he had later claimed. Nixon apparently was hoping to win an impeachment trial in the Senate, but on August 7 the leading Republican senators met with him to convey the message that he would badly lose such a trial. Faced with this reality, Richard Nixon on August 8 announced his resignation to a stunned nation. And on August 9, Gerald Ford, who had been appointed to the vice presidency only the year before, was sworn in as the thirty-eighth president of the United States.

To his credit, Ford made every effort to reassure the country and the world of the stability of U.S. policies. "We stand by our commitments," he told a joint session of Congress on August 12, "and we live up to our responsibilities in our formal alliances, in our friendships, and in our improving relations with potential adversaries." Perhaps most importantly, Ford announced that he would retain Kissinger in the dual role of Secretary of State and national security adviser, thus ensuring that a familiar figure would be carrying through on the previous administration's foreign policy.

Many people were surprised by the steadiness of American governmental institutions in this period of domestic crisis; this stability reflected conscious efforts by many political leaders. As Kissinger told the American Legion National Convention on August 20, 1974, in Miami, Florida: "The leaders of both parties in Congress deserve the nation's gratitude for having insulated our foreign and security policies from our recent domestic travails." But Kissinger later admitted that conducting the nation's foreign policy during the transition had not been easy. He was quoted in the December 18, 1974, *Newsweek*: "July to October was a period in which we could not act with decisiveness. Every negotiation was getting more difficult because it involved the question of whether we could, in fact, carry out what we were negotiating. Secondly, we were not in a position to press matters that might involve serious domestic disputes. And I think this affected to some extent the summit in Moscow in July. But it affected many other things in more intangible ways."

In fact, relations with the Soviet Union had peaked, though they were still benefitting from the momentum created during 1972 and 1973. The February 13 expulsion by the Soviets of dissident writer Aleksandr Solzhenitsyn seemed to indicate that the Soviets were taking a more humane attitude in such matters. After all, Solzhenitsyn could have been imprisoned or sent to a labor camp. Within the CSCE, the event was seen in this light. But his expulsion to the West also had the effect of calling attention to Soviet human rights practices in general and of crystallizing Western, particularly American, opinion on the subject.

When Nixon visited Moscow June 27–July 3, about one month before his resignation, his preference was still to deal with human-rights-related issues in private. The administration's language describing the objectives of detente with the Soviets increasingly alluded to the human rights issue, but in such muted tones that it did not satisfy human rights activists. In defining the president's objectives for detente on June 26 in Brussels, for example, Press Secretary Ziegler listed the aims of curbing the nuclear arms race, easing confrontations, and building East-West trade and cooperation which, he added, "may gradually ameliorate conditions in the East."

It was clear during Nixon's second Moscow visit that detente had lost its earlier dynamism. Nixon's position was weakened by the Watergate affair, and he could not afford to enter agreements that would provoke additional domestic controversy. The application of the SALT accord had not been fully satisfactory, and there were complaints of violations. The near-confrontation between the two superpowers over the Middle East, with the worldwide alert of U.S. forces, had made American officials more wary than before. And the inability of the U.S. administration to carry through on the 1972 U.S.-Soviet trade agreement provision on the granting of Most Favored Nation (MFN) tariff treatment left the Soviets dissatisfied with the benefits they were deriving from the relationship with Washington.

The results of the second Moscow summit reflected the more limited possibilities: a protocol reducing the number of antimissile sites permitted under the Antiballistic Missile Systems Treaty from two to one; a treaty on the limitation of underground nuclear weapons tests; and extension of bilateral cooperation to a number of relatively uncontroversial fields. Yet Nixon maintained his positive public attitude toward relations with the Soviets. "With this growing network of agreements," he said when he arrived back in the United States on July 3, "we are creating new habits of cooperation and new patterns of consultation, and we are also giving the people of the Soviet Union, as well as our own people in the United States, not just a negative but a positive stake in peace."

Following Nixon's resignation, Kissinger worked hard to ensure continuity in American policy toward the Soviet Union. In his August 20 speech to the American Legion National Convention, shortly after President Ford had been sworn in, Kissinger confirmed that the policies he had initiated would continue: "We have begun but not completed the journey from confrontation to cooperation, from coexistence to community. We are determined to complete that journey." Kissinger's visit to Moscow October 23–27 helped to ensure that relations were still on track and produced a surprise announcement that President Ford would meet Brezhnev in Vladivostok in November.

The Ford-Brezhnev meeting in the Soviet far east occurred following stops by the new American president in Japan and Korea. The Vladivostok summit, November 23–24, at first appeared promising. It confirmed that both the United States and the USSR intended to continue the relationship they had established. The joint communique signed November 24 stated: "The United States of America and the Soviet Union reaffirmed their determination to develop further their relations in the direction defined by the fundamental joint decisions and basic treaties and agreements between the two states in recent years . . . so that the process of improving relations between [them] will continue without interruption and will become irreversible."

The most important concrete result of the meeting was the joint U.S.-Soviet statement on the principles of a new SALT agreement; in addition, Brezhnev was invited to visit the United States in 1975. But times had changed, and this U.S.-Soviet summit turned out to be a disappointment. The new SALT agreement did not come to fruition, and Brezhnev never returned to the United States.

The root problem in the U.S.-Soviet relationship was human rights, and it was steadily growing as a domestic political issue in America. The debate had focused for more than a year on the relationship between granting of MFN trading status to the USSR, as promised in the 1972 trade agreement between the two countries, and the problem of restrictions on emigration from the Soviet Union. The proposed Trade Reform Act of 1973 would have given the president authority to grant MFN to the USSR, but an amendment proposed by Democratic Senator Henry M. Jackson of Washington and Democratic Representative Charles A. Vanik of Ohio prohibited granting MFN to communist regimes that restrict emigration. To find a way out, Kissinger had begun a series of sensitive negotiations with the Soviets on the one hand and key members of Congress on the other.

Kissinger, according to his testimony before the Senate Committee on Finance, December 3, 1974, discussed the emigration issue with Gromyko in Geneva in April 1974, in Cyprus in May, and in Moscow in July. As a result of these contacts, an exchange of letters between Kissinger and Senator Jackson was agreed, describing their understanding of what the Soviets might do in this area. The letters were exchanged on October 18, and many Congressmen thought the problem had been resolved; a waiver could now be granted so that the Soviets could receive MFN for an eighteen-month period, to be renewed on an annual basis.

But, during Kissinger's October visit to Moscow, Gromyko handed him a letter rejecting this approach: "When clarifying the actual state of affairs in response to your request, we emphasized that the question as such was entirely within the internal competence of our state. We gave a warning at that time that in this matter we had acted and would continue to act strictly in conformity with our present legislation on this subject."

On December 3, Kissinger warned in testimony before the Senate Committee on Finance that making a public issue of Soviet emigration practices would be self-defeating: "We believed, based on repeated Soviet statements and experience, that making this issue a subject of state-to-state relations might have an adverse effect on emigration from the USSR, as well as jeopardize the basic relationship which had made the steadily rising emigration possible in the first place."

As foreseen, the Soviets on December 18 publicly denounced the Jackson-Vanik amendment as "gross interference in the Soviet Union's internal affairs," and as contrary to the agreed principles of U.S.-Soviet relations and the terms of the bilateral trade agreement itself. The Soviet news agency Tass said the terms were "flatly rejected as unacceptable in leading circles in the USSR." Evidently thinking that the Soviet stance was solely intended for face-saving, Congress nevertheless passed the Trade Reform Act with the Jackson-Vanik amendment and the eighteen-month waiver for the USSR, and it was approved by President Ford on January 3, 1975. On January 10 the Soviets formally notified the United States that they would not put the 1972 trade agreement into effect because of the unacceptable conditions Congress had attached to it.

In philosophizing over this affair in a December 18 interview in *Newsweek*, Kissinger said, "There is no legal agreement we can make with the Soviet

Union that we can enforce. Whether the Soviet Union permits emigration depends on the importance they attach to their relationship with the United States and therefore on the whole context of the East-West relationship." These thoughts, and this episode, were also prophetic for the CSCE experience.

12 Those Who Must Negotiate
The Question of Germany

*Those who conduct a war are also those who must
negotiate to end it, for each is master of his own
interests, and only he can dispose of them.*

Hugo Grotius *The Law of War and Peace*

The fundamental argument against viewing the CSCE as a peace conference, and its Final Act as a peace treaty, is that the Second World War was with Germany, and a peace treaty, following the dictum of Grotius, should also be with Germany. Yet "Germany" no longer exists, and in its place there are two Germanies, which are ideological enemies and whose historical perspectives and objectives are profoundly different. There is no *interlocuteur valable* for the negotiation of a peace with "Germany," and until that "Germany" can be represented at the negotiating table, there can be no real peace treaty.

The absence of a "Germany" with which to negotiate also strengthens the theory that the Final Act of the CSCE was a form of tacit peace treaty, which implicitly concluded the war by accepting its results. Since there is little likelihood that it will be possible to negotiate with "Germany" at any time in the foreseeable future, the CSCE stands as a valid existing substitute for an explicit treaty of peace. Including the two Germanies among thirty-three other states was a way—in fact, the only way—of obscuring the fact that "Germany" had accepted the Conference results.

Whether or not the Final Act forms a tacit peace treaty, that essential non-participant—"Germany"—cast a long shadow over the Conference, a shadow which touched many aspects of the negotiations. To accommodate the ambiguities of the present German situation, and the views of the two German states themselves, the Conference twisted and turned through some labyrinthine problems.

To begin with, the basic objectives of the two German states with regard to each other were diametrically opposed. The German Democratic Republic was asserting through the CSCE its full, complete, and final independence, and the irreversibility of its communist form of government. "The German Democratic Republic would welcome it," said Otto Winzer, GDR foreign minister, at Stage I, "if the binding recognition under international law of the territorial realities that emerged from the Second World War and postwar developments in Europe were confirmed multilaterally by this Conference."

The Federal Republic of Germany, on the other hand, while recognizing the independence and equality of the GDR, wished to hold open the possibility of future German reunification. As Foreign Minister Walter Scheel said during the first stage of the Conference, "It is the political aim of the Federal Republic of Germany to help create a state of peace in Europe in which the German nation can regain its unity in free self-determination."

The German situation was also a central concern of the wartime allies—the United States, USSR, Great Britain, and France—who retain rights and responsibilities in Germany as a whole, and whose conquest and occupation of Germany is the foundation of the present-day status of the city of Berlin. The three Western powers supported the West German attitude in the negotiations, while the Soviets sought in CSCE to add to the barriers to eventual German reunification. For the USSR, acceptance of present-day frontiers in Europe meant the permanent division of Germany, and thus the elimination of the possibility of one day facing a new military threat from a united German nation.

In view of the sympathy and support that the two Germanies and the four powers could expect to receive from their allies, issues relating to Germany and Berlin were treated with great care. Although it was never mentioned publicly, and rarely discussed even in private, all of the delegates at the Conference realized that the CSCE was, in fact, about Germany, and that it would bear importantly on the status of that divided nation in the future.

The Existing Situation

To understand developments relating to Germany in the Conference, it is necessary to review briefly the political and legal situation of Germany at the outset of the CSCE, particularly three documents, sets of documents, or doctrines that relate most closely to the negotiations in the CSCE itself.

Four-Power Rights and Responsibilities

In the absence of a formal peace treaty, "Germany"—as opposed to the FRG or the GDR—remains a conquered nation, whose last sovereign act as a single and independent state was the signing of an unconditional surrender at Berlin in the early hours of the morning of May 9, 1945. The arrangements among the four occupying powers are based first on this unconditional surrender and the rights of conquest that it implies; second, on agreements reached among themselves at Yalta and Potsdam; and third, on practices that have grown up since the beginning of the occupation. Although the FRG and the GDR are now fully independent states, and the four-power rights and responsibilities thus have a greatly reduced significance on their territories, the situation with regard to Berlin is quite different. There, governing authority still depends on the four powers, and although the GDR has sought to incorporate East Berlin increasingly into the East German state, the rights and responsibilities of the four wartime victors still apply throughout Berlin, East and West. A modus vivendi has evolved, based on these rights and responsibilities and on a number of negotiated agreements: the FRG treaties with Moscow and Warsaw, the Quadripartite Agreement on Berlin, the basic treaty between the FRG and the GDR, and the Quadripartite Declaration of November 1972, on the occasion of the entry of the two Germanies into the United Nations. The working out of a satisfactory modus vivendi for Berlin, in the form of the Quadripartite Agreement, was a precondition of the NATO allies for entering the CSCE. The status of the city nevertheless remains ambiguous. East Berlin is being welded progressively to the GDR, while West Berlin has certain links to the FRG and certain attributes of a separate geopolitical entity.

Quadripartite rights and responsibilities are essential to the security and economic viability of West Berlin. It is a garrison of British, French, and American troops that would defend the city if it were attacked, since no FRG troops are permitted there. Physical access for the troops of the Western allies and their equipment is necessary to maintain this garrison. Similarly, access to the FRG is essential to the physical survival of West Berlin: food, fuel, and other products must be brought in and goods and services exported. All of this activity takes place through and across the territory of the GDR, a sovereign state except in relation to the rights and responsibilities of the nations that conquered "Germany" during the Second World War.

Prior to the opening of the CSCE, and at least partly because the Soviets were so interested in clearing the way for the beginning of the Conference, the Quadripartite Agreement on Berlin was negotiated; it was signed on September 3, 1971, and took effect in June 1972. This accord formalized a number of practical improvements in the status of Berlin, and served to reaffirm the more fundamental and far-reaching rights and responsibilities that the four powers had exercised since the war, and that were the basis for the agreement. These rights remain valid.

It was regarded as essential by the three Western powers and the FRG to avoid any downgrading of four-power rights and responsibilities through the CSCE. Since the Conference was not to produce a legal document, accomplishment of the objective of maintenance of four-power rights was primarily a political task, which entailed making it clear that these rights were unaffected by the CSCE. To do this, the Bonn Group powers undertook repeated clarifications and statements for the record. The first was made in Helsinki during the preparatory discussions, and this was repeated at the opening of the Stage II negotiations in Geneva. The statement entered into the record by the French delegate, and concurred in by the British and U.S. delegates, referred to and closely paralleled a similar disclaimer used at the time of entry into the United

Nations of the two German states. The statement read as follows: "As we participate in the work of the Conference on a Declaration of Principles, I would like to mention that joining in such a Declaration can in no way affect the rights and responsibilities of the Four Powers and the corresponding, related Quadripartite agreements, decisions and practices referred to in the Quadripartite Declaration of 9th November 1972."

However, this was not considered completely adequate for the full protection of four-power rights, especially since the Final Act contained strongly worded principles on the sovereign equality and territorial integrity of states, which could have been read as overriding such four-power rights as those permitting access to West Berlin. Language indicating that pre-existing rights and responsibilities would be unaffected by the results of the CSCE was needed in the Final Act. For this reason, the three Western powers (Britain, France, United States), with full support from the FRG and the acquiescence of the USSR (and, less willingly, the GDR), proposed inclusion of disclaimer language in the text of the Final Act. They wanted a "saving clause" that would clearly indicate the intact preservation of quadripartite rights.

This proposal was one of the most controversial of the Conference. Since it could not mention Germany or Berlin (this would have strongly implied limited sovereignty for the FRG and the GDR), the saving clause had to be phrased in a general way. Such generally applicable language was read by many delegations as implying acceptance also of the Brezhnev Doctrine that the sovereignty of communist states is limited by the overriding responsibility to perpetuate communism. The initial four-power proposal, for inclusion in the text of the tenth principle, was as follows: "The participating States note that the present [document] cannot and will not affect their rights, obligations or responsibilities nor the treaties, agreements or arrangements in conformity with international law which reflect them, previously entered into by those States or which concern them."

This language was strongly opposed by several neutral states, as well as Romania and many of the NATO allies. The mention of "responsibilities" of states and the phrase, "or which concern them," were particularly objectionable, since they seemed to imply obligations even in the absence of specific undertakings by the states themselves. Following intense negotiations, however, a phrase was accepted on July 5, 1975, which appeared to meet the needs of the German situation without recognizing the Brezhnev Doctrine. While this language is ambiguous, its purpose is political, not legal, and it was deemed sufficient to protect those rights on which Berlin depends: "The Participating States, paying due regard to the principles above and, in particular, to the first sentence of the tenth principle, 'Fulfilment in good faith of obligations under international law,' note that the present Declaration does not affect their rights and obligations, nor the corresponding treaties and other agreements and arrangements" (FA 72).

This saving clause, however, arguably applied only to the declaration of principles, and the FRG was concerned that the other, more concrete benefits of the CSCE might not be applicable to residents of West Berlin. The language of many sections of the Final Act refers to the citizens, firms, or other entities of the "participating states," and since the relationship of West Berlin to the FRG is subject to differing views, it could have been argued in the future that the document was not intended to cover persons or entities from West Berlin. To plug this possible loophole, the FRG proposed a clause that would extend the benefits of the CSCE "throughout Europe." This clause was known among delegates as the "Andorra clause" until the French justifiably protested this misnomer. (Andorra was adequately covered by the CSCE; its sovereignty has since 1607 resided jointly in the chief of state of France and the Spanish bishop of Urgel.) The "all-Europe" clause was accepted in July of 1975 as part of the opening phrases of the Final Act (FA 5).

An additional safeguard was added at the last moment with the objective of recording the four Bonn Group powers' interpretation of the Final Act's disclaimer language. In the Stage III speeches of the leaders of the three Western powers with responsibilities for Germany, the following phrase was included: "Subject to quadripartite rights and responsibilities, the Government of the UK [France, the U.S.] considers that the documents emerging from the Conference relate also to Berlin." This phrase was acknowledged and welcomed by West German Chancellor Schmidt in his speech to indicate the agreement of the Federal Republic.

The "Enemy States" Articles of the UN Charter
The United Nations Charter, drafted and approved in the immediate postwar period, contains the following articles:

> *Article 53* (1). The Security Council shall, where appropriate, utilize such regional arrangements or agencies for enforcement action under its authority. But no enforcement action shall be taken under regional arrangements or by regional agencies without the authorization of the Security Council, with the exception of measures against any enemy state, as defined in paragraph (2) of this Article, provided for pursuant to Article 107 or in regional arrangements directed against renewal of aggressive policy on the part of any such state, until such time as the Organization may, on request of the Governments concerned, be charged with the responsibility for preventing further aggression by such a state. (2). The term enemy state as used in paragraph (1) of this Article applies to any state which during the Second World War has been an enemy of any signatory of the present charter.

Article 107 Nothing in the present Charter shall invalidate or preclude action, in relation to any state which during the Second World War has been an enemy of any signatory to the present Charter, taken or authorized as a result of that war by the Governments having responsibility for such action.

These two articles are known together as the "enemy states clauses," and their existence was at the root of certain problems during the CSCE. Among the states participating in the CSCE, the two Germanies, Austria, Italy, Hungary, Romania, and Finland might have construed these clauses as applying to themselves until peace treaties ending the war had been signed. However, the status with regard to peace treaties was somewhat different in each case. Clearly, there was no peace treaty in the case of the two Germanies. In the other cases, peace treaties existed in one form or another, but both Romania and Italy shared to a certain extent the strong desire of the two Germanies to avoid reemphasizing these articles in the language of the CSCE Final Act. For the FRG, this was an especially delicate problem, since the West Germans were well aware that the enemy states clauses gave support to the claims of the three Western powers to the right of free access to the city of Berlin, a claim they had no interest in undermining.

Yet, most participants in the CSCE recognized that the United Nations Charter, the Declaration on Friendly Relations, and other UN documents, such as the Universal Declaration of Human Rights, were basic points of reference for the work of the Conference, and should thus be cited in the CSCE texts to place the documents produced in the broader context of world developments. This was, in fact, unavoidable, but any reference to the United Nations Charter immediately posed the problem of the enemy states clauses. While this may seem like a drafting problem over a point of detail, it raised fundamental issues, particularly the question of the relationship of the CSCE to the United Nations, to established international law, and to the world community. It also raised the question of whether the CSCE Final Act itself was to be accepted as a surrogate peace treaty, thereby ending the applicability of the enemy states clauses by meeting the condition of Article 107. For the four powers with rights in Germany the enemy states clauses provided an additional legal basis for those rights, while for the Romanians they represented yet another excuse that might some day be invoked by the Soviet Union to justify intervention in Romania.

The two Germanies and Romania were largely successful in eliminating references in the CSCE texts to the UN Charter as a whole. All such references in the Final Act, and there are several, are qualified in some way, except one, which states simply that the principles adopted in the CSCE are "in conformity with" the Charter of the United Nations (FA 21).

The FRG's Eastern Treaties

During the years immediately preceding the convening of the CSCE, the FRG, as part of Chancellor Willy Brandt's policy of ostpolitik, concluded treaties with the Soviet Union and Poland recognizing the postwar frontiers of those countries. In addition, the FRG concluded a basic treaty with the GDR, recognizing the East German state and its frontiers, and establishing a modus vivendi for relations between the two German states. A year later another Eastern treaty was signed between the FRG and Czechoslovakia. The language of these treaties with regard to frontiers is of some interest here:

> *FRG-Soviet Treaty (August 12, 1970)*
> They undertake to respect without restriction the territorial integrity of all States in Europe within their present frontiers;
>
> They declare that they have no territorial claims against anybody nor will assert such claims in the future;
>
> They regard today and shall in future regard the frontiers of all States in Europe as inviolable such as they are on the date of signature of the present Treaty, including the Oder-Neisse line which forms the western frontier of the People's Republic of Poland and the frontier between the Federal Republic of Germany and the German Democratic Republic.
>
> *FRG-Polish Treaty (December 7, 1970)*
> They reaffirm the inviolability of their existing boundaries now and in the future and undertake to respect each other's territorial integrity without qualification.
>
> They declare that they have no territorial claims whatever against each other and will not raise such claims in the future, either.
>
> *FRG-GDR Treaty (December 21, 1972)*
> They reaffirm the inviolability now and in the future of the frontier existing between them and undertake fully to respect each other's territorial integrity.
>
> *FRG-Czechoslovak Treaty (December 11, 1973)*
> In conformity with the objectives and principles defined above, the FRG and the Socialist Republic of Czechoslovakia reaffirm the inviolability of their common frontier, now and in the future, and undertake reciprocally to respect without restriction each other's territorial integrity.
>
> They declare that they have no territorial claim one against the other and that they will formulate no such claim in the future.

Taken together, these treaties constituted formal acceptance by the FRG of the frontiers of the GDR, Poland, the USSR, and Czechoslovakia that resulted from the Second World War. The document to be produced by the CSCE was not to have the status or force of a treaty, and it could not, therefore, add to or modify this acceptance. However, the special role of the CSCE as a kind of substitute peace conference made the West Germans uneasy that its concluding document would appear to place the final seal on the division of Germany. Also, and perhaps more importantly, by the time the Final Act was ready for signature, the political situation in West Germany had evolved considerably. Brandt was no longer in office; his departure had been soured by a spy case that underlined the less harmonious aspects of the FRG's relations with the East; Brandt's successor, Helmut Schmidt, was more pragmatic and less inclined toward detente for its own sake; public opinion had grown increasingly skeptical about the benefits of ostpolitik; and the opposition Christian Democrats were gaining strength.

For all these reasons, the FRG was especially sensitive to the language on frontiers that would be adopted by the CSCE, and insisted that such language should clearly keep open the possibility of future German reunification. In practical terms, this meant that the language on frontiers adopted by the CSCE should be at least as favorable to the FRG viewpoint as the language on this subject in the FRG's Eastern treaties. In view of the attitudes of the Soviet Union and the GDR, negotiation of this language promised to be extremely difficult, but it was central to the entire CSCE, and without a result that would be acceptable to all concerned, it was clear from the outset that the CSCE would fail.

13 The Application of Wills

Inviolability of Frontiers Is Agreed, January–April 1974

Every result, however small, will be progress, for it will be evidence of the application of our wills to a common purpose.

Michel Jobert Helsinki July 4, 1973

Although most delegates returned to Geneva in January of 1974 with a conviction that Stage II would be completed in the spring for Stage III in July, just one year after Stage I, the first days of the new session quickly revealed that the old disputes still hovered over the Conference. Each subcommittee in turn took the decision to enter the "drafting stage," thus closing down the "general debate" on which the Western countries had insisted and which had resulted in several months of delay. Somewhat fewer scheduled meetings took place, but these were supplemented by informal gatherings where the more serious business was transacted. The EC-Nine and NATO caucuses agreed early in January to table all their draft texts as soon as possible, in order to provide full material for the drafting process. But the transition from debate to drafting was often difficult to make, no delegation had dramatically new instructions, and the differences between the Eastern and Western approaches remained unchanged. Discussion continued as before, with the difference that it was now focused on actual texts.

In February the U.S. delegation received its third chief—Bud Sherer, the accredited American ambassador to Czechoslovakia. It was thought at the time he would need to spend only a few months in Geneva to wrap up the CSCE, and that he could therefore retain his full-time job in Prague.

One of the first casualties of the new year was the Swiss proposal for establishment of a system for the peaceful settlement of disputes in Europe. The Soviets launched an attack on the proposal in late January, and the Swiss correctly understood this to mean that it could not be approved at the Conference. From that point onward, the Swiss concentrated on negotiation of a mandate for a future meeting of experts to continue discussion of the idea of a peaceful settlement mechanism.

It was also during this period that differences among the NATO allies on questions relating to military confidence-building measures began to create a certain awkwardness, with the United States opposed to the idea of giving advance notification of major military movements (as opposed to maneuvers), which was backed by most other NATO states. There were also differences between the other allies and some NATO flank countries who wanted to include naval and amphibious maneuvers among those that would be subject to notification.

The southern Europeans pressed to allow the nonparticipating Mediterranean states to return to the Conference for questions and further explanations of their earlier written contributions. This idea was strongly opposed by the Soviets and viewed with quiet anxiety by many other CSCE participants, but was nonetheless accepted, since acceptance appeared to be the least problematical course of action.

Meanwhile, Basket III negotiations were stalled by continuing Soviet insistence that a preamble should be drafted before beginning work on substantive provisions.

These events helped to bring home to everyone in Geneva that the sheer complexity of the many interlocking problems and issues facing the Conference was almost beyond the capacity of such an amorphous group to resolve. This growing realization on the part of East, West, and neutrals slowly gave the CSCE a tenuous new element, an overall interest and objective that all delegates in Geneva shared: the successful completion of the negotiation.

In February Romania began to fall back from its unrealistic proposals for implementation of the principle of nonuse of force by presenting a revised paper on this subject; Britain, acting as NATO floor leader, tabled its draft of a Conference document on military confidence-building measures; and the director general of the United Nations Educational, Scientific, and Cultural Organization (UNESCO), Rene Maheu, addressed a joint meeting of the subcommittees on science and technology, culture, and education, offering the organization's facilities and services for CSCE follow-up.

It was during this slightly more promising phase of the negotiations that the USSR arrested Solzhenitsyn. The Soviet author's plight was uniquely symbolic for the CSCE, and every diplomat in Geneva understood this. For the Soviets, the problem of how to deal with the dissident author posed essentially the same question as the CSCE, or, in broader terms, the whole policy of detente: How much liberalization was the Soviet system prepared to accommodate in order to obtain full Western acceptance and the material benefits that could follow? The Solzhenitsyn case also symbolized the dilemma of detente for the West: What sort of human rights standards should the West demand from the Soviets as the detente relationship expanded, and what sort of behavior on the part of the Soviets would put that relationship in jeopardy?

The CSCE held its collective breath during the week of February 11. Most delegates at the Conference realized that trial and imprisonment of a man who for Western public opinion epitomized Soviet dissent would make a mockery of the ideals of human rights, fundamental freedoms, and the freer movement of people and ideas, which the West was seeking to have recognized in the CSCE. Should the Soviets have taken that course of action, the Conference might not have concluded for a very long time, if ever. To what extent this fact weighed in the Soviet government's decision to expel the author will probably never be known. But it is only reasonable to suppose that they understood the effect on the CSCE that harsher treatment of Solzhenitsyn would have had and that this factor was one of the considerations leading to the more humane action—expulsion—eventually taken.

The Solzhenitsyn incident passed, without seriously marking the work of the CSCE. In the week following his expulsion there were further signs of the increasing tempo and seriousness of the negotiations and indications that many participants were beginning to feel (overoptimistically as it turned out) that the end was in sight. Principal among these was a paper presented by the Netherlands after lengthy consultations with the Nine and the NATO allies. This paper displayed for the first time the Western concept of how the final texts of the CSCE should be organized into a single document. It was a draft of a framework for what eventually became the Final Act, which left the substance blank, but presented the form of a final act, with a preamble, four sections representing the four CSCE baskets (the existing three plus follow-up), a closing formulation, and signatures.

The Soviets, when they saw this paper, reacted with annoyance, particularly since they had hoped to frame the final texts in such a way as to give special status to the list of principles and to relegate Basket III to a lesser place. The Dutch document nevertheless contained elements of interest to the USSR. First, its presentation, especially by the stubborn Dutch, showed that the Western countries were indeed thinking about the conclusion of the Conference; second, although the principles were given no special status, the accepted organization of the Helsinki Blue Book had been followed, putting the principles first; third, the Dutch organization made room for preambles before each basket, thus making it possible for the Soviets to try to enter their caveats in these preambles; and fourth, and perhaps most importantly from the Russians' viewpoint, it committed the Western countries for the first time to a document that would be *signed*, a feature the Soviets badly wanted to enhance the historical status of the CSCE's final document. As Soviet Ambassador Mendelevich said when he saw the Dutch draft for the first time, "The most interesting word in this entire document is the last one." The last word in the draft was, of course, "signatures."

There were other signs of progress as well: the Coordinating Committee took a symbolic "decision" to speed up the work of the Conference (a decision virtually impossible to carry out, since each delegation blamed the others for the slowness of the work), and the long-awaited working group on Item IV of the agenda (on follow-up) was convened and held its first meeting on February 28. Six neutral states (Austria, Cyprus, Finland, Sweden, Switzerland, and Yugoslavia), in a politically significant first joint initiative, presented a draft resolution on military confidence-building measures, which attempted to find a middle path between some Eastern and Western positions, while maintaining maximalist goals on subjects of special interest to the neutral states. Presentation of the neutral draft committed these states to working together in a field that was already the most tightly structured in the Conference, since each of the military groupings, the Warsaw Pact and NATO, was particularly disciplined in this subject area.

By the end of February, the texts of one principle (sovereign equality) and several provisions of Basket II had been registered, and there was talk among some more optimistic delegates of putting together a "skeleton" of the final CSCE document before the Easter recess. Western and neutral delegations proposed in the corridors that this be done simply by bracketing unagreed language or areas of disagreement for later resolution, but the Soviets and their allies refused to accept such a procedure. The idea of a skeleton never got off the ground, but all delegations were beginning to feel the pressure of time, under the widespread assumption that Stage III would be convened in July of 1974. This hypothetical schedule left about ten weeks of working time and made every day count. An indication of the Conference's mood was the Coordinating Committee's approval of an intensified work schedule leading up to the Easter recess.

Meanwhile, all CSCE delegates pored over the results of the meetings between Brezhnev and French President Pompidou in Pitsunda, a tiny resort on the Soviet Black Sea coast. It was generally recognized that Pompidou was the key to a Stage III Summit, and that no other European leader was likely, in the final analysis, to refuse to go to Helsinki. On New Year's Day, Pompidou had said flatly that the level of the final stage "remained a problem." His reaction to Brezhnev's inevitable pressure on this point was therefore examined closely for clues to the real position of the man in the Elysee Palace. The official French view—that a Stage III Summit would depend on the results of the Conference—remained unchanged by the meeting with Brezhnev. But Pompidou told the press before returning to Paris that France was not "obstinately negative" on a Summit, a phrase interpreted by many as a cautious opening toward a more positive position. Coupled with the emphasis that the French president placed on CSCE in his remarks to the press, and his admission that the final CSCE document could "mark something important, decisive, or in any case significant, in the history of Europe," this seemed to suggest that the French were holding the door open for a Summit finale.

In early March the second of the ten principles (refraining from the threat or use of force) was provisionally agreed, and drafting began on a key Conference issue: inviolability of frontiers. The FRG opened the discussion of inviolability with a purposely conciliatory statement to the effect that this principle should be clear and unambiguous, consistent with the FRG-Soviet treaty, and not preclude eventual German reunification. This last phrase was an allusion to the FRG's desire to include language in the CSCE principle of inviolability that would specifically accept the possibility of peaceful changes of frontiers.

But the Soviets wanted an inviolability principle with no mention of peaceful change. Since the FRG-Soviet treaty did not mention the peaceful change concept, the Soviets saw no reason to recognize it in the CSCE. They were determined to have an inviolability text as ironclad as their treaty with Bonn; during the week of March 16, they began a major effort to obtain this objective. To move drafting forward they accepted some surprising textual adjustments, including language on territorial claims that excluded only claims where violence is implied ("demands directed toward seizure of part or all of the territory of any participating state," later rendered even more narrowly — see FA 32). This was a far cry from the kind of language the Soviets originally desired on claims, which would have barred all territorial claims, even those made and resolved peacefully.

To sweeten the deal and make Western delegations more willing to accept early registration, the Soviets also permitted registration of an agreed Basket III text on "Contacts and Regular Meetings on the Basis of Family Ties" (FA 430–433), which was a major element of the Western freer movement initiative. Nevertheless, the Western countries, aware that a clear inviolability principle was the single most important Soviet objective in the CSCE, were reluctant to agree on it unless the Soviets showed considerably more flexibility on subjects of interest to the West. In addition, the FRG considered adequate balancing language on peaceful change to be a sine qua non for conclusion of the Conference.

During the course of the week, a Spanish compromise suggestion for handling the peaceful change issue began to gain acceptance. Under this purely procedural solution, a formulation on peaceful change would be drafted on a separate piece of paper and registered simultaneously with the inviolability principle itself. It would be agreed that the peaceful change language would appear somewhere in the list of ten principles, and the fact that it appeared on a separate paper would not prejudice any delegation's view of where among the principles it would eventually be placed. This solution would permit registration of the inviolability principle, so that work could advance to drafting the next principle on the list, and theoretically would prejudice neither the Soviet view that the peaceful change language should be separated from the inviolability principle, nor the FRG position that it should be included in this principle. Most delegations recognized that acceptance of the separate-piece-of-paper solution meant tacit agreement that the peaceful change concept would be separated from inviolability and eventually placed elsewhere in the list of principles. Once it was broken off, it was difficult to see how it could be reintroduced into the inviolability principle. But the great majority of delegations considered that the Soviets were joining in a fair compromise by accepting a weakened inviolability principle plus peaceful change language somewhere else, and most were prepared to accept this compromise.

As March drew to a close the Soviets pulled out all stops in their effort to get a "crystal clear" principle of inviolability of frontiers agreed on paper before returning to Moscow for the Easter recess. In addition to accepting unorthodox procedures and making additional concessions on the inviolability language itself, the Soviets accepted an additional Basket III freer movement text, on dissemination of printed information, to demonstrate that progress on the specific provisions of Basket III was being made in parallel with work on inviolability. This further movement in Basket III encouraged some additional Western delegations to agree to the inviolability text.

Indications were strong that the CSCE was nearing a crucial breakthrough, and many delegates felt that everything would be easier once the inviolability principle, which the Soviets wanted so badly, had been settled. The Soviets, including delegation chief Kovalev, had for several weeks been broadly hinting that progress in Basket III would immediately follow agreement on inviolability. These hints were interpreted as assurances, even promises, by the Western delegates, who thought the leaders of the Soviet delegation had engaged their honor. The atmosphere of the Conference grew more animated as the delegates anticipated an important watershed in their work. This feeling was communicated to capitals as well, and the Finnish foreign minister took the cue to issue a statement, which was distributed by the Finnish delegation in Geneva, that Finland was prepared to organize Stage III of the Conference in July of 1974 and hoped it would be held at the highest level.

The principle of inviolability of frontiers was provisionally agreed at a late-night session on April 5, at the end of a week during which virtually all other Conference activity ground to a halt. Agreement was reached following an agitated day. The FRG delegation, the sole holdout, was pressed from all sides to accept registration of the peaceful change language on a separate piece of paper simultaneously with registration of the inviolability principle itself. Since the Western delegations could not agree among themselves on the optimum alternative placement for a sentence on peaceful change, the floating sentence idea seemed like the best interim solution. But Bonn was unhappy with this solution and accepted it only after making a series of formal reservations that would permit them to hold open the question of the phraseology and placement of the peaceful change language until much later in the negotiations.

On telephoned instructions from Bonn, the FRG delegation made the following reservations: "Before the FRG Delegation can give its consent to the final formulation of the principle of inviolability of frontiers, in particular to the words 'demand for' in the second sentence, agreement must have been reached on the following questions: (1) on the principle to which the formulation concerning 'peaceful change' will be attached; (2) on a precise formulation of 'peaceful change' in this new context; (3) on a precise formulation of the principle of 'self-determination'; (4) on a formula concerning the connection between the principles. (5) Furthermore, the German text of these principles must be satisfactory to the delegation of the FRG."

Agreement on inviolability/peaceful change was the most significant Conference breakthrough since the beginning of Stage II. Oddly, the Soviets appeared to have settled for less than they could have obtained, and evidently decided to make drafting concessions on the principle itself in order to register it immediately. They abandoned wording that would have implied immutability of frontiers, and accepted a formulation that strongly suggested that only violent changes in frontiers were excluded (see FA 30–32). Coupled with the phraseology on peaceful change, this gave a different coloration from that which had originally been intended by the USSR.

The Soviet delegation was apparently under high-level pressure to conclude this item before the Easter recess. The Soviets indicated informally on several occasions that Brezhnev himself was following the daily development of drafting on inviolability, and they were obviously satisfied with having achieved early agreement on a point that was of cardinal importance to the Kremlin. Coming immediately before the Easter recess, this progress also served to demonstrate to the participating governments that the CSCE could indeed reach broadly acceptable conclusions, and thus helped to form more positive judgments on the future of the Conference. Western delegations now expected the Soviets to make concessions on subjects of interest to the West, in order to assure an early Stage III at the highest level.

14 Progress So Slow
The Soviets Move Too Late and the
Summit Is Postponed, April–July 1974

At some moments in the course of the negotiations the
difficulties appeared so overwhelming and the progress so
slow that we may have had reason to believe we carried
on our shoulders the weight of the entire world.

Pierre Elliott Trudeau Helsinki July 30, 1975

The Conference reconvened on April 22, following the Easter recess. On that day, in Brussels, the CSCE delegation heads from the NATO countries met with the North Atlantic Council at alliance headquarters to review developments in the negotiations. It was clear from the discussion that, although results thus far were meager, both the EC-Nine and NATO groups anticipated more rapid progress than previously, leading to the probable conclusion of Stage II in the late spring and Stage III in July 1974. Those delegations that expressed themselves on the level of Stage III thought attendance by foreign ministers would be appropriate, as at Stage I.

It was also noted that NATO's spring meeting of foreign ministers, planned for Ottawa in June, would provide an opportune moment for assessing the progress of the Conference, and perhaps for taking a collective decision on level and timing of the final stage. Interestingly, this consultation among delegation heads also revealed that all NATO delegations thought the Conference would have to be followed up with some form of multilateral activity, and that this might imply an organizational framework of some kind, albeit minimal.

But the expected Soviet concessions were not made. Ignoring the assurances they had given in the buildup to agreement on inviolability of frontiers, the Soviet delegation returned to Geneva after the Easter recess with no new flexibility, and emphatically denied that it was now their turn to move forward on Basket III issues of interest to the West. In fact, Soviet delegation chief Kovalev, the only Soviet delegate with responsibility for both the principles and Basket III, was hard to find for several weeks after the recess and, when he did leave the Soviet mission, seemed to have completely forgotten that he personally had promised concessions in return for early agreement on the inviolability principle.

Of all the delegation heads in Geneva, Kovalev was probably the most influential within his own governmental system. He was a deputy minister of foreign affairs, responsible for policy planning, with direct access to Gromyko. And his work in the CSCE was followed closely by Brezhnev himself. In fact, there were times during the negotiations when it was clear that Brezhnev was receiving reports on the smallest details and that he alone could approve certain concessions. Kovalev thus was in a position to bring maximum influence to bear at the highest level of his government, a thing no other delegation head— certainly not the American one—could do.

Kovalev was a wily negotiator with a surprising personal style. He was dark-skinned, almost totally bald, and normally completely poker-faced. A chain-smoker (of American cigarettes), he spoke with a voice so soft it was almost inaudible. He rarely entered detailed discussions himself, but used his seniority among the delegates to bring pressure to bear on delegation heads whose subordinates were causing the Soviets difficulties for one reason or another. He had considerable patience and was willing to work carefully over long periods of time to obtain the results he desired. But when he lost patience, or felt that he had been tricked or deceived, a dark look would come across his brow, and he was capable of pouring forth criticisms with cold fury. He was also capable of labyrinthine conspiratorial plots to bring success, and sometimes this was necessary in view of the complexities of the negotiations and the apparent rivalry that existed between his principal lieutenants, Mendelevich and Yuri Dubinin.

In this case Kovalev had promised a great deal to obtain early agreement on the inviolability principle, but after his consultations in Moscow over Easter he returned to Geneva unwilling—or unable—to deliver. The Soviet delegation stonewalled throughout the April–May period, and the Conference ground to a standstill.

At the same time, the Soviets continued to press for a commitment by the Conference to an early date for the Stage III meeting. As Soviet representatives made demarches on this point in Western capitals, Kissinger and Gromyko met in Geneva April 28–29, and Gromyko once again urged Kissinger to bring his influence to bear in order to effect an early conclusion to the Conference.

The Coordinating Committee in early May discussed how the work of the Conference could be expedited. A variety of procedural suggestions were made: Kovalev suggested that all proposals being held in abeyance should be brought forward; the Polish delegation head proposed asking a working group for ideas to speed things up; the Romanian ambassador wanted to open immediately discussion of follow-up, the form of the final document of the Conference, and Stage III; the Greek representative thought more informal meetings were the answer; and the Swiss delegation head proposed two levels of negotiation, with delegation leaders reaching "political agreement" and experts concentrating on detailed drafting. But all delegates were well aware that new procedures would have little effect, and only the will of national governments to accept compromises would bring the CSCE to a conclusion.

That will was notably absent in the spring of 1974. Stung by the Soviet refusal to make concessions in return for Western agreement on inviolability, the Western delegations responded with stonewall tactics of their own, while seeking to place responsibility for the delay on the Eastern side. The West concentrated doggedly on detailed, even tedious, negotiations on the specific substantive Western proposals in Basket III and the military field, trying to get the wording of these clauses into as positive and concrete a form as possible. The result was mutual stubbornness, with the Soviets pressing for agreement on timing of Stage III but giving no concessions, and the West insisting on substantive progress before any commitments were made on the timing or level of Stage III. Week after week the pressure on both sides mounted.

By mid-May it was clear that the Conference was getting nowhere. The Swiss delegation chief, Rudolph Bindschedler, a respected professor of international law and a veteran of multilateral conferences, said flatly at a May 16 meeting of the Coordinating Committee that thus far the Conference had done nothing to add to security and cooperation in Europe. NATO caucus meetings were dominated by an atmosphere of deep pessimism. The Western side was perplexed by the Soviet tactic of pressing for an early conclusion while offering no concessions to obtain it. The Soviets were evidently aware that early June would include two events that could decisively affect the question of the timing of the conclusion of the Conference—the NATO ministerial gathering in Ottawa and a planned visit by President Nixon to Moscow—and yet they were not making an effort to influence Western judgments of the CSCE prior to those meetings.

While most Western delegates believed the USSR would make some concessions to obtain the Stage III conclusion they so ardently desired, it looked less and less possible for the Conference to complete its work in time for a July Stage III, even if the Soviets were to come up with last-minute concessions. Combined with this was the widespread feeling that the Soviet leadership was reassessing the Conference in light of the political changes in Great Britain, France, and the FRG, and in light of Richard Nixon's increasingly shaky position. Many Western delegates concluded gloomily that these various factors might combine to postpone the conclusion of the CSCE beyond the summer of 1974, with the possibility that it might then become institutionalized and never finish. The Conference of the Committee on Disarmament, which had met periodically in Geneva for about 12 years, was often cited as an example of how a conference could become perennial. An additional factor in the Western attitude was that no Western country wished to be blamed for what could mean a major reversal in the process of detente, and if the Conference were to be prolonged, each delegation wanted the responsibility to rest with the other side.

Speculation began to grow as to when a third stage might be convened if it proved impossible to agree in time for a July meeting, and more and more diplomats in Geneva began to think unenthusiastically in terms of September or October. Consideration was given within the EC-Nine and NATO groups to either provoking a crisis in the Conference by proposing adjournment sine die at the appropriate moment, or, if no serious progress were made by early summer, by proposing a lengthy recess, perhaps as long as two years. The Western delegations held intense consultations during this period to identify the options available to them. In view of the universally negative appraisal of Conference progress, virtually all of these options involved breaking off the negotiations, either temporarily or permanently, at a given moment.

The Western group was aware that the Soviets were probably deliberately setting up a situation in which a few minor concessions on their part would lead the West to conclude that important progress was being made. There was considerable effort to guard against such a euphoric reaction if and when the Soviet concessions should come. Consideration was given to the question of how best to convey to the Soviets a feeling of the depth of Western dissatisfaction and to inform the Finns, who were by this time becoming anxious to fix the dates for the Stage III gathering, that a July Stage III looked impossible.

By the beginning of June, despite registration of two more principles, on territorial integrity of states and peaceful settlement of disputes, even the neutrals had identified five options for the future of the Conference, including the possibility of adjournment sine die. A sense of resignation had replaced the concern of mid-May, and some delegates were beginning to make plans for a summer recess and resumption of work in the autumn.

A June 3 statement by GDR leader Erich Honecker gave a clue to Soviet tactics. Honecker said he was confident a July CSCE Summit was still possible because of the "soon-to-be-renewed dialogue" between Brezhnev and Nixon. Coupled with the tough Soviet stance in the negotiations themselves, this suggested that the Soviets were intentionally building up the political pressures, in the hope that these pressures would make it possible to clear away the remaining CSCE problems bilaterally with Nixon at the summit level. The Soviet delegation in Geneva also revealed that they believed the Nixon-Brezhnev meeting would bring other Western leaders to accept an early Stage III, with the brevity of the remaining time available for negotiations helping to squeeze out substantive proposals that were unpleasant for the USSR.

But the situation was more complex, and Western views more strongly held, than the Soviets apparently realized. The continuing buildup of a negative Western view of the Conference made it highly unlikely that the trend could be reversed by any understanding that might be reached in Moscow in late June. By then, European governmental thinking would have hardened and could not easily be changed, even if the American president, entangled in his own Watergate problems, had wished to undertake such an effort.

On June 7, CSCE delegation heads from the NATO countries again met with the North Atlantic Council in Brussels. The objective was to prepare the ground for the NATO ministerial session in Ottawa on June 18–19, and for the joint appraisal that would then be made of CSCE progress to date. The assessment in Brussels was gloomy.

The Soviets made their move on June 12, at an informal meeting of delegation heads organized by several neutral delegations in an attempt to promote frank discussion and break the deadlock. In a dramatic intervention after two months of stagnation, Kovalev announced three Soviet concessions: (1) The USSR would accept a reference to the possibility of subscriptions to foreign publications in a text on access to printed information. (2) The USSR would accept a clause stipulating that official fees in connection with family reunification cases should be "moderate." (3) The USSR was prepared to accept a commitment to notify other European states of major military maneuvers held within one hundred kilometers of frontiers in Europe, including those of the Soviet Union.

Kovalev's statement was carefully drawn to stress the importance of the Soviet moves and to indicate that it was now up to the West to move toward compromise. It also made it clear that there were limits on how far the Soviets would go, especially on Basket III topics, where the Soviets held positions of principle they would not compromise. Finally, the Soviet concessions were clearly offered as an incentive for early agreement on a date for Stage III.

These Soviet concessions had a certain importance in terms of the work of the Conference at the time. A reference to subscriptions to foreign publications was considered essential for the information section of the final document. (As a practical matter, it was not possible for ordinary citizens of the Soviet Union and some Eastern European states to subscribe to Western publications.) Negotiations in the information subcommittee had languished for several weeks because of the Soviet refusal to accept such a reference and Western insistence that there should be one. Likewise, a phrase on "moderate" fees for family reunification was a key stumbling block in the way of agreement on that crucial text in the human contacts subcommittee, since emigration fees from the USSR and some other communist states were exorbitant.

It was obvious to the experts handling these negotiations, however, that Soviet acceptance of the two words, "subscriptions" and "moderate," could not be considered a dramatic breakthrough, since the process of negotiation had already produced heavily hedged phrases into which these words would fit. Their value, while not negligible, was therefore limited. (See FA 437 and 490 for the final phraseology that includes these words.)

The Soviet acceptance of a hundred-kilometer border zone for prior notification of major military maneuvers was more concrete and was considered more significant by the Western group. It doubled the width of the border zone that the Soviets had previously been prepared to accept and, coupled with earlier Soviet indications of willingness to give notification one week in advance, as opposed to their previous position that five days was sufficient notification time, suggested a willingness to negotiate on military subjects that the USSR had not previously displayed in the CSCE.

Overall, the Soviet initiative did not match agreement on the inviolability principle in the scale of its importance, but it did breathe new life into the Conference. Although it was still generally considered impossible to finish the Stage II negotiations in time for a Stage III in the summer of 1974, it once again appeared likely that the Conference would eventually reach a satisfactory conclusion. Western and neutral comments during and after the June 12 meeting reflected this sense of relief and guarded optimism, and all ideas for adjournment sine die were dropped.

The timing of the Soviet concessions was obviously linked to the NATO foreign ministers' meeting, which was due to open in Ottawa six days later. The Soviets hoped their concessions would help to produce a more positive assessment of the CSCE by the fifteen NATO foreign ministers, which would, in turn, encourage movement toward an early conclusion. To reinforce this hoped-for effect, Soviet ambassadors undertook coordinated high-level demarches in CSCE capitals during the week of June 10–14 to stress the need for an early Conference conclusion at the highest level. The Soviets also suggested that the level of representation at CSCE be raised to facilitate the expected final decisions, an idea which, given the extraordinary amount of specialized knowledge required to negotiate in CSCE, stood very little chance of being accepted.

But the Soviets had seriously underestimated both the depth of disappointment of Western and neutral states in relation to their hopes and objectives in the Conference and the fact that the CSCE could not be moved simply by political decision. The recommendations for the NATO ministers' conclusions in Ottawa had been under preparation for some weeks, and a few relatively minor last-minute concessions could not fundamentally alter them. The Soviet move was too little and too late.

Nevertheless, Western delegations accepted the Soviet initiative as a sign of willingness to enter more meaningful negotiations, and began looking for equivalent Western moves that could be made in response. Pressure for such moves grew stronger in the military field when the Soviets, one week after their initial three concessions, again adjusted their position, stating that they could accept ten days as the timing for advance notification of major maneuvers.

Another boost was given to the general Conference atmosphere by the relatively uncontroversial subcommittee on the environment, which completed its draft document (FA 301–339) and adjourned on the understanding that it could be reconvened if required. This was the first CSCE working body to complete its work, a significant landmark in the slow progress of the Conference.

In the somewhat improved situation, the Italian delegation circulated its long-awaited draft "declaration" on the Mediterranean, the result of lengthy consultations within the EC-Nine and NATO caucuses. These consultations had been difficult because the United States had seen no need for a separate document on the Mediterranean, and thought suggesting such a device ran the risk of opening the Pandora's box of problems relating to the Arab-Israeli dispute. When the EC-Nine, seeking to demonstrate concern for their Arab neighbors, made the issue a point of principle, however, and raised the matter with Kissinger, U.S. objections were lifted and the draft was tabled. Circulation of the Italian draft prompted creation of a working group on the Mediterranean and subsequent joint submission of a more ambitious draft Mediterranean declaration by Cyprus, Malta, and Yugoslavia.

Despite these isolated signs of progress, the Western assessment of the Conference's results remained basically negative, as was shown by the NATO foreign ministers' communique of June 19, 1974: "The work has advanced unevenly. Some progress has been made on certain issues, but much work remains to be done, as for example on such key questions as the improvement of human contacts and the freer flow of information, as well as confidence-building measures and essential aspects of the principles guiding relations between states." The Canadian delegation head read this portion of the NATO communique to the full Coordinating Committee on June 20. In response, the ambassador of the GDR quoted from the communique of a recent meeting between Honecker and Brezhnev: "All the objective conditions are at hand to successfully complete the Geneva work at an early date and to hold Stage III at the summit level soon."

The last week of June produced some additional signs that the Conference was creaking forward. The British representative, as spokesman for the NATO group, responded to the Soviet moves on the prior notification of major military maneuvers by revising the Western positions on this subject by degrees that were considered roughly proportional to the importance of the Soviet changes. The NATO proposal for sixty days as the timing for notification was reduced to forty-nine days, and the level at which maneuvers should be notified was raised from 10,000 to 12,000 troops. The NATO side also indicated a willingness to accept fewer specifics in the content of the notification itself, and a readiness to discuss exceptions to the Western concept of "all of Europe" as the area of application for the provision on maneuvers.

At the same time, neutral delegations were working on a "package deal" intended to meet the Soviet demand for a preamble to Basket III, which continued to form the main obstacle to progress on freer movement.

The June 27 meeting of the Coordinating Committee had been set aside for a review of Conference progress and prospects for convening Stage III. The timing of the meeting coincided with President Nixon's arrival in Moscow, when he was certain to be under pressure from Brezhnev to agree to a date for

Stage III. With this coincidence looming over it, the Coordinating Committee's discussion took on an atmosphere of high drama.

The floor was taken first by the Finnish delegation chief, who stated that his government was prepared to welcome Stage III of the Conference in Helsinki in July, if that was the wish of the participating countries. The United States' response, given by Ambassador Sherer, had been approved by Washington. It was a somewhat surprising position in light of the Nixon-Brezhnev meeting that was beginning on that day. While the United States did not object in principle to a third stage toward the end of July, Sherer said, given CSCE progress to date this did not appear to be a realistic option.

The statement clearly annoyed Kovalev, who spoke after Sherer and expressed the opposite view. He was dutifully supported by the Bulgarian, Polish, Czech, Romanian, Hungarian, and GDR representatives. Norway, the FRG (speaking for the EC-Nine), Malta, Sweden, and Switzerland took attitudes similar to that of the United States. Kovalev was visibly angered by the Swiss intervention. He asserted that it was very strange to hear such comments from the Conference's host country, since they amounted to a call away from a successful conclusion. He suggested darkly that those who took this position would bear the "political responsibility" for the consequences and said there was no excuse for interrupting the work now, when there was a real possibility of completing it.

But Kovalev's threats did little to alter the situation. France and the Netherlands repeated the negative appraisal offered by the other Western and neutral representatives, and this view stood, despite the protests of the Warsaw Pact countries.

The message of the meeting was that a consensus could not be reached to convene Stage III in July of 1974. The Finns drew the necessary conclusions and made their plans accordingly. Stage III of the Conference had been postponed.

Nevertheless, the advancing work of the neutrals on their package deal to break through the Gordian knot of problems relating to the content of the Basket III preamble suggested that the CSCE was approaching another turning point, which would be achieved only when negotiating pressures built up on all sides.

The future work program itself became an issue. The Soviets insisted that there should be no recess; Stage II should continue until all its work had been completed. Other delegations did not wish to appear frivolous by seeking a holiday while there was much work remaining. But many Western and neutral delegations, especially the smaller ones, had a real problem. Given European vacation habits, there would be no responsible officials available in their capitals during the last week of July and most of August. This meant it would be difficult for them to obtain instructions even if Stage II were to continue uninterrupted. In the end, the vigorous objections of these delegations carried the day, and it was agreed that the Conference would recess from July 26 until September 2, with activity limited during the first week of September. Acceptance of a recess laid to rest any lingering hopes that Stage II might be finished during the summer and implied that Stage III could not be held until the end of 1974, at the very earliest.

The coup d'etat in Cyprus and the subsequent Turkish occupation of part of that island occurred at this time, but had a minimal initial effect on Conference activity. General statements of national views of the Cyprus problem were made by several delegations in the security committee, but by the time a scheduled meeting of this committee took place, a ceasefire had already been announced and reactions were muted.

The final weeks before adjournment saw a flurry of activity. Some ideas were, for all practical purposes, killed. The Soviets indicated that they could not accept a Swedish proposal for publication of information on defense spending, and the United States voiced its reservations on a British proposal for a CSCE magazine (which could easily have become a communist propaganda organ).

But other items were approved. The sixth principle, nonintervention in internal affairs, was agreed. The military subcommittee approved a confidence-building measure on exchange of observers at military maneuvers (FA 117–120), which would, of course, take on its full meaning only when the provisions on notification of these maneuvers were agreed. The subcommittee also approved a measure on exchanges of military personnel (FA 127), introduced earlier by Spain.

On the final day before the recess, the neutrals' package deal was accepted, after an intense series of informal and formal meetings, thus satisfying the Soviets' desire for a Basket III preamble and, theoretically at least, making it easier to negotiate substantive freer movement proposals.

In the slightly more optimistic atmosphere created by this compromise, the U.S. delegation introduced a revised version of the "floating sentence" on peaceful changes of frontiers. This action initiated the second part of the key negotiation on frontiers.

15 Obscure Skirmishes
The Conference Gets Back on Track after the Nixon Resignation, September–December 1974

Awful darkness and silence reign over the Great Gromboolian Plain on which the hundreds of negotiators involved in the Conference on Security and Cooperation in Europe have skirmished obscurely for 18 months.

The Economist June 1, 1974

Another year! No diplomat at the CSCE had contemplated that the Conference would last so long. These men (for they were almost entirely men) had come to Geneva for a temporary stay. They were without their wives and families; many lived in hotels; some—the lucky ones—commuted home to their capitals on weekends; but all were stuck. They had become indispensable experts on a project virtually no one else understood, and for them the only exit was the conclusion of the negotiation. True, some delegates were replaced over the summer, and there were a good many new faces when Stage II reconvened on September 3, but the great majority were returning to the corridors and meeting rooms in which they had berated each other day after day throughout the previous year; it was a joyless reunion.

Prospects for an early conclusion were bleak. In fact, the resignation of President Nixon had thrown an aura of doubt over the whole affair, and it was quite legitimate to ask whether the Conference could ever be brought to a conclusion. Had the detente "window," glimpsed in Helsinki the previous year, passed? Would the new American president, following his conservative instincts, shy away from participation in the spectacular Summit that would signal CSCE's success? At best it seemed there would have to be a delay while Gerald Ford accustomed himself to his new position and made at least one or two other overseas excursions first.

Perhaps just as important, there could be a delay while the Kremlin sized up the new situation. The Soviets could not be expected to commit their forces to an all-out effort to wind up the CSCE if the new terrain looked unfavorable. And the new terrain was considerably different; in a period of less than seven months, the leaders of all four Western powers had been replaced. The Portuguese revolution was in an uncertain phase, and Western anxieties were growing over the possibility of a communist takeover. In addition, the Turkish occupation of part of the island of Cyprus posed potentially difficult problems for which no solution was readily available and over which the superpowers had little, if any, control. There was indeed reason for reassessment.

The attitude of the Soviets toward the CSCE had become somewhat enigmatic. Previously, they had praised it consistently and unreservedly in speeches by officials from Brezhnev on down. But now speeches by Brezhnev and Soviet President Nikolai Podgorny omitted any reference to the Conference at all, and Brezhnev referred darkly to the "great many complex affairs" still to be resolved on the road to detente. The most hopeful comment by any Soviet delegate in Geneva was that Stage II might finish in early 1975, but he offered even this pessimistic (for a Russian) estimate half-heartedly and without any sign that he really believed it.

Thus it was that the CSCE reassembled slowly and unenthusiastically during the first two weeks of September, with the returning members getting to know their newer colleagues, and all delegates, East and West, watching each other, as well as the press, for indications of how the new East-West winds were blowing.

And these were not the only reasons for the slowness of the first weeks of this second autumn of negotiation. The Soviets had heard of the debate going on within the EC-Nine and NATO groups on what was "essential," and on the possibility of advancing more "reasonable" proposals. The Soviet delegation was not prepared to offer concessions of its own while there existed the prospect of bridging the negotiating gap on the basis of concessions from the Western side. The Russians maintained this attitude until they began to realize that because of Western solidarity, more realistic texts would not be advanced until the Soviets themselves showed some flexibility. In the circumstances, everything combined to produce a waiting game, and so the CSCE entered another of its periodic stalemates.

The Western side offered some concessions, both substantive and procedural, to get things going. In the negotiations on military measures Great Britain, speaking for NATO, indicated officially that there might be room for exceptions to the principle that these measures should apply to "all of Europe." This was important for the Soviets, who would not accept an obligation to give notification of maneuvers all the way to the Urals while the United States gave notification of no such activity on its own territory (U.S. and Canadian territory was excluded because the CSCE was a conference on Europe). The British delegate also hinted at further flexibility on the amount of notification time required, thus moving closer to the Soviet position on this point.

The Soviet reaction to these moves was to accuse the Western states of seeking military intelligence through their proposals in this field, a suspicion that had simmered just below the surface of Soviet and East European statements for some months, but whose public revelation did nothing to help the debate at this juncture. The Soviets pounced on a phrase used by an FRG delegate that the purpose of confidence-building measures was greater "transparency" in military activities. For the Soviets, "transparency" meant seeing through the veil of Eastern secrecy and obtaining valuable intelligence. They refused to respond positively to the Western moves.

In Basket III the Western countries also tried to be conciliatory. They agreed to discuss several subjects at the same time, a device the Soviets had urged and that the West had avoided in order to preclude a general Basket III trade-off. The EC-Nine tabled draft texts on all their proposals in Basket III and announced that they would make no further demands in this subject area. As a further sweetener, agreement was reached on a paragraph for a preamble to Basket II making the provisions under this heading, like those of Basket III, subject to the principles on relations between states. But, despite all these Western moves, the Soviets would not budge from their unyielding positions in the areas of interest to the Western participants.

The Soviet position remained ambiguous until September 24, when Gromyko, in a speech at the UN General Assembly, once again indicated that the USSR was interested in an early conclusion to the Conference. In a long section of his speech, which claimed significant progress had already been made in the negotiations, Gromyko said, "The Soviet Union attaches paramount importance to the successful conclusion of the CSCE. This is now the number one question in European political life . . . The Soviet Union is convinced that it is possible to conclude the Conference within a short time . . . The Soviet Union will continue to do everything it can to ensure the complete success of the Conference . . . to include agreements at the highest level which will provide a legal framework for peace and cooperation on the scale of the entire continent." This was the first high-level public commitment by the USSR to pursuit of the CSCE project since Nixon's demise, and seemed to suggest that the Soviets had completed their review of the situation and were again prepared to move ahead with the Conference. The commitment of the Soviets was essential, since without it they would have made no concessions, and the Conference would have expired in failure.

Despite the implications of Gromyko's speech, however, the Soviets in Geneva were evidently not ready to move. They continued their stubborn tactics for another two weeks. In early October their attitude appeared to change slightly, probably less because the post-Nixon review had been completed than because Kissinger was due to visit Moscow and a major debate on the CSCE had been scheduled in the Bundestag in Bonn. The Soviets obviously hoped to ensure that the Conference would be viewed in the most favorable light. Whatever the reason, the CSCE saw progress again for the first time since it had reconvened.

An important text on circulation of and access to printed information (FA 483–492) was provisionally registered, the first registration of any text under the information heading since the previous March. The Soviets also indicated informally that they could accept application of CSCE military measures to "all of Europe," as the West wanted, provided exceptions to this rule could be negotiated. (The Turks promptly told the NATO allies that they, too, would insist on exceptions applicable to Turkey, a position that proved difficult to reconcile with the eventual compromise solution to this issue.) In addition, a text on the publication of the Final Act (eventually included as FA 671) was informally agreed.

These were all significant steps, and the Soviet delegates appeared to be more active and cooperative, even mildly positive in their approach to the discussions. What was more unusual was that they agreed to certain minor language and textual points without referring these questions to their superiors, a phenomenon that had rarely been seen in CSCE.

Any hopes that these signs indicated a major shift in Soviet tactics faded quickly, however, as the Soviets returned to their stonewall tactics immediately after the Bundestag debate and Kissinger's departure from the USSR. The Soviet delegation promptly withdrew its tentative agreement on publication of the Final Act. Once again, Soviet strategy apparently was to apply political pressure for an early conclusion without giving any concessions in the negotiations themselves. Podgorny, on a visit to Helsinki, repeated the call for a Stage III Summit "at an early date," but in the Conference itself the only text agreed was a single phrase (FA 657) intended to begin the resolution on follow-up to the Conference, as meaningless as any text the CSCE had registered since it began.

It was at this time that the linkage between the conclusion of the CSCE and Soviet plans for convening a conference of European communist parties became evident. In an article datelined Warsaw, where a preparatory meeting for the European communist parties' conference was taking place, Le Monde reported that it might not be possible for such a conference to be convened until after the CSCE had been completed. This linkage surprisingly was confirmed by Boris Ponomarev, a ranking official of the Soviet party, in a speech to the Warsaw meeting. How the linkage had originated was open to speculation, but it did appear logical that the Yugoslavs and Romanians, as well as many Western communist parties, would want to have a CSCE document, which they could use to justify their independence from the Soviet party, in hand to offset their attendance at a conference that, by definition, would express their loyalty to Moscow. Such a linkage was of great interest to Western countries because it multiplied the strong reasons the Soviets already had for an early and successful CSCE conclusion, thereby increasing the leverage that the timing of the Summit gave the West in the Geneva negotiations.

Throughout October the Soviets stonewalled, and when a group of key neutrals began taking soundings on the acceptability to all sides of an attempt by them to put together another package deal in Basket III, the Soviets discouraged such an effort, which they thought would be difficult to control. Another month passed in general stagnation.

But a series of high-level meetings, among Western leaders and between East and West, was in the offing. President Ford's first meeting with Brezhnev was scheduled for November 23-24 in Vladivostok. The EC-Nine foreign ministers were due to assemble in Brussels on December 2-3. This was to be followed by a Brezhnev visit to Paris and Rambouillet on December 5-6 for his first discussions with the new French president, Valery Giscard d'Estaing, while West German Chancellor Schmidt was simultaneously visiting Washington for talks with Ford. An EC-Nine summit December 9-10, a NATO foreign ministers' meeting December 12-13, and a Giscard-Ford summit in Martinique December 14-16 added up to a very full agenda during which CSCE would repeatedly be discussed.

The Soviets made a special effort to demonstrate to Western leaders on the eve of these meetings that the CSCE was making progress. They knew that the more positive the current appraisal of the Conference, the more inclined these leaders would be to begin fixing dates for the Stage III meeting.

On November 20, there was a major step forward as the principle of "Respect for Human Rights and Fundamental Freedoms, Including the Freedom of Thought, Conscience, Religion, or Belief," the seventh of the ten CSCE principles (FA 48-56), was provisionally registered. The principle, which had taken longer than any other to negotiate (fifty-six negotiating sessions), was a solidly worded Western achievement. On November 28 the document on family reunification (FA 434-443), one of the most important and politically charged of the Western freer movement proposals, was informally agreed; it was registered on December 3, after more than eight months of patient effort.

These steps seemed to inspire some Conference participants. The Maltese delegate, reflecting the hopes of many of the diplomats in Geneva, proposed in the Coordinating Committee that March 1 be set as a deadline for the conclusion of the work of Stage II, in order to make Stage III possible in April or May of 1975. Most delegations firmly believed such a timetable was now possible, even though many, especially those of the Western countries, were unwilling to accept a deadline, however moderate or informal, that would enable the Soviets to refuse further concessions.

No deadline was set, but hopes continued high as the work of the Conference moved ahead comparatively smoothly, and reports from the Rambouillet summit meeting between Brezhnev and Giscard indicated that further East-West compromise agreements might be possible. The French delegation exhibited a more active interest in an early conclusion following Rambouillet, and a more forthcoming attitude toward the Conference overall. It was generally assumed that this attitude reflected a more positive view of the CSCE on the part of the new French president than that held by his predecessor. It had been widely believed that Pompidou did not want to attend a Stage III Summit that would place him in a secondary role alongside Brezhnev and the U.S. president. Had Stage III been held during Pompidou's lifetime, it seemed possible that France would have been represented by its prime minister. Giscard's attitude was more realistic; he had emphasized the need for France to be present at, and to participate in, major diplomatic events. Rambouillet appeared to signal Giscard's willingness to attend a Summit conclusion, provided satisfactory results could be achieved. This was a key factor for the USSR; no other major European power appeared likely to resist the idea of a Summit, and Kissinger's continued presence in the State Department ensured that Ford would abide by Nixon's earlier commitment. The apparent French conversion, therefore, meant that the idea of a Stage III at the Summit was now tacitly accepted all around.

These developments had a stimulating influence on Conference work as the Christmas recess approached. The eighth of the ten CSCE principles, on "Equal Rights and Self-determination of Peoples" (FA 57–60), was informally agreed, as well as the Basket III sections on "Marriage between Citizens of Different States" (FA 444–447) and the study of "Foreign Languages and Civilizations" (FA 637–646). The Basket III text on "Cooperation in the Field of Information" (FA 498–504) was provisionally registered. The French delegation tabled a revised draft of the tenth principle that included a clause designed to protect four-power rights and responsibilities in Berlin and Germany.

The rush of work just before adjournment on December 20 brought another difficult item into closer focus. Romania tabled a new version of the key paragraph of its proposal for giving effect to the principle of nonuse of force. The Romanians had originally hoped to prohibit even the stationing of troops in another country, but had met objections from both East and West. Their revised paragraph had the more limited objective of prohibiting the use of armed force against another state. Though this was modest enough for most delegations, it was still too strong for the USSR, which immediately blocked it, prompting the Romanian delegation to block registration of the eighth principle in retaliation. Extended private negotiations were required between the USSR and Romania to reach an acceptable compromise on the Romanian paragraph (FA 80).

The pace of work was up, to match the pace of high-level interest in the Conference, and the CSCE had now reached tentative agreement on large sections of its final document. But the two major issues—frontiers and human rights—remained unresolved. In each case, only part of the final result had been agreed. The toughest negotiations on both questions still lay ahead.

16   The Inevitable Conclusions
Inviolability and Peaceful Changes
of Postwar Frontiers

The hour has struck for the inevitable collective
conclusions to be drawn from the experience of history.
Leonid Brezhnev Helsinki July 31, 1975

If the Final Act has a claim to being a substitute for a peace settlement following the Second World War, it is principally because of the agreement it contains
on frontiers in Europe. This compromise between the concept of inviolability
of frontiers and the possibility of peaceful change is a carefully balanced one
and is the CSCE's attempt at a rational approach to the territorial questions left
over from the war. In declaring that the present boundaries of states in Europe
are inviolable, the CSCE confirmed multilateral acceptance of the changes resulting from the war; the geopolitical status quo in Europe was accepted with a
number of unresolved issues left intact. At the same time the peaceful change
language preserved positions of principle about future revisions; the possibility
of a physical evolution of the territorial situation was thus also accepted, provided it occurs peacefully.

Despite the fact that none of the participants in the Conference considered
its results legally binding, this multilateral accord was an important new factor
in the postwar political development of Europe. It was the first such general
and agreed pronouncement on frontiers of states throughout Europe since the
Versailles treaty in 1919. It was both appropriate and inevitable that the final
compromise on this subject would be concluded privately at a high level between the two superpowers, just as the principal decisions of the Peace Conference of 1919 were made in camera by the four allied powers.

For the Soviets, the principle of inviolability of frontiers was—in the private
words of one of their delegates—"the key to European security," since it would
permanently fix all European frontiers, particularly the division of Germany.
Not only would this protect the status of the GDR, the USSR's strongest ally;
it would also prevent a united Germany from again threatening the Soviet
Union, and would facilitate the growth of Soviet influence in Western Europe.
The Soviets also had an interest in obtaining language recognizing their incorporation of the Baltic states (Latvia, Lithuania, and Estonia) into the USSR.

The Soviets regarded as a major achievement the agreement reached during the Helsinki preparatory talks to include inviolability as a separate and distinct principle in the list of ten principles to be drafted during Stage II of the Conference. The nearest precedent for the CSCE principles, the UN Friendly Relations Declaration, contains the following language on inviolability of frontiers: "Every State has the duty to refrain from the threat or use of force to violate the existing international boundaries of another State. . . ." However, in the UN document this phrase is contained in the principle of refraining from the threat or use of force, and is not a separate principle.

From the outset of the Geneva phase of the CSCE, the Soviet delegation stressed the need for a "crystal clear" principle of inviolability and asserted that they would not budge from their own proposed language on inviolability: "Inviolability of frontiers, in accordance with which the participating States regard the existing frontiers in Europe as inviolable now and in the future, will make no territorial claims upon each other and acknowledge that peace in that area can be preserved only if no one encroaches upon the present frontiers."

In addition to the Soviet-proposed version of the inviolability principle, there were also FRG and French versions, which were very similar and had U.S. support, and a Yugoslav draft. The key element in the FRG (and French) draft was inclusion, in the inviolability principle itself, of language specifying that peaceful changes in frontiers were not excluded and were in keeping with international law: "The participating States have the duty to refrain from the threat or use of force against the existing international frontiers of another participating State or for the settlement of territorial disputes and questions relating to State frontiers. The participating States regard one another's frontiers, in their existing form and irrespective of the legal status which in their opinion they possess, as inviolable. The participating States are of the opinion that their frontiers can be changed only in accordance with international law, through peaceful means and by agreement with due regard for the right of the peoples of self-determination."

Like the establishment of inviolability as a separate principle, the inclusion of language specifying that peaceful change is possible was a novel idea. No such language appears in the Friendly Relations Declaration, which because of its universal acceptance was regarded as a model for work on the CSCE principles.

When the drafting of the principles began in early February, 1974, the Soviets undertook a concerted drive for acceptance of their inviolability language. The inviolability principle was the third in the list of ten, and drafting on it began in March, after completion of drafting on the first two principles. This timing was unfortunate for the FRG; their leverage would have been stronger if this key Soviet desideratum had come under negotiation later, simultaneously with other major Conference issues.

As drafting work proceeded, it became clear that the Soviets would accept language on peaceful changes of frontiers provided it was separate from the principle of inviolability. The first of several key negotiating compromises on the inviolability/peaceful change issue came as the result of the Spanish suggestion that language on peaceful change be drafted on a separate piece of paper simultaneously with drafting of the inviolability principle itself. The text of the principle, as it emerged from the final drafting process, was brief: "The participating States regard as inviolable all one another's frontiers as well as the frontiers of all States in Europe and therefore they will refrain now and in the future from assaulting these frontiers.

"Accordingly, they will also refrain from any demand for, or act of, seizure and usurpation of part or all of the territory of any participating State" (FA 31–32).

The floating sentence on peaceful change read as follows: "The participating States consider that their frontiers can be changed only in accordance with international law through peaceful means and by agreement."

The FRG had no problem with the first paragraph of the inviolability language; Bonn accepted that frontiers should not be altered by force, that they were therefore "inviolable," and that they should not be "assaulted." The second paragraph, too, was generally acceptable; the FRG, like other CSCE participants, agreed that there should be no "act of seizure or usurpation" of territory. But the inclusion of the phrase, "any demand for" seizure and usurpation was less clear. It was thought that this phrase might be read as excluding even reiteration of the FRG's position of principle that the reunification of Germany should one day be possible in peaceful circumstances.

To clarify the point, the German delegation sought Soviet views on the meaning of the phrase. On the final day before agreement, after difficult discussions, the question was put to Kovalev: What was the Soviet interpretation of the significance of the phrase "demand for"? Kovalev's response was rambling and ambiguous. He was then pressed to cite an example of what the Soviets would view as a "demand for" seizure and usurpation of territory. Finally, Kovalev gave an example: an "ultimatum" would, in Moscow's view, constitute a "demand for" territory.

The German delegation told Kovalev that the Bonn government would record this interpretation with their negotiating history of the inviolability clause, and if there were ever a dispute on the issue, the FRG would publicly cite Kovalev's example as the accepted Soviet definition of what constituted a "demand for." (An abridged account of this episode is contained in an article by Götz von Groll, a member of the FRG delegation to the CSCE, in *Aussenpolitik*, Volume 26, of August 1975, p. 252.)

This information was conveyed by phone to Bonn. Most senior officials were unreachable, and final authorization to accept the compromise was difficult to obtain. Late in the evening, telephonic instructions were given, including the five conditions that were later met, and the principle of inviolability, along with the "floating sentence" on peaceful change, was approved.

Agreement was "subject to subsequent decision on location in final document/documents and to agreement on texts as a whole." This meant that the phrase on peaceful change could theoretically be included in any one of the ten principles, including inviolability of frontiers.

The Western delegations felt that the inviolability language as agreed conveyed the idea that only violent changes in frontiers were excluded and that, with the phrase on peaceful change to be inserted in the list of principles providing specific acknowledgement of the possibility of peaceful change, an acceptable balance had been struck. The word, "assaulting," was particularly thought to convey the sense of the type of violent change that should be excluded, even though this word was translated into Russian as *posegat*, which conveys a less violent impression.

At the time of the Helsinki Summit, certain journalists thought the inviolability language also constituted European and American recognition of the USSR's far eastern frontiers, which are contested by China and Japan. The Chinese, who ridiculed the Conference throughout its existence as a form of appeasement toward the USSR, ignored such implications, but the Japanese informed themselves carefully as to the interpretations of key delegations on this point. In fact, however, the nature of the CSCE as a conference on Europe, the negotiating history of the inviolability language, and the views of the negotiators themselves all support the interpretation that the Final Act is not intended to settle existing border disputes between participating states (the United States and Canada, for example, have at least one such dispute), much less disputes with nonparticipating states in other parts of the globe.

As for the Baltic states issue, the Western delegations insisted on insertion of a paragraph that would protect their positions of principle—essentially that they do not recognize the incorporation of these states into the USSR as legal. The third paragraph (FA 36) of the principle of "Territorial Integrity of States" reads as follows: "The participating States will likewise refrain from making each other's territory the object of military occupation or other direct or indirect measures of force in contravention of international law, or the object of acquisition by means of such measures or the threat of them. No such occupation or acquisition will be recognized as legal." While the tense of this phraseology makes it somewhat ambiguous, it was interpreted by the Western negotiators as preserving their position of principle. This was especially important for the United States, and on July 25, 1975, prior to traveling to Helsinki, President Ford issued a statement reaffirming the U.S. position on the Baltic states and the U.S. government's interpretation of the Final Act language.

Following registration of the principle of inviolability of frontiers and the enunciation of the FRG's reservations, Chancellor Schmidt and Foreign Minister Hans-Dietrich Genscher, perceiving that the FRG's negotiating position with regard to language on peaceful change had been considerably weakened, approached Kissinger seeking active American assistance in negotiating a peaceful change clause that would more effectively balance the inviolability language and preserve the FRG's position of principle on German reunification.

The FRG felt that the "floating sentence" on peaceful change was satisfactory only if it were to be included in the principle of inviolability of frontiers. In that principle, it would appear as the single exception to the general rule that frontiers would not be altered by force. But the fact that the "floating sentence" had already been separated from inviolability meant that it would be very difficult to reinsert it into that principle. If the "floating sentence" were to be included in another principle, the most likely candidate was the principle of sovereign equality, which listed the attributes of sovereignty. The possibility of altering frontiers in agreement with a neighboring state could be included there as another attribute of sovereignty. But in that case the existing sentence was not satisfactory, because it was worded negatively, as an exception. The FRG, therefore, preferred to reword the peaceful change sentence more positively, principally by deleting the word "only."

The United States could hardly refuse such a request from a key ally, and agreed to put forward the FRG's preferred peaceful change language as a U.S. proposal. This "U.S." proposal on peaceful change was tabled in the full CSCE on July 26, 1974: "In accordance with international law, the participating States consider that their frontiers can be changed through peaceful means and by agreement." About four months had passed since registration of the so-called "floating sentence" on the same subject.

The "U.S." formulation was intended for placement elsewhere than the principle of inviolability of frontiers, probably in the principle of sovereign equality, and it was therefore necessary that the phraseology be similar to that of the other attributes listed; it could not be phrased negatively by inclusion of the word "only," since the other attributes were phrased positively and such a juxtaposition would have stressed the fact that peaceful change can occur solely in certain narrow circumstances.

The Soviet reaction to the U.S. proposal was decidedly cool, not only to the substance of the new phrase, but also to the fact that the United States was acting on behalf of the FRG. The Soviets became even more annoyed when they tried to discuss this new language and were referred back and forth between the West Germans and Washington.

The U.S. action set off a series of contacts and exchanges on the peaceful change sentence, which was a subject of discussion at or on the fringes of virtually every high-level U.S.-Soviet or U.S.-FRG meeting during the following six months, in New York, Moscow, Vladivostok, Washington, and Geneva. The Soviets produced an alternative text that was very close to the "floating sentence" phraseology, and the United States, again acting with and for the

FRG, presented another variant to the Soviet embassy in Washington in January 1975: "The participating States consider in accordance with international law that their frontiers can be changed by peaceful means and by agreement." The Soviets rejected this new variant in mid-February.

On February 17, Kissinger arrived in Geneva on short notice for one of his periodic meetings with Gromyko. This two-day visit would dramatically affect the negotiation on frontiers.

Both men wanted to resolve the peaceful change issue. It had become important to Kissinger because of his promise to the Schmidt government in Bonn to attempt to obtain Soviet agreement to language that would balance inviolability of frontiers. It was important to Gromyko because, ever since the inviolability language had been agreed, the FRG had maintained that it would not go to a Stage III Summit without a satisfactory phrase on peaceful change. Although the United States and the USSR were close to finding a formulation that would satisfy them both, the precise phraseology remained elusive.

In agreement with the FRG, the United States handed the Soviets yet another version of the peaceful change language on February 17: "The participating States consider that, in accordance with international law, their frontiers can be changed by peaceful means and by agreement."

The new formulation was delivered to the Soviet mission late in the morning and was handed immediately to Gromyko. When he met Kissinger for lunch, Gromyko scribbled two changes on the proposed formulation. He suggested moving the phrase, "in accordance with international law," so that it would appear after the word "changed," and wanted to reintroduce the word "only." The phrase then read: "The participating States consider that their frontiers can be changed in accordance with international law only by peaceful means and by agreement."

At a meeting with Kovalev after lunch, the U.S. side told the Soviets that inclusion of "only" was not possible, since it would appear to restrict the circumstances in which frontiers can be changed. This was especially true if the sentence were to be fitted into the principle of sovereign equality. (The other possible placement discussed was in the principle of territorial integrity of states.)

It was agreed that the other suggested change would be tried out on the FRG. Both sides were to reflect on the situation.

Kissinger and his party left Geneva in the afternoon, but Gromyko remained one day longer. At nine in the evening Kovalev asked to see U.S. delegation chief Sherer. The meeting was arranged for ten o'clock. Kovalev handed over a new formulation, similar to Gromyko's latest suggestion, but without the word "only": "The participating States consider, that their frontiers can be changed in accordance with international law, by peaceful means and by agreement." (Placement of the first comma in this version may have been a simple punctuation error by the Soviets in their use of English.)

The FRG's reaction to this language was that, though elimination of the word "only" was significant progress, the sentence still had faults. As now drafted, it would make peaceful changes in frontiers subject to three conditions: they should be (1) in accord with international law, (2) by peaceful means, and (3) by agreement. Bonn felt that peaceful change was by definition in accordance with international law and that the text should reflect this fact.

To stick as closely as possible to the compromise sentence that was now emerging, the FRG suggested simply moving the erroneously placed first comma so that it would appear before the phrase, "in accordance with international law." The phrase would then read as though it was taken for granted that peaceful change was in accordance with international law: "The participating States consider that their frontiers can be changed, in accordance with international law, by peaceful means and by agreement."

This change was proposed to the Soviets, who made a swift and dramatic decision: they accepted it. Two weeks later the U.S. delegation announced to a surprised NATO caucus that agreement had been reached with the Soviets on this key Conference issue. "I would like to extend my congratulations to the negotiators," said the Canadian delegate, "whoever they may be."

On March 17, 1975, the U.S. delegation tabled the revised version of its earlier peaceful change proposal. The new compromise version had the support of the FRG and the USSR, as well as practically all other delegations. But it was not possible to reach agreement on it immediately for procedural reasons and because the Romanians were not prepared to agree until some time later. There was also a sticky dispute over the German translation.

When it was finally accepted by the full CSCE, the peaceful change sentence was included in the principle of sovereign equality, and it appears in FA 25 as negotiated between the United States and the Soviet Union. To complete the balance between the inviolability and peaceful change formulations, it was also thought necessary to insert a phrase somewhere in the principles stating that all the principles are of equal weight. Such a phrase appears in FA 70: "All the principles set forth above are of primary significance and, accordingly, they will be equally and unreservedly applied, each of them being interpreted taking into account the others."

When Kissinger, in a press conference on February 25, 1975, referred to issues in the CSCE that had "become so abstruse and esoteric" that they depended on the placement of a comma, he was referring to this episode, but while the issue of peaceful change had indeed become somewhat abstruse following lengthy and esoteric negotiations, it was, and remains, the heart of the territorial compromise that made it possible for the Conference to reach agreement.

Part IV
1975   Human Rights

17 Adjusting Illusions
Detente Unravels and the U.S. Attitude Stiffens

*We must give up the illusion that foreign policy can
choose between morality and pragmatism.*

Henry Kissinger   Address to American Society of
Newspaper Editors   April 17, 1974

The change in presidents and the evolution of events led to a revised set of
priorities for the United States. Richard Nixon's dream of a "structure of
peace," by his own declaration his primary objective throughout his years in
the White House, seemed to fade in importance when compared with the
immediacy of the growing economic crisis, which was being felt not only in
America but throughout the industrialized West. Triggered by a sharp rise in
oil prices following the Middle East War of October 1973, the crisis was, by
the beginning of 1975, reflected in rising unemployment, inflation, recession,
and a rapidly growing budgetary deficit.

In his state of the union address in January of 1975, President Ford told the
nation starkly that "the state of the Union is not good." Ford referred to a
global economic crisis and stressed the need to get the U.S. economy moving,
rather than the building of good relations on the international scene. "A re-
surgent American economy," said Ford, "would do more to restore the confidence of the world in its own future than anything else we can do."

Ford proposed a number of new programs and controls on federal spending
to meet the challenge. "America needs a new direction," he said, and enunciated a series of priorities: to put the unemployed back to work; to increase
real income and production; to restrain the growth of federal spending; to
achieve energy independence; and, last, to advance the cause of world understanding.

There was no question that the American people were shaken from their
recent experiences and concerned over their economic well-being, and the early
months of 1975 would plunge them further into a period of introversion,
guilt, and doubt. Communist guerrillas and units of the North Vietnamese
army were advancing toward Saigon as the U.S. administration struggled to
obtain congressional authorization for needed military assistance. By the time
Ford gave his state of the world address on April 10, the situation was becom-

ing desperate, and Ford's dramatic language sought to rouse Congress to respond: "Who can forget the enormous sacrifices of blood, dedication, and treasure that we made in Vietnam?"

Ford reported that "a vast human tragedy has befallen our friends in Vietnam and Cambodia." And, indeed, events were moving so quickly that almost no assistance the United States could provide, short of massive intervention, could have saved the situation. Virtually the entire North Vietnamese army was on the offensive in South Vietnam, and communist rebels were on the outskirts of Phnom Penh. On April 12 American personnel were evacuated from Phnom Penh, and on April 17 the Khmer Rouge occupied the city. In Vietnam, town after town fell to the North Vietnamese, and the government in Saigon ordered evacuation of whole regions. On April 21 President Nguyen Van Thieu resigned, as communist forces closed in on Saigon. On April 29, with the Saigon airport so overrun by would-be evacuees that planes could no longer land, the United States began a desperate evacuation of Americans and Vietnamese who had worked with the United States. Eighty-one helicopters evacuated thousands from Than Son Nhut airport and the U.S. embassy. By April 30 it was over, and North Vietnamese forces entered the capital. The White House spokesman read a presidential message to a packed press briefing room: "This action closes a chapter in the American experience. I ask all Americans to close ranks, to avoid recrimination about the past, to look ahead to the many goals we share, and to work together on the great tasks that remain to be accomplished."

The breadth and depth of the effect of this final Vietnam experience on the American people cannot be overestimated. It left a wound that would not be completely healed for a generation or longer. Its effects were immediately visible in the administration's policies and in public and congressional attitudes toward U.S. engagement on the world scene. Henry Kissinger, addressing the American Society of Newspaper Editors on April 17 in Washington, observed the effect on the nation: "We are now going through a period of adversity," he said, during which the American people were suffering from "deep and chronic self-doubt." For Kissinger, who had personally negotiated America's exit from the Vietnam conflict, the pill was bitterest. "There are not many provisions of the Paris agreement that are still relevant," he said in a press conference on April 29.

Kissinger's reaction was to apply the lessons of the Vietnam experience to other aspects of American foreign policy, and particularly to relations with the Soviet Union. The result was a much more realistic and limited attitude toward detente than had been evidenced previously. As he told the newspaper editors: "We must continue our policy of seeking to ease tensions. But we shall insist that the easing of tensions cannot occur selectively. We shall never forget who supplied the arms which North Vietnam used to make a mockery of its signature on the Paris accords."

In the same April 17 speech he drew another direct lesson from Vietnam: "One lesson we must surely learn from Vietnam is that new commitments of our nation's honor and prestige must be carefully weighed."

The revised attitude toward detente was colored also by the administration's experience in seeking congressional approval for the Trade Reform Act. What that experience had shown was that the American people, and the Congress, demanded a policy toward the USSR that was based publicly on the American view of human rights. Kissinger's revised view of detente took account of this feature; the Vietnam experience stirred bitterness toward the Soviet Union and encouraged U.S. leaders to give human rights principles more prominence. Kissinger conveyed the spirit of a lesson learned when he told the newspaper editors: "We must give up the illusion that foreign policy can choose between morality and pragmatism. America cannot be true to itself unless it upholds humane values and the dignity of the individual. . . . The American people must never forget that our strength gives force to our principles and our principles give purpose to our strength."

Under Kissinger's "radically new agenda," relations with America's traditional allies came first, followed by: meeting the economic and energy crises, standing up for America's ideals, meeting regional responsibilities, stopping the nuclear arms race, meeting the world's food needs, reducing conflict with America's adversaries, and cooperation in the oceans and space. This list of priorities moved two detente-related points down (to fifth place for stopping the nuclear arms race and seventh place for reducing conflicts with adversaries), and moved up three objectives that were related to traditional American values and responsibilities (relations with allies to first place, standing up for ideals to third place, and regional responsibilities to fourth place). By any measure, this was a significant change, and its effects were felt within the CSCE as in other elements of U.S. foreign policy.

One of the first manifestations of the new mood of the Ford administration following the fall of Saigon was its reaction to the attack on an American merchant ship, the SS *Mayaguez*, in international waters near Cambodia on May 12. The *Mayaguez* was captured by a military vessel of the new communist Cambodian regime, and its crew taken prisoner. Following two days of fruitless efforts to communicate with the Khmer Rouge leadership on the incident through third parties while the *Mayaguez* and its crew were taken to the Cambodian island of Koh Tang, President Ford ordered a bold rescue operation by U.S. naval and marine units. The action was accomplished successfully, and the *Mayaguez* and its crew were liberated, but the price was high: fifteen American servicemen were killed, three missing, and fifty wounded.

The more realistic appraisal of the possibilities of detente proved prophetic in another area of the world. In the midst of a revolution, and in large measure because of it, Portugal decided to grant independence to its two most important African colonies, Angola and Mozambique. The date for Angolan independence was fixed for November 11, but a civil conflict was raging among the factions within Angola, each of which hoped to control the country at the moment of independence. Beginning in August and continuing during the autumn months, Soviet and Cuban support for the leftist Popular Movement for the Liberation of Angola (MPLA) grew steadily, reminding the world that the Soviet interpretation of detente did not exclude backing for revolutionary movements. When Angola became independent, the MPLA was in control of Luanda, the capital, and claimed the right to form the government.

During these months, domestic criticism of U.S. policy toward the Soviets became more vocal, and President Ford repeatedly felt obliged to define what he understood by detente. In a speech to the American Legion National Convention in Minneapolis on August 19, Ford made a major attempt to do this, while at the same time extending a plea for support in his efforts to resist cuts in defense spending.

"Detente means moderate and restrained behavior between the two superpowers," said Ford, "not a license to fish in troubled waters. It means mutual respect and reciprocity — not unilateral concessions or one-sided agreements." Ford was reflecting the same revised priorities Kissinger had expressed when he added: "Peace is crucial, but freedom must come first. . . . The American people are still dedicated to the universal advancement of individual rights and human freedom."

One of the few major foreign policy pluses in a generally bleak year was Kissinger's success in putting together a further Egyptian-Israeli disengagement agreement, which entailed a second Israeli pullback in the Sinai. After one Middle East shuttle mission March 6–23 had failed to produce results, Kissinger seemed pessimistic. But in August there were new opportunities, and Kissinger once again undertook a shuttle mission. This time it produced a new agreement, initialed in Jerusalem and Alexandria on September 1, and signed in Geneva on September 4. The new agreement took the significant step of returning the Abu Rudeis oilfields to Egyptian control, and established a buffer zone between Egyptian and Israeli forces that was easier to monitor.

The economic and energy crises, the setback in Vietnam, the increasing disillusionment with detente, all had the effect of pushing the United States back toward its traditional allies. The NATO summit meeting, in Brussels, May 29–30, which was originally intended to demonstrate allied solidarity before the CSCE Summit in Helsinki, became, in the circumstances, an occasion for a broader reaffirmation of alliance values, as well as a joint redefinition of detente. In his May 29 statement at the summit, Ford conveyed the new U.S. attitude: "Let us cooperate in developing a productive and realistic agenda for detente, an agenda that serves our interests and not the interests of others who do not share our values."

Ford specifically warned of the need to ensure that the agreed provisions of the CSCE were actually carried out: "One item on [the allied agenda for detente] must be to assure that the promises made in the CSCE are translated into action to advance freedom and human dignity for all Europeans. Only by such realistic steps can we keep CSCE in perspective, whatever euphoric or inflated emphasis the Soviet Union or other participants may try to give it."

The joint communique at the end of the NATO meeting picked up this same point in its reference to the as-yet-unfinished Conference: "An advance along this road [toward understanding and cooperation] would be made if the CSCE were concluded on satisfactory terms and its words translated into deeds. The Allies hope that progress in the negotiations will permit such a conclusion in the near future."

Allied relationships were also reinforced in November, when, on the invitation of French President Giscard d'Estaing, the first Western economic summit meeting was held at Rambouillet. This new institution attempted to address the economic problems that had assumed first place on everyone's list of priorities. The economic summits have since then become annual events.

Relations with the USSR remained a major preoccupation, and efforts toward detente, though more realistic, were still an active part of Western policy. As Ford put it in his state of the world address on April 10, 1975: "There should be no illusions about the nature of the Soviet system, but there should also be no illusions about how to deal with it."

The U.S. administration still hoped to conclude a SALT II agreement with the Soviets, though such hopes dwindled in the course of 1975. "We hope," said Ford in the state of the world message, "to turn the Vladivostok agreements into a final agreement this year at the time of General Secretary Brezhnev's visit to the United States." (Brezhnev, of course, did not return to the United States, and the Ford administration did not conclude a second SALT agreement with the Soviets.)

Moreover, there was still considerable momentum from the earlier days of detente. This was epitomized by the Apollo-Soyuz linkup in space on July 17, which resulted from a project originally agreed in 1972. The same was true of the Helsinki Summit and many of the actions and statements surrounding it. There were several events that recalled earlier attitudes. In the Soviet Union, Andrei Sakharov, the nuclear physicist who was a leader of the dissident Soviet human rights movement, was awarded the Nobel Peace Prize, but was prevented by the Soviet government from traveling to the West to receive it. And in the United States, shortly before the CSCE conclusion at the Summit, Ford refused to receive Solzhenitsyn in the White House. These remnants of an earlier period were incompatible with the commitments that would be contained in the Helsinki Final Act. The Soviet action in prohibiting Sakharov's travel was a sad omen of how well the USSR would respect those commitments.

18 Reaching Imperfect Decisions
The Effort to Engage Negotiations on Human Rights and Freer Movement

Decisions reached under a consensus procedure are unlikely to be perfect.

Anker Jorgensen Helsinki July 31, 1975

During the first year and a half of the Conference, work on the human-rights-related issues of Basket III had advanced slowly, barely keeping pace with work on other CSCE subjects. The West and the major neutral delegations patiently sought to engage the Soviets in discussion of their specific freer movement proposals and to identify areas where agreement was possible. In response the Soviets posed a perplexing mix of procedural and substantive obstacles to slow down and deflect the Western effort and to render the Western-proposed texts as meaningless as possible.

The Soviet Basket III chief, Yuri Dubinin, was an urbane diplomat whose several years' service in Paris had given him a taste for good food and wine. But he was an intense and monolithic negotiator who refused the most elementary flexibility. He was capable of sticking to a point indefinitely, with considerable disdain and even rudeness toward his negotiating partners. Provoked, he would fly into a rage of belittling and insulting language. He seemed not only to disagree with, but actually to despise many of the principles of a free society for which the West was seeking recognition. In the face of Dubinin's unsophisticated and unbending negotiating style, Western negotiators became stubborn, and progress was measured in terms of words agreed. Each noun, verb, and adjective was disputed.

The first obstacle Dubinin fixed was the notion of a preamble for Basket III, and the position that drafting on subsequent points could not begin until the principle of a preamble had been agreed; then, that drafting of the preamble would have to precede drafting of the substantive elements of Basket III. The preamble really represented the fundamental issue of the extent to which the specific freer movement agreements of Basket III would be subject to Soviet caveats that would rob them of any meaning. The caveats that the USSR sought to introduce in the preamble were essential to the defensive Soviet strategy in this part of the Conference, and Dubinin's basic attitude was that he would not discuss specifics until he knew that he would be able to include the Soviet caveats in a preamble.

The Bulgarian delegation acted on behalf of the Soviets in Basket III, and tabled a draft preamble that, if it had been accepted, would have made the provisions of Basket III subject specifically to the principle of nonintervention in internal affairs, to respect for the sovereignty of each state, and to "observance of the laws and customs of the participating states." Such a solution would have given overriding importance to one of the principles over the others, in particular the principle of nonintervention over the principle of human rights, and would have made it impossible to seek compliance with Basket III. Basket III provisions would have been formally established as "internal matters" subject to local "laws and customs." A result of this kind was unacceptable to the West.

The question of how the provisions of Basket III would relate to existing national practices was considered basic to the significance of the Western freer movement proposals. Since the West was seeking improvements in Soviet and East European behavior, there had to be some commitment in the agreed text that its provisions would be put into practice, not that previous practices would continue. During the Helsinki preparatory talks the same issue had arisen, and the Western countries had agreed that the drafting of Basket III would be accomplished in "full respect for the CSCE principles." Now, the Soviets were reopening a debate that the West thought had been settled during the preparatory session and were proposing that caveats eliminated at that time should be reintroduced in the final CSCE document.

The Western and neutral states were prepared to accept in the preamble to Basket III a general reference to all the principles, along the lines of the formulation used in the Helsinki Blue Book, but were not prepared to single out the principles of national sovereignty and nonintervention in internal affairs as having special application to Basket III, much less to make Basket III subject specifically to national "laws and customs."

At the beginning of 1974, Western Basket III delegates realized that they would have to find a way to meet Dubinin's point and bring him to negotiate. Discussions of the principles, which the Soviets considered the most important section of the Conference agenda, were moving ahead smoothly, and there was a risk that Basket III would be left behind and its substance squeezed out in a rush to finish the negotiations. There was no way to force progress in Basket III without accepting the concept of a preamble.

In February a procedural compromise was accepted under which drafting of a preamble would proceed parallel to drafting of the concrete provisions of Basket III. The West thus accepted in principle that there would be a preamble to Basket III (without any agreement as to its content) and obtained Soviet agreement to enter drafting of Basket III specifics. Adoption of this arrangement did not, of course, resolve the issue. It yielded few positive results, and the basic dispute continued.

Later in the spring, Finnish Ambassador Jaako Iloniemi attempted to find a substantive compromise that would satisfy the Soviets' desire to subordinate Basket III to the internal "laws and customs" of the participating states, without giving any one of the principles primary importance. Under Iloniemi's two-part proposal, the preamble to Basket III would contain a phrase similar to the formulation already adopted in the Helsinki Blue Book (see HR 43), indicating that the provisions of that basket would be carried out in full respect for all ten CSCE principles. At the same time the principle of nonintervention in internal affairs, which was then being negotiated, would include a statement, derived partly from the language of the UN Friendly Relations Declaration, that the participating states would "respect the political, economic, and cultural foundations of other participating states, as well as their right to determine their own legislative and regulatory systems." Iloniemi explained that the two parts of this proposal should be seen as an attempt to find a solution to the question of nonintervention in relation to Basket III and thus to break the impasse in that area of the Conference. While there were concerns about the wording and placement of the Finnish language, and tactical considerations about accepting it, the Finnish package deal, as it came to be known, was received with cautious interest.

Finnish delegation head Iloniemi, who subsequently became political director of the foreign ministry in Helsinki and ambassador to Washington, was one of the most intelligent and understanding of all the delegation heads at the CSCE. Coming from a small country with a deep interest in establishing a regularized CSCE forum to help protect Finland's neutrality, Iloniemi's objective was an outcome to the negotiations that would be satisfactory to all concerned and make a continuation of the CSCE process possible. He worked diligently and responsibly for compromises to bring this about, but he never forgot the Western principles on which his country's democratic system is based. An unprepossessing, totally bald man with a dry, sometimes caustic, sense of humor, Iloniemi was one of the handful of diplomats who not only understood the CSCE, but also made it work.

In considering the Finnish package deal, the Western group reasoned that a general reference to the principles was acceptable because it would mean Basket III should be carried out not only with respect for the principles of national sovereignty and nonintervention in internal affairs, but also in keeping with the principles of respect for human rights and fundamental freedoms, and fulfillment of international obligations (which would include such obligations as those of the Universal Declaration of Human Rights, for example).

Four neutral delegations (Austria, Finland, Sweden, and Switzerland) correctly perceived that here was the basis for a compromise: a general reference to the principles and language placed somewhere in the principles to satisfy the Soviet desire to strengthen the nonintervention idea.

The neutrals continued over a period of several weeks to build on the Finnish package deal. They were attempting to find the right balance for a compromise by mixing into this proposed package various other elements of substance and procedure to satisfy East and West and to safeguard the interests of all concerned. As the Conference moved into July, work on the principles and Basket III was largely held in suspense while neutral delegates conducted soundings on this complex arrangement.

The neutral delegations proceeded cautiously in view of the complexity of achieving adoption of such a broad device, involving work in one committee and several subcommittees. To lay the groundwork, neutral delegates first contacted key delegations privately, then formulated their proposal. They presented a first draft to separate, informal gatherings of Eastern, Western, and independent delegations, then sought to improve on their draft to make it fully acceptable. Both East and West moved reluctantly; the East because such a compromise would blur the kind of clear caveat they wished to introduce in Basket III; the West because they preferred a Basket III with no caveats and because they suspected that once the overall Soviet caveat was eliminated, the Soviets would simply try to introduce more specialized caveats in the introductory language, sometimes referred to as "minipreambles," that would precede each section of Basket III.

The role of the neutrals was essential in situations like this. Unconstrained by the need to stay in step with a large grouping, and with a perceived interest in moving the negotiations forward, they were able to formulate compromises when Eastern and Western sides were unable to move. Several neutral delegates had major roles in the Conference because of their talent for finding solutions to difficult negotiating problems. The most active was the deputy head of the Swiss delegation, Edouard Brunner, a brilliant innovator and indefatigable maneuverer who was constantly probing for devices to advance the Conference's work. Brunner was mistrusted at various times by each Conference faction, but this was the inevitable lot of one who took on the responsibility of compromise-finder. The best testimony to the role of Brunner and many other neutral diplomats was that whenever the Conference got tangled up in a seemingly unsolvable problem, delegates of all political persuasions went looking for them.

The package the neutrals put together attempted to meet the concerns of all sides. They proposed a general reference to the principles for inclusion in the Basket III preamble (FA 419), in a context that arguably made it apply only to "new ways and means" (presumably other than those agreed in the CSCE itself) (FA 418). To satisfy the Soviets, the neutrals picked up the Finnish idea to include language in the principles recognizing that each state had the right to choose its own "laws and regulations." The neutrals suggested including this phraseology as an aspect of national sovereignty in the principle of sovereign equality (last sentence of FA 24). To satisfy the Western fear that this would render Basket III meaningless, the neutrals suggested balancing the "laws and regulations" language with a specific statement, in the principle of fulfillment of international obligations, to the effect that the participating states would implement the provisions of the final document of the CSCE (FA 68). Furthermore, to ensure that more specialized caveats would not subsequently be substituted in the minipreambles of Basket III, the neutrals proposed that the whole package be tentative until negotiation of these minipreambles and much of the substance of Basket III had been completed.

This was the most complicated deal that had yet been attempted in the CSCE, and it took several weeks before all delegations were prepared to accept it. In the interim, most work was blocked, either because it depended directly on resolution of the package deal, or because one side or another was unwilling to compromise and decrease its bargaining leverage.

Acceptance of the neutral package deal on the final day before the summer recess, July 26, 1974, was the most promising movement in the CSCE since agreement on the principle of inviolability of frontiers, and appeared to make progress on Basket III specifics easier. But the Soviet hostility to Basket III and the primitive negotiating tactics that Basket III chief Dubinin continued to use promised further delays and slow progress at best.

With the Soviets forcing Basket III to concentrate on the preambular issue, few concrete freer movement provisions were agreed in the first half of 1974. The only significant exception was the important text on "Contacts and Regular Meetings on the Basis of Family Ties" (FA 430–433), which was registered in mid-March during the buildup to agreement on inviolability of frontiers and was undoubtedly a calculated Soviet sweetener. This text was the first, and least sensitive, part of the Western "family package" of proposals to be agreed. The "family package" was a key set of freer movement proposals designed to obtain a commitment to permit freer contacts between families separated by national borders, easier marriage between persons of different nationalities, and the possibility of reunification of divided families.

In the autumn of 1974, however, following agreement on the Finnish package deal, a number of additional texts were registered, including the two remaining parts of the "family package," on "Reunification of Families" (FA 434–443, registered on December 3 after eight months of negotiation) and "Marriage between Citizens of Different States" (FA 444–447, registered in late December). The basic text on freer circulation of and access to printed information (FA 483–492) was registered in October, and the text on "Cooperation in the Field of Information" (FA 498–504) was agreed in December. The landmark principle of "Respect for Human Rights and Fundamental Freedoms, Including the Freedom of Thought, Conscience, Religion, or Belief"

(FA 48–56) was registered on November 20, following a record fifty-six negotiating sessions.

But as 1974 ended, Western negotiators were reminded once again of the difficulties they faced. Even before the neutral package deal was approved, the Soviets had shown that they would indeed seek to make up for loss of the "laws and customs" caveat by introducing individually tailored caveats in the minipreambles to the sections of Basket III. A Bulgarian proposal for language introducing the human contacts section included a phrase stating that the provisions of that section should be carried out under "mutually acceptable conditions." This phrase, known in Conference parlance as the MAC clause, became symbolic of the specific caveats with which the Soviets hoped to pepper Basket III.

This particular MAC clause was subsequently the subject of private negotiations between the French and Danish delegations, as the Western floor leaders on human contacts, and the Soviets, Bulgarians, and Poles. Following agreement among the delegations, two different versions of the text were tabled. One version was in Russian and was sponsored by Poland; the other, in French, was sponsored by Denmark. These texts, which purported to be the same, were manifestly different in a number of places. They were politically sensitive because they attempted a compromise between opposing ideological approaches to the relationship between human rights and detente. The Soviets wished to indicate in this text that progress in the field of human rights was dependent on progress toward detente. Such a concept was anathema to the Western countries, for which human rights represent an essential principle of human existence not dependent on the state of relations between national governments. The West felt, on the contrary, that progress toward detente should depend on progress in respecting human rights (the eventual compromise text appears as FA 422–429).

The Soviets were convinced that, since two Western negotiators had accepted the linguistic discrepancy, the other Western nations would also swallow it. But there was resentment among Western delegates over what they perceived as Franco-Soviet bilateralism, an apparent result of the short-lived "spirit of Rambouillet," which derived from the summit meeting between Giscard and Brezhnev in December. More importantly, conscious acceptance of two different versions of the same text would have been a precedent with broad implications for the CSCE. Both Western and neutral countries balked at the idea of eventually submitting for the signature of their leaders differing language versions of the same document. The dispute remained unresolved as the delegations left Geneva for their Christmas vacations.

19   Who Has the Right?
Nonintervention in Internal Affairs and Human Rights

No one should try to dictate to other peoples on the basis of foreign policy considerations of one kind or another the manner in which they ought to manage their internal affairs. It is only the people of each given state, and no one else, who have the sovereign right to resolve their internal affairs and establish their internal laws. A different approach would be perilous as a ground for international cooperation.

Leonid Brezhnev Helsinki July 31, 1975

One of the most perplexing issues underlying the CSCE was the question of what kinds of interference in internal affairs of other states should be prohibited, and how. The CSCE principles, like the UN Friendly Relations Declaration, separate the concept of interference in internal affairs from the concept of threat or use of force against another state. Each concept is recognized under a specific principle; both activities are prohibited.

Yet states *do* attempt to influence the internal affairs of other states in a variety of time-honored ways. Political leaders offer their views on events in other countries; diplomats seek to influence officials or key parliamentarians prior to important votes in national legislatures; overseas information offices circulate their government's propaganda; etc. Between the threat or use of force on the one hand and these legitimate and accepted efforts to influence events in other countries on the other, there lies an additional area of unacceptable interstate activity. It is this area of activity that is covered by the concept of nonintervention in internal affairs. The activities of private persons, publications, or organizations, over which a government has no control, are not, in the Western view, affected.

But even within this narrow scope, it is difficult to establish what is meant by intervention, especially when the definition must be acceptable not only to Western countries, but also to governments whose philosophy is based on Marxism-Leninism. For Western countries the support of a revolution in another state clearly constitutes intervention in the internal affairs of that state.

But for a Marxist, who is ideologically committed to world revolution, this is not always the case.

Ideological differences of this kind underlay virtually all the debates in the CSCE, and the language finally agreed is therefore subject to differing interpretations. Consider, as another example, the concept of self-determination of peoples. In the West self-determination evokes the mechanism of pluralistic elections, with the will of the people expressed by a majority of the voters. The Marxist, however, has another way of looking at it. For him, self-determination evokes not the "bourgeois" concept of majority rule, but the desires of the proletarian class, which are not always clear to the workers themselves. The CSCE principle of self-determination, like its counterpart in the Friendly Relations Declaration, firmly proclaims self-determination, but says nothing to prejudice either of the above viewpoints.

The concept of nonintervention, even within its narrow limitations, was subject to similar differences in ideological interpretation during the CSCE. And even ideological considerations were at times outweighed by concrete national interests. Both East and West had dual, and at times conflicting, objectives with regard to nonintervention.

For the USSR it was desirable to obtain language in the CSCE final document that would preclude Western nations from pressing for compliance with the principle of human rights and the freer movement provisions of Basket III. Noninterference in internal affairs, as suggested by Brezhnev in the quotation cited at the beginning of this chapter, was the primary defense envisioned by the USSR against possible use of Basket III by the West. At the same time it was essential for the Soviets that the agreed language not inhibit interventions that they might consider necessary to prevent Eastern European regimes from being overthrown or modified, as in the case of Budapest in 1956 or Prague in 1968.

The Western countries faced a similar dilemma. They wished to obtain Final Act language that would contradict the Brezhnev Doctrine and help prevent repetitions of Budapest and Prague. They also preferred language that would commit the Soviets to refrain from efforts at subversion in other countries. But the West could not accept language seeming to imply that human rights were subordinate to national laws and practices, or indeed that they were subject to limitation by any governmental authority. In the Western view human rights are God-given and cannot be altered by national laws. As the American Declaration of Independence asserts: "All men are . . . endowed by their Creator with certain unalienable rights." The West wished to avoid language that could be used to preclude active support for human rights in other countries, or that would inhibit active pursuit of implementation of Basket III.

The concept of nonintervention was especially relevant to the situations of Romania and Yugoslavia, each of which wanted the strongest possible expression of the idea of nonintervention to complement passages on refraining from the threat or use of force, so as to provide an additional inhibition against possible future Soviet interventions in their countries. Since they were less interested than the Western countries in an active pursuit of Basket III implementation, the Romanian and Yugoslav delegations did not face the kinds of dilemmas that confronted the Soviets and the West.

A further complicating factor, especially after the Turkish occupation of part of Cyprus, was the difference in the views of the situation in that country that were held by the Greeks, the Turks, and the Cypriots themselves. These delegations did not have a strong influence on the drafting of the nonintervention principle, but at times sidetracked the discussion as they made conflicting points for the record.

The compromise found to meet the requirements of these different factions was a complex one involving several parts of the Final Act.

The main elements of the compromise were included in the so-called neutral package deal, described in the previous chapter. As a result of this deal, the preamble to Basket III (FA 419) states that "this [Basket III] cooperation should take place in full respect for the principles guiding relations among participating States" (this sentence is also included in the preamble to Basket II— FA 148). The package also introduced the following sentence into the principle of sovereign equality (FA 24): "They will also respect each other's right freely to choose and develop its political, social, economic and cultural systems, as well as its right to determine its laws and regulations." Finally, the neutral package placed this sentence in the principle of "Fulfillment in Good Faith of Obligations under International Law" (FA 68): "In exercising their sovereign rights, including their right to determine their laws and regulations, they will conform with their legal obligations under international law; they will furthermore pay due regard to and implement the provisions in the Final Act of the Conference on Security and Co-operation in Europe."

Complementing this package are two statements that all the principles are of equal value (FA 22 and 70). Finally, the section on conference follow-up (FA 661–664) and the preamble and closing phrases of the Final Act (FA 5 and 674) reiterate the commitment to implement its provisions.

This interrelated series of clauses and provisions comes closer to the objectives of the West than it does to the interests of the Soviet Union. Basket III is not subject only to certain of the principles, such as nonintervention in internal affairs, but to all the principles, including the principle on human rights, and there are several strong commitments to carry out the provisions of the Final Act. At the same time human rights are established as a separate principle of interstate behavior as important as other such principles, a status they do not have in the Friendly Relations Declaration. Furthermore, the principles of sovereign equality, refraining from the threat or use of force, territorial integrity, nonintervention, and equal rights and self-determination of peoples contain concepts and language that fundamentally contradict the Brezhnev Doctrine. The principle of nonintervention itself, while somewhat ambiguous, implies that the types of intervention excluded are those entailing some measure of force. The very use of the term nonintervention, instead of noninterference, was deemed to narrow the applicability of the principle to actions involving force.

However, the differing ideologies of the signatories to the Final Act impose different filters through which these provisions are viewed. If there was any doubt as to the communist view of the effect of the Final Act on the Brezhnev Doctrine, it should have been dispelled by the language of the GDR–USSR Treaty of Friendship, Cooperation, and Mutual Assistance of October 7, 1975, just two months after the Final Act was signed. This treaty contains language that echoes the USSR-Czechoslovak treaty of 1970, in which the doctrine of a national sovereignty limited by the overriding need to defend the socialist revolution was first included. The GDR–USSR treaty baldly reasserts the Brezhnev Doctrine: "[The USSR and the GDR] declare their readiness to take the necessary steps to protect and defend the historic achievements of socialism."

Just as the balance between inviolability of frontiers and peaceful change was the central CSCE compromise with respect to the post-World War II territorial situation in Europe, so the complex arrangements on nonintervention and human rights, including Basket III, were perhaps the central political compromise. The balance is a fine one, and the positions of principle of both East and West are preserved. But it is clear that the new element introduced by the CSCE is the dynamic concept that respect for individual rights is a legitimate aspect of relations between states and that discussion of human-rights-related issues is therefore not a form of intervention in internal affairs.

20 What Talleyrand Said
The Negotiations Begin to Move,
January–March 1975

*Our Conference must not be allowed to mark time, nor
should become applicable to it what Talleyrand said about
the foreign ministers at the Congress of Vienna: Too
frightened to fight each other and too stupid to agree.*

Walter Scheel Helsinki July 4, 1973

When negotiations reopened on January 20, 1975, following a five-week
recess, they did so once again in an atmosphere of uncertainty. Rumors of
Brezhnev's failing health surfaced in diplomatic circles and the press; the Soviet
leader had disappeared from view for an unusually long time. Coupled with
the Soviet cancellation on January 10 of the U.S.-Soviet trade agreement because of the Jackson-Vanik amendment to the Trade Act of 1974, this again
raised the possibility that Soviet interest in an early conclusion to the Conference might be downgraded, with all this would signify in terms of the
Kremlin's willingness to make the concessions necessary to satisfy Western
participants.

The Soviet delegates went out of their way to dispel the impression that a
slowdown in U.S.-Soviet relations might affect the CSCE. The day after the
Conference reconvened, Kovalev took his U.S. counterpart Sherer aside in the
midst of a crowded committee meeting to say that "trade questions" should
have no effect on the CSCE. The intention was at least partly to convey this
message through Sherer to other Western delegations, who could be counted
on to ask the U.S. delegation leader what Kovalev had said.

The NATO group offered a new element in negotiations on military
confidence-building measures during the first week of the new session, specifying for the first time a numerical figure—700 kilometers—for the border
zone in the USSR within which, as an exception to the general "all of Europe"
formula, military maneuvers would be subject to notification. This vastly simplified the negotiation on the area of application by reducing it to a straight
numerical problem, since the Soviets had already offered a hundred-kilometer
zone.

There were also a few isolated advances, especially in Basket II, and a handful of new texts were agreed. A paragraph was registered on double taxation and repatriation of profits (FA 260), and the Basket II section on tourism (FA 354–375) was finalized and arranged in order, a step that virtually completed work on this subject in Basket II. But these were items of secondary importance, and in the main areas of negotiation—military subjects and Basket III—the Soviets stubbornly resisted any concessions and complained aggressively that the West should moderate its more ambitious proposals.

In Basket III there was a proliferation of informal negotiating groups focused on specific topics and limited to representatives of a few interested delegations. Soon, there were small informal groups working sporadically on the introduction to human contacts and the texts on travel, tourism, youth contacts, audiovisual information, and working conditions for journalists. The composition of each of these groups was different, and meetings were organized on an ad hoc basis whenever a new development was anticipated.

The creation of numerous informal groups gave the Conference a strange, hollow appearance. Formal meetings convened and immediately adjourned; it was necessary to maintain the facade of formal meetings, even though everyone realized that the real work was going on elsewhere. (The interpreters became seriously annoyed at the lack of meetings. Despite the fact that they were paid for full working hours, they felt they would grow rusty and lose their skills if the lack of meetings continued.) The lobbies and corridors of the CSCE were vacant, as delegates met for private sessions at their national missions. There was also an illusory air of mystery, since the usual information channels had dried up. Delegates became anxious to find out what was "really" happening. But in the first weeks of 1975, very little of significance was happening.

The lack of progress on confidence-building measures was so disturbing that a number of Western and neutral delegations, and particularly Yugoslavia, warned the Soviets that progress would have to be made in this subject area as well as the others if the Conference was to be successfully concluded. A meeting of the military subcommittee was cancelled by Western and neutral delegations to demonstrate the need for new Eastern concessions.

In Basket III feelings ran even stronger. The dispute over the differing French and Russian versions of the introductory language to the human contacts section (FA 422–429) continued and became a bitterly contested issue of principle. The Soviets remained adamant and privately stressed that they did not care what the Western language versions of this text said; the Russian version would not be changed.

The cavalier Soviet attitude alerted all delegations to the need to ensure that the various language versions of the CSCE document would be identical. This was a monumental task for genuine linguistic experts, of whom there were very few at the CSCE, but responsibility for ensuring complete agreement among texts could not be left to the Conference secretariat.

The Swiss secretariat had made translations into the six official Conference languages as work progressed, but most national delegations were required by their governments to assure for themselves that all language versions were identical. This was difficult not only because of limitations on the language capabilities of individual delegations, but more importantly because in some cases language differences covered differing political nuances of meaning. Tampering with linguistic compromises therefore risked reopening some of the Conference's most delicate issues. As Kovalev put it, this problem was a "time bomb ticking away beneath the Conference." Eventually, a team of U.S. linguists was brought to Geneva to check all language versions to ensure agreement among them.

The lack of progress resulted in gradually increasing pressure on all delegations. Most Western governments now hoped for an early conclusion to the Conference, but could not agree to a less-than-satisfactory result. The Soviets continued to be interested in an early Stage III, but would give no concessions to move toward that goal. Their intransigence had a visible effect on the Western group, some of whom began to look for "compromises," even when the result would have been highly unsatisfactory. The EC-Nine and NATO caucuses were looking at some of the issues on which fallback positions — taboo until now — would have to be considered if the CSCE was to be brought to an end. Among these were the Mediterranean declaration, notification of military movements, and follow-up to the Conference. On each of these issues there was a sharp division of views among the Western allies, which served to complicate further negotiations on them.

The negotiating equation on follow-up, in particular, began to come into focus. The Soviets pressed for a reference in the follow-up document to the possibility of holding a new conference or conferences in the future, leading many delegations to wonder whether the Soviets were not more interested in a loose commitment to a new conference than they were in a more precisely defined continuing follow-up mechanism, which had previously been one of their assumed CSCE goals. Speculation on an evolution in the Soviet view of follow-up was fed by the Romanians, who said privately that the Soviets had been so disappointed by the way CSCE had come out that they no longer wanted a follow-up mechanism that could be used by the West to put pressure on them to carry out the provisions of Basket III. The Romanians sought through use of this argument to interest Western delegations in their own concept of periodic follow-up meetings. Lipatti, the Romanian delegation chief, was an extremely able and articulate spokesman for continued CSCE meetings. One of the cleverest negotiators at the CSCE, he had spent many years in France, and was a convincing advocate of a permanent forum that would permit Eastern countries such as Romania to follow a more independent foreign policy. An urbane and cultivated man with an attractive actress wife, Lipatti was also one of the chief philosophers of the Conference. "Europe," he would say, "is here in this Conference; this is Europe!"

At the same time, NATO caucus discussions of the possible final outcome of negotiations on follow-up revealed important conceptual differences among the allies. Some believed regular follow-up meetings to be genuinely in the Western interest, while the French insisted that they would not agree to anything beyond the existing Danish proposal for a single meeting after two or three years to review implementation of the Conference results. The French were evidently as wary of giving the United States a permanent role in pan-European affairs as they were of giving the USSR an increased opportunity to meddle in Western European business. It was clear that this issue would entail a tight negotiation, and that a solution would only be found at the very end of the Conference.

The pressures from national leaders to be able to plan ahead for a Summit conclusion continued to mount. Finnish Ambassador Iloniemi discreetly pointed out to other delegation leaders that a Stage III Summit would take considerable planning. Such a unique event would require advance agreement on scenario, timing, and a variety of practical matters that could not be left to the last few weeks of the Stage II negotiations, since consensus would be needed on every detail. A tedious all-day meeting of the NATO Council in Brussels on February 7 with NATO delegation heads from Geneva did little to resolve allied differences or to advance CSCE work.

The growing pressures and the lack of concrete progress on specifics gradually conveyed to Western delegates that the situation had evolved during two short months and was now different from what it had been at any previous time in CSCE. It was evident that their contacts with Western leaders in the last few months of 1974 had convinced the Soviets that a Stage III Summit in the late spring or early summer of 1975 was virtually in the bag. The Soviets had apparently concluded that a few concessions by them at the right moment would assure final acceptance of the Summit by all Western leaders. Since the general assumption at the Conference itself was that the negotiating stage would be wound up in about May or June, the Soviets were taking a tough position in order to derive the maximum impact from their concessions when they made them.

The Soviet tactic depended on reversing the time pressure the West had previously sought to use against Moscow, and applying it as leverage against those countries that theoretically had less interest than the Kremlin in an early conclusion. The Soviets' possibilities for success in this attempt depended on the varied Western political investments in detente in general and CSCE in particular, but these were considerable.

The Soviet tactics had some effect. Their discipline and patience made it easier for them to outwait the Western delegations, which were burdened by family separations and catch-as-catch-can staffing. While the Western countries stuck to their proposals, most were willing to settle for less, and all were anxious to end the affair. At the same time, no Western leader could go to Helsinki without a satisfactory result, and this required wringing a number of further concessions from the USSR.

It was in mid-February that the Conference began to change from a detached, gentlemanly, rather obscure debating society to the high-pressure negotiation it became in its final months. The mood had been there since late December, a curious tension as the delegates in Geneva sensed the awakening of political interest in the Conference. There was an air of expectation, of suppressed excitement, of a growing perception that finally, after almost two years of dreary discussions, the CSCE was approaching its denouement.

The second week of February began with promise. The Romanians and Soviets had completed their difficult private negotiations in Bucharest and Moscow and had agreed on phraseology for the key fourth paragraph of the Romanian proposal on refraining from use of force (FA 80). This paragraph commits the signatories "to refrain . . . from invasion of or attack on" the territory of another participating state and was considered by the Romanians as a major achievement imposing an important new restraint on Soviet temptations to repeat Budapest or Prague in Bucharest.

With agreement on this paragraph, the Romanians gave their consent to the registration of the text of the eighth principle on equal rights and self-determination of peoples (FA 57–60), leaving only two of the ten CSCE principles to be drafted. One of these, the ninth principle on cooperation among states, was already nearing completion, and the realization that the subcommittee drafting the principles would soon begin work on the last of the decalogue brought home to everyone in Geneva that the end of the long tunnel was really in view.

But this was not the only news that week. The subcommittee on industrial cooperation removed the remaining brackets in its text (FA 200–229), agreed on the ordering of paragraphs, and asked the secretariat to print the final version of this section of the final document.

Other lesser progress was also noted: a further paragraph on working conditions for journalists and the introductory text for the education section of Basket III were informally agreed, and the Swiss circulated compromise language intended gracefully to end discussion of their proposal for the establishment of a system for peaceful settlement of disputes in Europe. Under their new plan, the Conference would simply be asked to agree that at some future date a meeting of experts would continue consideration of the idea.

The Cyprus problem again looked as though it might affect the work of the Conference, as the Turkish Cypriot community issued a separatist declaration. This incident prompted another bitter Turkish-Greek-Cypriot exchange and led the Turkish delegation to mutter darkly in the corridors that they might formally question the credentials of the Cypriot delegation if they concluded that it was not fully representative of the interests of the Turkish Cypriot community. The CSCE had never had credentials problems, and in view of its consensus system it was difficult to imagine how the Conference could proceed if credentials should be challenged. Fortunately, the wise and prudent Turkish delegation leader, Ambassador Ozdimir Benler, never carried out this threat.

Although work on some subjects, such as military confidence-building measures and human contacts, remained stuck, overall Conference momentum continued. A clause on distribution of official information bulletins by embassies was agreed (FA 492), completing the section on printed information (FA 483–492), and another paragraph on working conditions for journalists was set. The Western group presented the Soviets with a slightly revised version of the introduction to human contacts, intended to settle the difficulties over the two differing language versions, which the Soviets proceeded to try to whittle down, point by point. In the compromise version eventually agreed, the "mutually acceptable conditions" phrase (FA 426) follows a clause regarding further efforts (after the CSCE) in the field of human contacts and arguably applies only to such post-CSCE activities.

Elsewhere, a sensitive paragraph was registered in the Mediterranean working group indicating that the participating states would conduct their relations with the nonparticipating Mediterranean states "in the spirit of" the ten CSCE principles (FA 406). The working group on follow-up to the Conference registered the final two paragraphs of the preamble to the follow-up section of the Final Act (FA 659–660), when the Soviets in successive weeks dropped their insistence on references to a future CSCE and to the primacy of the CSCE principles.

On February 21 the Swedish delegation proposed creation of a working group on the organization of the final documents of the Conference and the practical arrangements for Stage III. The Swedish idea was enthusiastically supported by the Soviet bloc and virtually all the neutrals, but the Irish delegation head, speaking in Ireland's capacity as the president of the EC-Nine, responded that the proposal would have to be discussed further in the Coordinating Committee before a decision could be taken.

Soviet behavior suggested that Moscow had decided to move ahead in areas of the Conference in which they did not have major difficulties, in order to generate a more positive atmosphere, while digging in on issues such as military confidence-building measures and many specific points in Basket III, where they had real difficulty. At the same time they were moving behind the scenes to eliminate the few remaining major obstacles standing in the way of a third stage summit, such as the peaceful change clause that was a sine qua non for the FRG.

The Soviets were as selective as ever in choosing subject areas in which to permit progress, but the movement that did take place was sufficient to rekindle a widespread desire to focus Conference attention on Stage III. Some

Western delegations were inclined to accept the Swedish-proposed working group on Stage III immediately. Their eagerness reflected the growing interest of the political levels of their governments in holding the Stage III Summit as a demonstration that the policy of detente was working. All Western delegates realized that beginning joint consideration of Stage III would generate greatly increased pressures for moderation of the remaining Western proposals, but most were prepared to take this risk, especially since the list of Western desiderata was being steadily diminished as the Soviets offered one concession after another to reach agreement on individual paragraphs, sentences, and phrases.

By the end of February, the central question before the CSCE was the extent to which the participating countries together judged that the Conference was coming to its end. As a practical matter, this question was posed in the form of two procedural issues: the Swedish proposal for establishment of a working group on Stage III, and whether the CSCE should take an Easter recess.

The Soviets tried hard to create a favorable atmosphere, but remained inflexible on most key questions. The West reacted prudently, prepared to be reasonably flexible in order to move toward agreements, but unwilling to give up the basic elements of their proposals or to water them down unacceptably. The Western delegations wished to avoid being put in the position of seeking an early conclusion. This was sometimes difficult for them, since their political leaders were in many cases pressing for progress and could not understand why a single phrase or even a single word should stand in the way of the Helsinki Summit. All the Western delegates knew that the timing of the Summit was still the best leverage they had to squeeze concessions from the Soviets. Like racers, they were unwilling to start the sprint first. But privately, in the Western caucuses, the final fallback positions, the few remaining compromises, were quietly being prepared.

The first week in March was a marathon debate on the two procedural issues that would indicate the collective judgment of the Conference on progress toward the Summit. The Soviets pressed for establishment of a working group on Stage III, and angrily insisted that there should be no Easter recess whatsoever. The debate culminated in an unusual two-day meeting of the Coordinating Committee. The Soviets, smelling blood, pulled out all the stops. They ordered their ambassadors to put pressure on foreign ministries in Western capitals, ridiculed those who opposed them, made personal threats, and stated flatly that they "knew" certain delegations were ignoring their own instructions.

The U.S. and other Western delegations opposed creation of a working group on Stage III until it was really justified. Most Western delegations were prepared to accept a long weekend instead of an Easter recess, in order to create the best possibilities for progress. But the smaller delegations, who depended on consultations in their capitals for instructions, insisted on an Easter break and were supported on principle by some Western delegations.

The result was a compromise under which it was agreed that the Coordinating Committee would hold further discussions of the final document (or documents) and Stage III, and would establish a working group on these subjects when all delegations agreed the time was right. The Easter recess was arranged through a complex phasing of committee and subcommittee meetings permitting most delegates to get away for about one week, while the Conference continued at half-speed.

In two short months the CSCE had become a tough poker game, and the stakes—the Helsinki Summit—were high.

21 Agreement Despite
Breakthrough on Freer Movement,
March–May 1975

*Clearly we have not assembled here to approve one
another's ideologies or state and political systems. The
peoples we represent expect us to reach an agreement
despite actually existing ideological and political
differences.*

Janos Kadar Helsinki July 31, 1975

In early March Brezhnev wrote to the principal Western heads of government,
proposing that the Stage III Summit begin on June 30. The letter represented a
further investment of personal prestige by the Soviet leader, and for diverse
reasons it had a significant impact in the West. At a meeting in Dublin the
heads of government of the nine Common Market countries issued a communique that included the most positive language yet developed by a Western
group on the possibility of a Stage III Summit. Many officials in Geneva regarded it as a collective commitment to a Summit, leaving only the question of
timing to be arranged.

The more forthcoming Nine position was based at least in part on the
belief, which was widely held in Western political and diplomatic circles at the
time, that Brezhnev was seriously ill, even perhaps dying. It was speculated that
the struggle for his succession had already begun, and many Western Sovietologists argued that it was desirable to strengthen the hand of Kremlin moder-
ates at this key juncture by giving Brezhnev his CSCE Summit. The Brezhnev
letter focused attention on his health, and the Brezhnev factor undoubtedly
played a part in Western decisions on the Summit.

In any event, the negotiations themselves seemed to be moving forward, and
the atmosphere within the Conference during March was as positive as it had
been at any previous time. With a peaceful change clause agreed among the
United States, the FRG, and the USSR, one of the key remaining issues had
essentially been resolved.

The U.S. delegation, as sponsors of the provision on peaceful change,
undertook an elaborate series of contacts with Western and neutral delegations
to obtain their support for, or at least acquiescence in, the agreed language. On

March 17, the United States tabled the new peaceful change language formally in the subcommittee on the principles, explaining that it was a revision of the earlier U.S. proposal on peaceful change. Despite the Americans' advance preparations, immediate acceptance of the language was blocked by the French, who linked resolution of this issue to two others: language protecting quadri-partite rights on Berlin and a clause assuring the equal value of all the principles. The Romanian delegation, which was unhappy with the peaceful change language for its own reasons, also blocked immediate approval on procedural grounds. The Romanians explained privately that they did not wish to open up possibilities for revisions of their borders, but were probably equally interested in developing further leverage for acceptance of their own pet ideas.

Another problem arising immediately in connection with the U.S. peaceful change formulation was the German-language translation. No sooner had the new U.S. text been distributed in the six official languages than the FRG delegation objected to the German version as translated by the Swiss secretariat staff. The U.S. delegation asked the secretariat to withdraw the German version, whereupon the Soviet delegation warned that they would vigorously object to such a step. A serious dispute was avoided when the FRG agreed to take up their objections at a later date.

Several other Conference issues also moved forward. The Soviets announced that they could accept notification of military maneuvers to all CSCE partici-pating states, instead of only to neighboring states. They added a condition, however: The military confidence-building measures must be on a "voluntary basis." At first this position caused consternation, since the automatic conclu-sion of Western and neutral delegates was that the Soviets did not intend to carry out their commitments in this field. After further consideration, however, the Western and neutral negotiators concluded that, as the CSCE would not produce a legally binding document, all commitments in it would be "volun-tary" anyway. Their conclusion was that the Soviet condition could be satisfied in some fashion, provided the wording was carefully negotiated (the "volun-tary basis" phrase as finally agreed appears in FA 105). Despite its shortcomings, the Soviet position was seen as evidence of a desire to get negotiations on military aspects moving.

Further progress was also evident in Basket II, where the sections on market-ing (FA 192–198), business contacts and facilities (FA 167–176), economic and commercial information (FA 177–191), harmonization of standards (FA 245–250), and arbitration (FA 251–256) were put in final form, with all remaining brackets eliminated. Basket III showed some progress with agreement on a resolution on meetings among young people (FA 459–466) and another para-graph of the section on working conditions for journalists. And at the end of March the ninth principle, cooperation among states (FA 61–65) was agreed, permitting the subcommittee on principles to take the symbolic step of begin-ning their work on the tenth, and last, CSCE principle.

The Coordinating Committee was trying to come to grips with the difficult questions of the organization of the final document (or documents) of the Conference and the arrangements for Stage III. All delegations realized that work on these issues would have to begin at an early date because of their complexity and the need for advance preparations for printing the final document(s) and setting up the Helsinki meeting. Yet the very fact of beginning work on these questions was politically sensitive, since such a step would indicate the approach of the Conference's conclusion.

The first session of the Coordinating Committee formally devoted to these issues illustrated the delicacy of the new terrain. In discussing arrangements for Stage III, it was proposed that President Kekkonen of Finland be invited to preside over the opening session. Most delegations were ready to accept this proposal, and open opposition to it would have appeared as a rebuff to the Finns. However, approval would have signaled acceptance of a summit-level Stage III, something the U.S. and other Western countries were not yet prepared to do. To slip out of this ticklish situation, the U.S. delegation privately suggested to Finnish Ambassador Iloniemi that it was too early to consider the question. Iloniemi thanked those delegations that had expressed themselves positively on the idea and indicated that a formal decision would be premature until all the arrangements for Stage III had been clarified.

The Coordinating Committee heard Kovalev explain that the Soviets wished to have the Conference issue four final documents, one for each of the baskets plus one on follow-up, and to have each one signed "at the highest level." If the Soviet proposal had been adopted, the Helsinki Summit would have witnessed 140 signatures! This fact led some Western delegates to conclude that the Soviet intention was to have Brezhnev sign the principles and then leave some other official to sign the rest. Kovalev also proposed initialing of the documents by delegation heads in Geneva and advance negotiation of a brief Stage III communique to avoid any problems in Helsinki. The Soviet preference for four documents/four signatures contrasted with the view of the Western and neutral delegations (and Romania) that there should be a single document with single signatures, in order to ensure the unity and equality of all the baskets. The West also felt strongly that the final document should make clear that it had no legal status, to avoid the appearance of a World War II peace treaty. The Coordinating Committee, approving the earlier Swedish proposal, established a working group to tackle these questions after the brief Easter break.

After Easter, however, the atmosphere changed, and the Soviets once again became uncooperative. Throughout the month of April, Basket III was stalemated. The Soviets had evidently sensed that acceptance of the Summit by Western political leaders was already a fait accompli and that no further concessions were necessary to obtain it. They dug in stubbornly and resisted every effort to move Basket III further. As the West Europeans apparently lost their will to continue standing up to Soviet pressures, the United States stepped in to shore up the Western side.

The firm U.S. position was appreciated by the Western and neutral delegations, but infuriated the Soviets, who undertook a carefully organized probing operation to determine the extent of senior level support for U.S. positions on Basket III and to locate weak points. U.S.-Soviet differences were evident on all the remaining sensitive issues in Basket III: improved working conditions for journalists, freer travel, freer access to radio broadcasts, and the introductory texts to the sections on human contacts and information, which would set out general freer movement objectives.

Soviet interest in concluding Basket III was demonstrated by their numerous requests for urgent private meetings with key Western delegates and the long hours they insisted on spending methodically going over the texts and portions of texts still in dispute. Moscow was anxious to conclude, and the Soviet delegation in Geneva was aware that the mountain of work remaining to be done meant it would be difficult to meet the desired time frame. Yet the Soviet delegation made no concessions to advance Basket III. The situation made the Soviet delegates nervous and quick to show their tempers.

Their anxiety was understandable, for the Eastern media had followed the Brezhnev letter with public suggestions of dates for concluding the Conference. Dr. Siegfried Bock, head of the GDR delegation, predicted in a radio interview that Stage III would be convened at the end of June or the beginning of July. At about the same time (April 18) an article in *Izvestiya* said most CSCE participants "are inclined to conclude its work in the summer of 1975 in Helsinki at the highest level." Since August is not suitable for major international events in Europe, this meant holding Stage III before the end of July.

Other major conference issues were ripening to maturity. The French, on behalf of the three Western powers with responsibilities for Berlin and Germany as a whole, began private consultations with the neutrals on the disclaimer required to eliminate any inference that the declaration of principles would contradict or override quadripartite rights and responsibilities. The need for such a saving clause was understood by the Western allies (and presumably by the Warsaw Pact countries), but was unfamiliar to the neutrals, who felt it had nothing to do with them. Sweden and Switzerland, having been neutral during the war, asserted that they could not now associate themselves with its results. In addition, the neutrals (and some NATO members, plus Romania) were unhappy with the general character of the original draft saving clause as agreed among the four powers (United States, USSR, Great Britain, and France) because it could be read as giving support to the Brezhnev Doctrine. Delegates from these countries made it clear that their political leaders would never go to Helsinki to sign a document that appeared to recognize the Brezhnev Doctrine. The consultations held by the French during April convinced the three Western powers that the draft saving clause would have to be modified considerably to make it generally acceptable, and careful consideration of fallback positions began at a series of Bonn Group lunches in the private upstairs room of a suburban Geneva inn.

The new working group on the organization of the final document(s) and Stage III opened its work by listening to a presentation by the prospective executive secretary of Stage III on technical preparations for the Helsinki meeting. The Finns had made it clear that, while they were prepared to host Stage III at any time, the end of July would be far more expensive than the beginning of that month because of the need to recall technical and security personnel from their vacations, etc. They also insisted that a minimum of thirty days' notice was required to organize this meeting. Despite the Finnish appeal for early planning, this working group made little headway, and sharp East-West differences over how the final document(s) of the Conference should be organized and signed finally led to this issue being set aside as too sensitive for open discussion. There was tacit agreement that after a cooling-off period the question should be settled quietly in the corridors.

In the military subcommittee the Soviets were trying to bring the state of work up to the level of the other subject areas. They pressed for acceptance of the "voluntary basis" concept, but also made concessions on the parameters for notification of military maneuvers. They stated formally that they would accept the formulation "all of Europe" as the area in which notification should be given, provided a large amount of Soviet territory was exempted. Acceptance in principle of the "all of Europe" concept was considered important by Western negotiators, even if an exception had to be made for the USSR. Significantly, this concession followed an earlier one (acceptance of notification to all CSCE participants) before any comparable counterconcession had been made by the West. Toward the end of April a Czech representative for the first time expressed numerically the size of maneuvers that should be notified, using the figure of 40,000 troops instead of the "army corps" description used previously by the Warsaw Pact countries to indicate the threshold for notification.

The tenth (and last) principle was agreed in mid-April (FA 66–69), and the principles subcommittee went on to discuss such issues as the transitional phrase between the preamble and the principles themselves, which could affect their legal status (e.g., the Soviets preferred, "The participating States . . . solemnly declare:").

The Conference continued to move forward—texts were agreed on development of transport (FA 341–353) and tourism (FA 455–458)—and as April passed, pressures mounted. The Western press began to rediscover the Conference after almost two years of eclipse. The gap in coverage meant there was a widespread lack of understanding of the Conference among journalists, or that their information was out of date. Several articles criticizing the U.S. delegation's low profile, for example, would have been valid in 1973–74, but were seriously out of date in the spring of 1975.

By the end of the month, both sides were playing it very tough, especially in Basket III. Almost every delegation wanted to wind up before August, but the Soviets needed this much more than anyone else. Looming up at the end of May was a summit meeting of leaders of the NATO countries. This rare event was designed to demonstrate a renewed commitment to the North Atlantic alliance before the anticipated conclusion of the CSCE. Everyone in Geneva assumed that the progress of the Conference would be discussed and that a position would be taken, publicly or privately, on the timing and level of Stage III. The more progress that took place before the NATO meeting, particularly on subjects of importance to the West, the more likely it was that the fifteen Western leaders would come to positive conclusions. Thus, every detail settled before the Brussels meeting was significant, and the Conference worked feverishly to accomplish what it could.

The Soviets began to show more flexibility in these circumstances; they accepted a French compromise offer on a phrase describing the equal value and interrelationship of the principles (FA 70). This was a key breakthrough in the work on the principles, since it helped work on a number of other issues move forward and left agreement on the quadripartite rights and responsibilities saving clause the single most important issue remaining to be settled in the principles declaration.

The Soviets hinted they could accept a longer time period for advance notification of military maneuvers — thirteen or fourteen days instead of ten days. In addition, they proposed reopening bilateral discussions with the Dutch delegation concerning a Dutch proposal on contacts between authors and publishing houses in other states (known among Western delegates as the "Solzhenitsyn proposal"), which had remained at an impasse for many weeks.

The Western countries were also trying to move things forward. The Bonn Group delegations received more flexible instructions on the wording of the quadripartite rights saving clause after personal study by French Foreign Minister Jean Sauvagnargues, an expert on Germany. The Dutch delegation tabled a revised paper setting out an alternative framework for the organization of the final document(s), suggesting a brief cover note, which would be signed, followed by unsigned annexes. The Soviet response to this proposal was relatively mild and conveyed the impression that some compromise might be possible. The Soviets reiterated their desire for four to five signatures, but accepted the idea of a single volume. One week later the Swiss offered a compromise suggestion: one volume, including all documents, with signatures at the end.

It was at this time that the British delegation conceived the idea of offering the Soviets the possibility of concluding the negotiations on the two most sensitive subheadings in the CSCE: human contacts and information. The British idea was to put together complete documents on these subjects, including all the bits and pieces that had already been agreed, together with unagreed portions, drafted to represent an overall compromise offer. These draft documents would be presented to the Soviets with a careful explanation that they indicated the price for which the West was prepared to settle. The offer was not to be a take-it-or-leave-it one. It would be explained that the Western countries would be willing to discuss a few minor changes in the documents—but not to negotiate every point in them. If the Soviets sought such negotiations, the Western offer would be withdrawn and negotiations would proceed subject-by-subject, as before.

The implications for the Soviet side would be clear: if they accepted the Western offer with only minor changes, the key half of Basket III, including what the West considered the most politically important subjects in the Conference, would be concluded before the NATO summit, and the way to Helsinki would be open. If not, the detailed negotiations on individual subjects would drag on through the summer, and Brezhnev's cherished dream of the conclusion in the Finnish capital would once again be postponed.

The NATO caucus worked diligently to prepare the papers for this initiative, which was designed to "globalize" the negotiations on these subjects and was therefore dubbed the "global initiative." The allies reduced their demands by cutting where possible, but retained the essential elements of the Western proposals on which agreement had not yet been reached.

With authorization from capitals, the global initiative was handed to the Soviets at an informal meeting on May 15. The NATO delegations were joined by Austria and Switzerland, who gave their support to the initiative. The Soviets, surprised and wary of being outmaneuvered, were angry and resentful, but studied the document with apparent interest, well aware of what it could mean for them.

The global initiative was a dangerous tactic because it contained an overall balance—numerous Western concessions were offered in order to obtain points considered essential, such as the freer movement concept of "wider travel" and a strong text on working conditions for journalists. The Soviets undoubtedly would try to pocket the concessions and negotiate all the other points, thus putting the West in the position of negotiating downward from minimal texts. To ward off this danger the Western side insisted that the initiative be treated as a whole and agreed among themselves not to enter negotiations on any specific point until the Soviets gave an overall reaction. If the Eastern response was so different that reconciliation seemed impossible, the Western group was determined to go back to negotiating subject-by-subject, on the basis of their former positions.

The Soviets took almost a week to respond to the global initiative. Meanwhile, little was accomplished in the work of the Conference, and delegates of every political persuasion grew increasingly anxious over the rapidly diminishing amount of time available to complete the negotiations for a summer Summit.

The only real progress while the West awaited the Soviet reply in Basket III was in the military area. The Soviets, trying to accelerate work on confidence-building measures to bring it into line with other subjects, accepted that the definition of the threshold for notification of maneuvers should be expressed solely in numerical terms and lowered their proposed figure from 40,000 troops to 35,000. In return the Western allies offered to reduce the width of the border zone in the Soviet Union that would be covered by the notification provisions from 700 to 500 kilometers, to diminish the time for advance notification from six to five weeks, and to raise the threshold from 12,000 troops to 15,000. The negotiation on this subject was now vastly simplified, since the gap between positions of East and West had become a clear numerical one.

The only other movement of note was that, following agreement on a preamble for the Mediterranean declaration (FA 399–404), the Maltese delegation introduced its anticipated extreme demands for phraseology in the operative section of this declaration. The Maltese proposal was even more extreme than anyone in the Conference had expected; it called for special links between the Mediterranean states and the Arab world and the gradual withdrawal of U.S. and Soviet forces from the Mediterranean area. This explosive suggestion, which was not taken particularly seriously at the time, came back to haunt the Conference several weeks later.

Meanwhile, another key turning point in the development of the negotiations was taking place elsewhere: Kissinger and Gromyko met in Vienna on May 19 and 20. The discussion of CSCE between the two foreign ministers was different on this occasion from what it had been before. For the first time, Kissinger was better informed on the details of the CSCE situation than Gromyko, whom Kissinger had always referred to jokingly as the world's greatest expert on CSCE. Kissinger had been carefully briefed by the Assistant Secretary of State for European Affairs Arthur Hartman. The American secretary of State was tempted to reach a bilateral accommodation with Gromyko, something that would have been deeply offensive to the West Europeans, but was warned by Hartman not to try this.

When he met Gromyko, Kissinger took the offensive and pressed for a full response to the Western global initiative. Gromyko sought to negotiate particular texts, but Kissinger insisted on the global nature of the proposal and suggested that specifics be taken up in Geneva. Gromyko was surprised and put off balance. Not only did Kissinger's attitude signify that the global initiative was a serious proposal with which the Soviets would have to deal; it also indicated that the tougher U.S. stance on Basket III that they had probed for several weeks was a firm position, with strong backing at the highest level in Washington.

Gromyko, for his part, conveyed to Kissinger a new set of parameters (the "Vienna parameters") for notification of military maneuvers, which the Soviets hoped would settle this issue. The new parameters (30,000 troops—

eighteen days' advance notification—150-kilometer border zone in the USSR) represented a major Soviet step forward. But the most significant result of the Vienna meeting as far as the CSCE was concerned was that the Soviets went away impressed that they faced a solid Western position on Basket III and would have to make further concessions to get their Summit.

The Soviets gave their response to the global initiative on May 21, which probably signified that it had been prepared before the Kissinger-Gromyko meeting. It entailed about fifty proposed changes in the texts as put forward by the Western group. In the meeting at which this reply was handed over the Soviet Basket III negotiator, Dubinin, became personally abusive, accusing the Western negotiators of "trickery."

The NATO caucus on May 22 decided unanimously that the list of Soviet changes was too long. But there were also indications that Dubinin was trying to be tougher than his instructions required, and that even within the Soviet delegation he was acting independently. The allies, therefore, agreed that they would not take dramatic action and would instead express disappointment to the Soviets, point out that their position would seriously prolong the negotiations, and press for a more positive response.

On May 23, when this message was received by Soviet delegation chief Kovalev, he reacted sharply, asking for an immediate meeting with American Ambassador Sherer. Kovalev, extremely agitated, spent three hours threatening Sherer and myself (I had taken over the Basket III negotiations on human contacts and information in April) about the "political implications" of the Western position and the possible prolongation of the Conference. In response Sherer said the Western side was simply disappointed that the Soviets had not taken advantage of a fair compromise offer that would have enabled the Conference to conclude within the time frame the Soviets themselves had set. Kovalev, losing his cool for the first time in the Geneva negotiations, said the global initiative was not a compromise but an ultimatum. He and his colleagues were tense, emotional, and frustrated—obviously under great pressure from Moscow to wind up the negotiations and faced in the closing days with a firm and united Western position on the most politically sensitive subjects in the Conference.

But the required Soviet concessions were not long in coming. On May 28 Gerard Andre, the French ambassador, gave a luncheon in a private room at the elegant restaurant in the Parc des Eaux Vives. This luncheon was ostensibly to discuss tactics for further negotiations on the quadripartite rights saving clause, and Andre had invited the delegation heads and their deputies from France, Great Britain, the United States, and the Soviet Union. Discussion focused initially on the quadripartite rights problem, but quickly petered out since there were no new developments on that subject. Conversation then turned to Basket III. Kovalev was nervous and sullen, smoking even more than usual and apparently reluctant to speak.

Midway through the main course Kovalev was called away from the table for a phone call. When he returned, he spoke privately to Dubinin in agitated tones. Several minutes later Dubinin's deputy arrived and handed Kovalev a rumpled piece of paper. Kovalev excused himself and asked for a "recess" in the luncheon. The Soviet group huddled in a corner of the ornate drawing room in which the lunch was taking place, while the Westerners looked on curiously. After some minutes of animated discussion, the Soviets returned to the table and Kovalev indicated that the lunch could continue.

He began to speak immediately in tones that were a mixture of triumph and spiteful anger. He spoke first of the ultimatum that had been presented and of the unreasonable demands of the Western delegations. By contrast, he said, the Soviet delegation was flexible and accepted the need for compromise. As a generous "gesture of goodwill," therefore, the Soviets were prepared to make several concessions in order to open negotiations on the global initiative and thereby conclude the human contacts and information sections of the work of the Conference. Kovalev then rapped out in defiant tones the concessions the Soviets were prepared to make:

(1)   The Soviets dropped their suggestion for a troublesome addition to the text on travel and accepted the text as presented by the West (FA 448– 452), including the key freer movement concept "to facilitate wider travel," and were prepared to reserve a place for a Vatican-proposed clause on travel by religious leaders, provided precise language could be agreed.

(2)   The Soviets accepted a Western paragraph affirming that journalists will not be expelled from the country in which they are assigned for the legitimate pursuit of their profession (FA 515).

(3)   The Soviets were prepared to accept a paragraph on facilitating the dissemination of radio broadcast information and would not insist on inclusion of language reflecting the concept of government responsibility for the content of programming.

(4)   The Soviets accepted the Western-proposed sequence of subjects, as well as all Western subtitles except one, which could nevertheless be negotiated, and agreed that the subtitles could be given prominence in the layout and printing of the final documents, as the Western delegations wanted.

(5)   The Soviets made a forthcoming compromise offer to settle the one remaining problem in the family reunification text.

Kovalev knew perfectly well what he had done; he had provided the concessions needed to keep the global initiative alive. Not only did this mean the final negotiations on human contacts and information could begin; it also meant a positive signal would be conveyed to the NATO summit, meeting in Brussels the very next day.

The NATO caucus on May 29 decided on the basis of the new Soviet concessions to open negotiations on the remaining thirty-odd Soviet changes in the Western global initiative paper, in a small group under Austrian-Swiss coordinators, with the West represented by Britain, Denmark, Ireland, and the United States. The first session was set for that day. On the following day, May 30, the Soviets announced their "Vienna parameters" for notification of military maneuvers. A common appraisal flowed through the Conference like an electric current: We were on our way to Helsinki!

An Interlude

We had discussed, fought, and laughed together for two years; we had shared triumphs and frustrations; we had grappled with some of the most complex problems diplomats have ever faced. Despite our differences, was it not the most natural development of all that we had become a village, even a kind of family? On May 31, in the village church of Collonges-sous-Saleve, in that corner of France nestled between Geneva and the Mount Saleve, the CSCE *family gathered for the wedding of two of its members, a young Spanish diplomat and a Dutch interpreter, both of whom had been with the Conference since its very beginning in Helsinki. Like all of us, they had met at* CSCE; *unlike the rest of us, who would soon go our separate ways, they had decided to remain together permanently. And so we gathered—Russians, Germans, Yugoslavs, Frenchmen, Bulgarians, Norwegians, Romanians, Portuguese, and even Americans—all the nationalities of our sprawling Conference—to witness this unique family event.*

The marriage was performed in Spanish, Italian, and Latin by our village priests, the delegation of the Vatican. And afterward, at the Chalet des Roses, amidst mild showers of warm, dew-like rain, and the late spring wild flowers of the French countryside, we toasted this symbolic couple, our village, and our two-year life together.

22 What They Want
Human Rights and Basket III

Detente means little if it is not reflected in the daily lives of our peoples. There is no reason why in 1975 Europeans should not be allowed to marry whom they want, hear and read what they want, travel abroad when and where they want, meet whom they want.

Harold Wilson Helsinki July 30, 1975

The history of the CSCE is filled with ironies, and of these perhaps the most complete — and most significant for East-West relations in Europe — lies in the saga of human rights in the Conference. The principal trade-off in the Final Act was between a qualified general recognition of the geopolitical status quo in Europe and an equally qualified agreement that human rights are a legitimate element of East-West relations, without which detente cannot advance.

There had to be a human rights component in the Final Act; otherwise, it would not have been possible for Western leaders to sign it. In fact, human rights are dealt with in two ways in the Final Act: as a theoretical matter in the seventh principle, "Respect for Human Rights and Fundamental Freedoms, Including the Freedom of Thought, Conscience, Religion or Belief" (FA 48– 56), and as a very practical matter in the first two sections of Basket III, human contacts (FA 421–470) and information (FA 471–515).

The text of the human rights principle is not exceptionally innovative. Although it contains some interesting new points, it draws largely on pre-existing documents, such as the Universal Declaration of Human Rights adopted by the UN General Assembly in 1948. The most important aspect of the human rights principle was that it was included at all. Here we have a part of the Final Act entitled "Principles Guiding Relations between Participating States," and one of these principles is respect for human rights. Thus, a major East-West document, signed by the leaders of European and North American states and applicable to relations among them all, recognizes that respect for human rights is a principle of international relations; that the way in which states treat their own citizens is an element of their relations with other states. The inclusion of human rights in this list of principles is the heart of the broad compromise mentioned above, and it is of considerable importance.

Moreover, inclusion of a principle of human rights in a landmark East-West document was a major evolution; in the "Basic Principles of Relations between the United States of America and the Union of Soviet Socialist Republics," for example, signed by Brezhnev and Nixon with great fanfare in May 1972, there is no mention of human rights whatsoever, whereas the Final Act's principle is a full elaboration of human rights norms as they are generally accepted in the West. The text of the seventh principle is the longest of all the principles in the Final Act.

The Final Act also adds a principle of "Equal Rights and Self-determination of Peoples" (FA 57–60), which amplifies certain rights, and goes on to establish a principle of "Fulfillment in Good Faith of Obligations under International Law" (FA 66–69), which specifically reiterates the obligation to implement the provisions of the Final Act. No doubt the Soviet leadership was extremely reluctant to accept these texts. They did so to obtain the compromise result that led to the Helsinki Summit.

Of course, just as the major Soviet gain in the Conference (recognition of frontiers) was qualified by a provision on peaceful change, and by other clauses in the Final Act, so the principle of human rights is also qualified. The human rights principle follows a principle of nonintervention in internal affairs (FA 43–47), which is given equal weight with the human rights principle. A clause of the preamble to the principles (FA 22) states that all the principles "are of primary significance"—that is, are of equal importance. The Western interpretation of the nonintervention principle is that it refers to interventions involving some form of coercion. The Western side attempted to make this clear in negotiating the text, but was only partially successful, and the principle remains ambiguous on this point. The Soviets are correct when they argue that the Final Act contains a commitment not to intervene in the internal affairs of other states. But the Western countries are equally correct when they argue that there is nevertheless an obligation to respect human rights and that this has equal weight in relations among states as any other aspect of state-to-state relations. This is the basis on which the Western countries have the right to raise questions of human rights in the Soviet Union or the countries of Eastern Europe.

The sections of Basket III relating to human rights are much more original in their ambitions and implications. The notion of international recognition of human rights as a theoretical matter was fairly well established before Helsinki, dating back to the UN's Universal Declaration and before, and the CSCE principle of human rights fits into this traditional treatment of the subject. It is a restatement of static norms of governmental behavior that are broadly accepted, at least pro forma, while being subject to widely differing interpretation and application.

Basket III, on the other hand, reflects a Western attempt to define more closely how human rights principles should be applied in practice to certain specific areas of governmental responsibility, and to obtain international agreement on these guidelines. The types of situations chosen for this entirely experimental negotiation were carefully selected according to a number of (unspoken) criteria: (1) some international aspect that made them more acceptable as subjects for negotiation among states; (2) immediate application to existing cases of human hardship; (3) sufficiently limited scope to make them negotiable; and (4) continuing applicability.

For example, "family reunification" was chosen rather than "emigration," because at least two countries have a legitimate interest in reuniting a family separated by national frontiers. The more general problem of emigration, of which family reunification is a part, is arguably the sole responsibility of the state from which persons wish to emigrate. The family reunification problem had immediate and continuing application, and its scope was small enough to have given some hope that a solution would be negotiable.

The Western side put forward a sizable number of specific proposals of this nature. They all sought to advance beyond static human rights principles (for example, the notion in the Universal Declaration that "everyone has the right to leave any country, including his own, and to return to his country") and to create a more dynamic concept of human rights, applicable to the real situations in which real people find themselves in today's world. The implication of agreement on the specific provisions in Basket III was that agreement was legitimate, and possible, on many others that had not yet been taken up.

There is no doubt that the Basket III experiment (or more properly, the experiment represented by the first two sections of Basket III, since the second two sections, on educational and cultural exchanges, are a traditional area of state-to-state negotiation) was the most original element of the CSCE negotiation, and it was concluded with relative success. Some Western proposals were inevitably dropped along the way, such as a Dutch proposal on guaranteeing the privacy of personal correspondence. Other proposals were watered down in the negotiating process. The communist countries introduced meaningless or self-serving texts to render the final results more palatable from their viewpoint or to obscure passages with which they were uncomfortable. A number of caveats were insisted on by the USSR in an attempt to undercut any commitment made, but these were rendered textually ambiguous at worst, and the overall political message of the inclusion of the texts on "Reunification of Families," "Marriage between Citizens of Different States," "Travel for Personal or Professional Reasons," and "Improvement of the Circulation of, Access to, and Exchange of Information" was clear: these areas would become barometers for the state of detente.

The ironies surrounding the treatment of human rights in the Conference began at the very outset of the negotiating process. It seems clear from the text of the basic principles of U.S.-Soviet relations, negotiated by Henry Kissinger and signed by Richard Nixon, that public recognition of the principle of human rights was not for them a primary consideration in America's relations with the Soviet Union. (This approach may have been fruitful on a practical level. During the Nixon administration Jewish emigration from the USSR was allowed to reach record high levels.) Not only is the concept of human rights not mentioned in that text, but the notion of noninterference in internal affairs, which is the USSR's chief defense against Western efforts to encourage improvements in Soviet human rights practices, is mentioned in several places. Take, for example, the following phraseology, part of the first "principle" in the U.S.-Soviet document:

> Differences in ideology and in the social systems of the USA and the USSR are not obstacles to the bilateral development of normal relations based on the principles of sovereignty, equality, noninterference in internal affairs and mutual advantage.

Or later, in the third "principle":

> Accordingly, they will seek to promote conditions in which all countries will live in peace and security and will not be subject to outside interference in their internal affairs.

While Nixon and Kissinger were agreeing to these principles in Moscow, in May 1972, lower-level U.S. negotiators were participating at NATO headquarters in Brussels in preparations for the forthcoming CSCE. Among the projects under discussion was a draft declaration of principles for signature by the CSCE participants, and a key element of this declaration was to be a principle of human rights. The allied diplomats working on this project were keenly disappointed that the United States would agree with the Soviets on principles of interstate behavior that omitted human rights and gave prominence to concepts for which the Soviets could be expected to seek recognition later in the CSCE.

Moreover, the allies were at the time also discussing proposals of a humanitarian nature for possible use during the CSCE. These were to flesh out the concept of "freer movement of people and ideas," which the NATO allies had insisted be a subject of discussion at the forthcoming Conference. The United States was a leader in formulating such suggestions as the proposal on family reunification, which later became central to the Western negotiating effort.

The differences between U.S. activities in the CSCE and, on higher diplomatic levels, in bilateral relations with the USSR became even more apparent when the Conference began, and the "low profile" became the caricature description of the U.S. delegation's role. At the beginning of the negotiation, the U.S. delegation exercised considerable prudence in taking positions on human-rights-related subjects. They knew that Kissinger's view of the CSCE as part of a vast negotiation between the United States and the USSR meant he was prepared to trade a strong U.S. position in the Conference against Soviet concessions in areas he considered more important. The delegation nevertheless tried to give low-key support to Western positions on human rights.

Another irony is that, though Kissinger evidently found human rights issues largely irrelevant to superpower politics, it was he who, in Vienna in the spring of 1975, took up the remaining unresolved issues in Basket III with Gromyko, thus impressing the Soviets with the need to make sufficient concessions in this area to make it possible for Western governments to accept a summit-level conclusion. Though Kissinger was motivated partly by a growing political need to be seen dealing toughly with the USSR, this was one of the most important turning points in the Conference. Kissinger's key role in breaking the deadlock on the last issues is little known and largely obscured by the erroneous notion that the United States played no important part in the CSCE.

But an even more unexpected irony was that what Kissinger, or any other political leader, thought about the Conference did not always have an enormous effect on the textual results achieved. The questions were so complicated, the number and variety of countries and national interests so broad, and the various interrelated negotiating problems so tangled that only the negotiators themselves, on the spot in Geneva, could see through to possible solutions. In such a situation, it was the unity and solidity of the Western position that brought the desired results. It was genuinely inspiring, in the midst of all the usual Conference trivia, to observe that on questions such as human rights, which touched the very basis of our civilization, the Western negotiators were in fundamental agreement. This group of middle-grade career diplomats understood instinctively and unanimously the concepts they could not, under any circumstances, compromise. Sometimes their judgment necessarily turned on the nuance of an adjective or the sequence of a series of phrases; in each case, the limit was clear. The agreement among these rather junior negotiators was mutually self-reinforcing and resulted in a Western position that was extremely tough indeed. Since few people outside the Conference could possibly have understood what was going on within it, and since the political leaders who eventually signed the Final Act could not even have read it, we probably owe a great deal to this anonymous group of diplomats, who acted for the most part on the basis of their own collective best judgment.

The dominant role of the relatively low-level negotiators in the CSCE contained another irony: it may have made agreement on sensitive subjects such as human rights possible, and certainly made it easier. This factor was particularly valid with regard to the U.S.-Soviet relationship in the Conference and has been demonstrated since the Helsinki Summit by the Soviet reaction to revised American attitudes toward the CSCE. As the degree of public, high-level U.S. political interest in the CSCE mounted after Helsinki, Soviet willingness to participate in meaningful negotiations on human-rights-related subjects declined proportionately. The Soviets find it extremely difficult to make concessions when they are publicly under pressure. Applied to the CSCE itself, this apparent rule of Soviet behavior suggests that, had the United States pursued the csce negotiations at a highly visible political level, it would have been much more difficult to obtain Soviet agreement on human rights and other sensitive issues. Such a U.S. attitude would, in Soviet eyes, have guaranteed continued political pressures on these issues following the Conference.

As it was, the Soviets were confronted with an array of first, second, and third secretaries arguing about nuanced shades of adjectives whose meaning was hidden in a vast tome few would read. Such negotiators appeared to represent a low level of political interest in Western capitals. The Soviets concluded that the results of negotiations conducted at such a level would be quickly forgotten and that U.S. political figures had no interest in maintaining human rights pressures. It is deeply ironical that the very lack of interest of Nixon and Kissinger in this affair enhanced the possibility of lower-level negotiators to achieve positive results, while the Soviets concluded that these results would not cause them problems.

The ironies surrounding human rights in the csce continued at the time of the Helsinki Summit itself. Far from congratulating often-courageous negotiators for a Western achievement, the Western press almost universally vilified the Final Act. The view of the American press on President Ford's participation in the Helsinki Summit was typified by the title of an editorial in the *Wall Street Journal*: "Jerry, Don't Go!"

One of Kissinger's errors was in not perceiving the potential political importance of the csce. He downplayed its significance and official U.S. interest in it publicly and privately. Thus, when it was announced that President Ford was going to Helsinki to sign a Final Act of which Americans had never heard, the general conclusion was that this was another Munich, or at best a favor Ford was giving to Brezhnev, in return for something else. Rather than read the document to see what it might contain, the press trumpeted the very interpretation the Soviets wanted them to pick up: that the Final Act was nothing more than a confirmation of existing European frontiers. The human rights content of the document, and all its implications, was entirely overlooked.

But the ironies do not stop there. Gerald Ford's failure to understand the human rights implications of the document he had signed may have been one of the elements in his electoral defeat by Jimmy Carter. His inability to provide the right response when challenged on Helsinki during a televised debate with Carter, leading him to make his peculiar assertion that Poland was not controlled by the USSR, seemed to many to confirm Ford's public image as inadequate for the presidency, and was specifically offensive to some important ethnic groups.

To bring this ironic saga full circle, it only remained for Jimmy Carter and (quite separately) a few members of Congress to see the csce's human rights significance that Nixon, Ford, and Kissinger had overlooked, and its political appeal to Jewish and other American ethnic groups and others interested in human rights in the Soviet Union and Eastern Europe. Republican Representative Millicent Fenwick of New Jersey drafted a bill setting up a special joint committee to monitor implementation of CSCE commitments, chaired by Democratic Representative Dante Fascell of Florida. Carter picked up the CSCE as a ready-made part of his human rights policy, and the Soviets concluded that they had made an important miscalculation. Soviet treatment of dissident members of the Helsinki Watch Group in the USSR demonstrates better than any Western analysis the discomfiture the Final Act's human rights language eventually gave the Soviet government. Ironically, it was the United States, which had under another administration followed a low profile on CSCE, that led the West in seeking to use the Final Act to further its human rights objectives.

Underlying all these ups and downs in the analysis of the human rights content of the CSCE by politicians, the press, and the public has been the most basic irony of all: the Final Act has rarely, if ever, been seen for what it really is—a serious and important, if qualified and unsensational, contribution to the long, slow process of building more positive relations between the two halves of Europe.

Part V
To Helsinki

23 The Washington Parameters
Trying to Agree on Military Issues
and a Summit Date, June 1975

Decades of confrontation are not replaced overnight by
an era of cooperation.
Helmut Schmidt Helsinki July 30, 1975

The Conference was racing toward its conclusion. The Soviet concessions in
Basket III had led to the opening of negotiations on the Western global initiative. The Soviets continued their rapid-fire concessions, and within a week
virtually all the major remaining issues in the human contacts and information
sections had been resolved. The working group on Stage III, inspired by the
sudden breakthrough and acting in the belief that the Helsinki Summit was
now in sight, began serious discussions of the new issues associated with the
Summit meeting: timing, level, duration, guests, communique, and an agreed
method for establishing the speakers' list.

There was no question now that the Soviets were out to nail down the
summer Summit they wanted—and that they were willing to make substantial
concessions to achieve this. Their agreement on human contacts and information plainly was designed to ensure a decision in favor of the Summit. The
Soviets were also aware that the other Western interest was confidence-
building measures, and the Western side expected a Soviet drive to complete
work on this subject. If the Soviets could succeed in concluding work on
confidence-building measures as well, Stage III would be virtually inevitable.

The Soviet drive on confidence-building measures opened in Washington.
On Sunday morning, June 8, Mendelevich telephoned Sherer. "Have you
received your new instructions yet?" he asked. We had not. "You will, you
will," he laughed. He was right; we received telegraphic instructions that same
day to tell the Soviets and our allies that we could accept as parameters for
notification of maneuvers a threshold of 30,000 men, a border zone of applicability of 250 kilometers in the Soviet Union, and a time of notification of
eighteen days. Kissinger had told Soviet Ambassador Anatoly Dobrynin in
Washington that we could accept these figures. We dubbed them the "Washington parameters."

We met with Kovalev that same evening to convey our instructions, but indicated that we did not believe the other Western allies would accept these figures, and that insistence on them would only prolong the Conference. We sent the same message to Washington.

On June 9 Sherer told British Ambassador Sir David Hildyard of our instructions. The Englishman, usually a model of understatement, said his reaction was one of "stupefaction and horror." As allied floor leader on military subjects, he had been in tough negotiations with Kovalev, insisting on a threshold of no more than 20,000 to 22,000 men, a border zone of no less than 300 kilometers and a time of twenty-one days. We told Washington of the British reaction.

Our indications of allied reactions evidently caused some concern in the upper reaches of the State Department. On June 10 we received telephone instructions to tell the allies that our acceptance of the "Washington parameters" had been conditional on acceptance by our allies. If they did not like the "Washington parameters," the United States would tell the Soviets flatly at a high level that these parameters would not sell. At a NATO caucus that afternoon, we repeated all this to the allies. The allies were strongly opposed to the "Washington parameters" and deeply resentful that their negotiating position had been undercut. We conveyed this reaction to Washington, too. The situation remained tensely frozen throughout the week.

On Friday, June 13, while we were lunching with the Czechoslovak delegation head at the handsome Czech mission, we received an urgent telephone call; a "flash" message had arrived requiring immediate attention. We cut lunch short and hurried back to the U.S. mission. The telegram contained a reversal of our previous instructions: the "Washington parameters" were out. We were instructed to inform the Soviets and our allies immediately that the NATO allies could not accept the "Washington parameters," that the Soviets should be flexible and find a compromise, and that a neutral compromise formula then in preparation (25,000 men, 300 kilometers, twenty-one days) might be the basis for early agreement. Sherer called on Kovalev to give him this bad news, while it was conveyed simultaneously to the British ambassador. The Englishmen subsequently met with Kovalev to say that their earlier negotiations on the parameters could be resumed only on the basis of the figures in use before the "Washington parameters." The Russian reiterated that he could go no further than 30,000 men, 250 kilometers, and eighteen days, but the negotiation was back on track and the United States had recovered from a serious error, which could have developed into a major split with our allies.

Meanwhile, other subjects had advanced. The subcommittee on science and technology completed its work and registered its section of the final document (FA 261–300) when the Soviets withdrew a list of proposed changes. The subcommittees on culture and education came close to completion, and the Soviets indicated that they could accept the Swiss proposal for a single signature at the end of a single final Conference document. This reasonable compromise for the format of the Final Act was essentially the same as the original Dutch proposal.

In mid-June, Brezhnev wrote to several Western leaders proposing that the Helsinki Summit be convened on July 22. It was commonly assumed in Geneva that August was not suitable for a thirty-five-nation Summit because European vacation habits would pose practical and political problems (technicians on long-planned holidays and the public off at the beaches). September was also a difficult month, since foreign ministers would be involved at that time with the UN General Assembly. October seemed very far away, especially if the work of the negotiations should be completed during July—a long interval ran the risk that some government might have second thoughts, or indeed might change; succeeding leaders might feel no commitment to go to Helsinki.

The bind was growing tighter all the time. Late July appeared to be the only possible time frame for the Summit, in view of the Finnish requirement for four weeks' notice, which implied a decision by the end of June, but there were too many outstanding substantive problems, and consensus on a date was unlikely until they were settled.

The Soviets argued energetically that early agreement on a date would make it easier to find compromises on the remaining issues. But the Western delegates (as well as Romania, Malta, and Yugoslavia) knew that if they agreed on a Summit date their negotiating leverage would be gone, and the pressure now on the Soviets would abruptly shift to them. They knew that the only compromises that would come after agreement on a date would be unsatisfactory ones.

The Swedish delegation, taking the part of the Finns, pointed out to the Coordinating Committee on June 19 that a decision on timing would have to be taken the following week. Absence of a decision would, in reality, constitute a choice by the Conference not to hold a Summit in July. But the inventory of major unresolved issues was still very long. Among them, the parameters for a confidence-building measure on notification of maneuvers was the most important; if the Western allies obtained satisfaction on this point, most would consider that the major Western objectives had been attained. Other unresolved issues were important, too: a saving clause for quadripartite rights in Berlin and Germany, and the form of Conference follow-up. There were also many special problems representing the particular national interests of Yugoslavia, Romania, Malta, Turkey, and others. Everyone at the Conference was hoping for rapid progress so that a date could be agreed during the Coordinating Committee meetings set for June 26 and 30.

The Conference was moving relentlessly forward, but the speed of its progress seemed maddeningly less than what was required by the circumstances. On June 20 the neutral group tabled its compromise parameters for the maneuver confidence-building measure (25,000 men, twenty-one days, 300 kilometers), which looked as though it could form the basis for a final solution on this problem. The French, who had been resisting any change, agreed to a new formulation for a quadripartite rights saving clause, which was aimed at satisfying the objections raised by several delegations to the original version. This new text was tabled in the full Conference on June 27, but immediately ran into difficulties. An informal working group was constituted under Swedish chairmanship to put together a compromise on the issue of follow-up to the Conference. The Western countries joined the Soviets in accepting the Swiss compromise proposal to have one signature at the end of a single final document to be approved at the Stage III Summit, with a disclaimer (yet to be negotiated) on the nonlegal nature of the final document.

The time pressure encouraged Maltese Prime Minister Mintoff, who felt his increased leverage, to make unreasonable demands. His representatives, who had become isolated within the working group on the Mediterranean, insisted more and more adamantly on a paragraph for the Mediterranean declaration calling for broad cooperation between Europe and the Arab world and gradual withdrawal of the U.S. and Soviet fleets from the Mediterranean. Despite the emerging consensus on timing, it appeared that Malta might withhold agreement until its special interests were satisfied, and that Mintoff intended to provoke a dramatic last-minute showdown.

Over the weekend of June 21–22, the Soviets offered Great Britain, as NATO floor leader on confidence-building measures, a new package on parameters for notification of maneuvers: 25,000 men, twenty-one days, and 250 kilometers; they also accepted inclusion of their Baltic and Black Sea coasts as border zones subject to notification requirements. Great Britain wished to close the deal on parameters of 25,000 men, twenty-one days, and 300 kilometers; then 275 kilometers. Despite the fact that this did not work, the two sides were obviously extremely close.

All of this was taking place in an atmosphere of feverish activity. Many delegates took their meals at the Conference hall, even, at times, on trays in the meeting rooms themselves. On one occasion the Conference hall restaurant refused to serve a meal to a Soviet negotiator — Mendelevich — at the Conference table where he was meeting. Mendelevich, exhausted by round-the-clock negotiation, flew into a rage and sent for the manager, who appeared, bowing obsequiously. "I am the ambassador of the Soviet Union," shouted Mendelevich, "and you will serve me when and where I choose." The manager served the meal himself.

Beginning on June 23, the attention of the Conference zeroed in on the question of timing. The Soviets were pressing hard for acceptance of the July 22 date proposed by Brezhnev, and many neutral and Western delegations favored reaching agreement on timing. However, the Common Market Nine, and other Western countries, held to the position expressed by the foreign ministers of the Nine at their June 24 meeting in Luxembourg: a Stage III in July was possible and desirable, but work on the key issues would have to be completed before a date could be accepted.

This work was progressing rapidly. The FRG-GDR dispute over the German-language translation of the peaceful change clause was resolved when the GDR withdrew its objections. The Vatican text on religious travel and contacts (FA 454) and the U.S. text on radio broadcasting (FA 497), the last problems in the human contacts and information sections, were agreed, the broadcasting text the result of a long and bitter negotiation, conducted mainly between the U.S. and Soviet delegations. And the informal working group on follow-up to the Conference produced a single draft of a possible compromise text on this difficult issue.

At the Coordinating Committee meeting of June 26, the Soviets cited this real progress and formally proposed that the Helsinki Summit open on July 22. The Swedish delegation proposed July 28 as an alternative, which was immediately accepted by the USSR. These proposals set off an acrimonious debate, which lasted most of the day but failed to reach any conclusion.

Another Coordinating Committee meeting on the following day also failed to reach agreement on a date and left the Conference in a state of considerable suspense. The Finns were agitated and seriously concerned. The Summit represented a sizeable investment for them, both in terms of political prestige and actual cost. To put on a Summit, they would have to cancel police and army leaves in the middle of the vacation period, as well as commandeer hotel space at the height of the tourist season.

A further session of the Coordinating Committee on June 30, exactly four weeks before the end of July, also reached no agreement. A majority in favor of Stage III in late July was clearly emerging. While several issues still needed to be resolved, they could be concluded at any moment. A complete consensus would probably not be possible until very late, but a broad tendency toward fixing a date at the end of July might permit the Finns to begin preparations for Stage III and create pressures on the holdouts to join the consensus as their special interests were satisfied. It began to look as though Stage III could indeed be held during the last week of July.

24   If States Knew More
Military Security in the CSCE

The Military balance, which is generally considered a guarantee of peace, could be maintained at a lower level if states knew more about one another's preparations and intentions. Confidence would deepen. Over-reaction and arguments based on "worst case" assumptions could be avoided.

Olof Palme Helsinki July 31, 1975

Negotiation of the section of the Final Act covering military aspects of security (FA 93-137) was sufficiently different from that of the rest of the negotiations to merit a detailed explanation. The experience of this part of the CSCE may also be useful in other arms control negotiations, since it was a rare example of a successful multilateral negotiation on a military subject.

The interests of the participating states in this aspect of the CSCE were such that the negotiating equation was unique from the very beginning. The NATO allies wished to include some military content in the CSCE because a conference on security that did not address issues relating to the military confrontation in Europe would have made a mockery of its name. However, the allies did not wish to bring basic military questions of weaponry and force levels into the CSCE forum. Negotiations on strategic weapons were already under way in the SALT talks, and the allies had obtained Soviet agreement to the opening of Mutual Balanced Force Reduction discussions in early 1973. The MBFR forum was more limited in its geographic scope, since it covered only the Central European area, and in membership, with only NATO and Warsaw Pact countries participating. As a bloc-to-bloc negotiation, it appeared to be a simpler forum for achieving some kind of agreement on the fundamental issue of force levels. Moreover, the MBFR negotiations were aiming for a formal agreement of some kind, whereas the CSCE seemed destined to produce a nonbinding declaration.

For these reasons the military content that the allies agreed should be added to the CSCE was limited and relatively achievable. The idea of confidence-building measures, a concept closely related to the Western concept of "collateral constraints" to accompany force reductions in MBFR, was viewed as the most appropriate military content for the CSCE. The allied objective in advancing proposals on this subject was similar to the underlying objective of the Western proposals in other CSCE subject areas—to obtain agreement on a limited number of concrete steps designed to improve security and cooperation in Europe. In the case of the military aspects of security, there was a corollary: to keep CSCE from complicating or detracting from the allied negotiating effort in MBFR.

Within the allied bloc there were varying degrees of enthusiasm for the confidence-building measures concept. The U.S. position in particular was lukewarm, despite the fact that many of the ideas originated with the United States. From a military point of view the confidence-building measures appeared to U.S. planners to have marginal value, at best. At worst, they could conceivably have become hindrances on the freedom of action that might be required in some future emergency. The United States supported the confidence-building measures concept more for reasons of allied solidarity than because of anticipated military or arms control benefits.

Soviet objectives with regard to military subjects also flowed naturally from their overall approach to the Conference. The Soviets wished to have a Summit meeting that would create the atmosphere of detente in Europe and would confirm the existing European geopolitical situation. They were not interested in substantive agreements in CSCE that would go beyond this broad political statement. The military aspects of security should, from the Soviet point of view, have been treated only in political generalities, as part of the confirmation of the status quo that the CSCE was supposed to produce. In short, the Soviets wanted no concrete military negotiations in the CSCE. This position paralleled that of the NATO allies insofar as it stressed that the primary locus for military negotiations in Europe should be the MBFR talks. However, the Eastern position was more negative than that of the NATO allies in that it sought to exclude even the limited military content foreseen by the West—the confidence-building measures.

The position of the neutral and nonaligned European states was different from that of either of the military blocs. The neutrals had no role in MBFR and thought they should have a say in any such negotiations, which could affect their own security. In their view the only really proper forum for discussion of European military subjects was one in which their own interests would also be reflected. They saw the CSCE as a more legitimate forum for military negotiations than MBFR, and sought to make the most of it. Underlying this thinking was the idealistic notion that the two military blocs might someday be replaced by a European-wide security system based on something like the CSCE. Swedish Prime Minister Olof Palme expressed the basis of this concept in his speech at Helsinki. "It is not axiomatic," said Palme, "that the present pattern of European security will remain unchanged in the long run."

The neutrals' objectives, which were loosely shared at first but grew more harmonious as their coordination became more active during the course of the

CSCE, were twofold: to inject as much military content as possible into the CSCE in order to enhance the Conference as an arms control forum; and to create some form of linkage between CSCE and MBFR, which would suggest that the results of an arms control negotiation among a limited number of European states were also of legitimate interest to the other European countries.

One of the unique and interesting features of the CSCE negotiations on military subjects was that Romania for all practical purposes split off from the Warsaw Pact group and sought the same objectives as the neutrals, for its own national reasons. Another feature was the position of Spain, which was neither a member of a bloc, nor neutral or nonaligned, but which was seeking through CSCE as elsewhere to reestablish a legitimate role in European affairs. Denied such a role in Basket III because of the repressive Franco regime, and unable to develop a constructive position for themselves in Basket II, the Spanish concentrated on Basket I and the Mediterranean as areas where they could contribute positively. Thus, they took an active part in the military negotiations, aligning themselves largely with the neutrals.

The preparatory talks in Helsinki produced agreement that the CSCE itself would concentrate its work on three confidence-building measures. The agenda for the Conference (HR 23) stated: "Committee/Subcommittee shall submit to the Conference appropriate proposals on confidence-building measures such as the prior notification of major military manoeuvres on a basis to be specified by the Conference, and the exchange of observers by invitation at military manoeuvres under mutually acceptable conditions. The Committee/Subcommittee will also study the question of prior notification of major military movements and submit its conclusions."

The notification of major military movements was accorded a lesser status in this agenda; whereas "appropriate proposals" were required on notification of major military maneuvers and exchange of observers, the question of notification of movements was simply to be "studied," and the "conclusions" to be reported. This wording in the agenda reflected the opposition of the Soviet Union to a confidence-building measure on notification of movements, which had already been made clear during the drafting of the agenda. While consideration of the issue remained possible, the chances of successfully negotiating a confidence-building measure on notification of movements were severely limited from the very beginning.

It was also understood from the beginning that the confidence-building measure on exchange of observers would relate closely to that on notification of maneuvers. Since observers would in any case be invited only to maneuvers for which states had given notification, the nature of the confidence-building measure on maneuvers would also control the scope of that on observers.

Thus, the principal substantive military negotiation focused on notification of major military maneuvers. Soon after discussion of this question began, it became apparent that the significance of the confidence-building measure would be defined by its parameters. These could be broken down into the following specific points of definition: the type of maneuvers to be included; the geographic area within which notification would be required; the size of the maneuvers considered "major" and thus subject to notification; the amount of advance notification time to be required; and the content and modalities of the notification. The two-year negotiation concentrated on these specific points.

The USSR at the opening of the CSCE apparently hoped to avoid any detailed agreement on confidence-building measures. The original Soviet draft for the military portion of the final document, tabled in September of 1973, simply stated: "The participating states . . . deem it of great importance that the States concerned . . . should notify each other in advance on the basis of agreed procedures, of major military manoeuvres in specified areas."

The details presumably were to be worked out after the Conference by "the States concerned," evidently bilaterally. Soviet intentions were revealed even more clearly later, when they insisted that notification need be given only to neighboring states. Under the Soviet concept, the USSR would have given notification of maneuvers only to its Warsaw Pact neighbors and, if maneuvers were held in the areas near their frontiers with Finland or Turkey, to those countries as well.

Great Britain, as floor leader for the NATO group in the military subcommittee, tabled the Western position in a paper dated February 4, 1974. This paper took the opposite approach; detailed decisions were to be reached during the CSCE itself. The British paper proposed that notification be given bilaterally to all CSCE-participant states of any maneuver, including a division or more of troops (about 10,000 men) held "in Europe," sixty days in advance of the maneuver. Britain also proposed that notification include details of the name and nature of the maneuver, the number of troops taking part, the time frame, and area involved.

These proposals represented the negotiating terrain within which a compromise would have to be found. But this compromise was difficult to identify. When the Soviets began hinting at the parameters they might accept, they were radically different from those proposed by the British. Rather than notification of maneuvers in "all of Europe," the Soviets suggested giving notification only of maneuvers taking place in border zones of fifty kilometers; instead of sixty days' notice, they preferred five days; and in place of a notification threshold of one division, they offered the level of army corps—generally interpreted to be three divisions or larger (somewhere between 30,000 and 50,000 men).

It was not until June of 1974 that the Soviets slightly modified their position on the parameters: to hundred-kilometer frontier zones and ten days' advance notice. In response the NATO allies reduced their demands to seven weeks' notice, and a threshold of 12,000 instead of 10,000. The NATO group also hinted that they would be willing to negotiate exceptions to the "all of Europe" definition of area.

In September of 1974 the Soviets hinted they might accept "all of Europe" as a definition of area, provided exceptions that would apply to the USSR could be agreed. The Soviets reasoned that the Soviet Union was an enormous country stretching into Asia, and it was therefore unfair to insist that maneuvers throughout the USSR's European territory be notified. There was also another argument suggested privately but not used publicly: United States and Canadian territory, because it is not in Europe, was exempted, and the Soviets wished to balance this fact without claiming that they themselves were not European. (When the Soviets asked for an exception on the basis of their Asian territory, the Turks also asked for an exception on the same basis.)

In late January of 1975 the NATO group specified that they could accept a 700-kilometer border zone in the USSR as an exception to the "all of Europe" area formula.

In mid-March, the Soviets accepted notification to all CSCE participant states instead of neighboring countries only, but insisted that the text of the military section of the final document indicate clearly that notification would be given on a "voluntary basis." The Western countries gradually accepted this concept as the Soviet position on parameters improved. They reasoned that all the undertakings in the Final Act would be voluntary anyway. The text reflecting the "voluntary basis" concept (FA 104–105) nevertheless indicates that the participating states accept "the responsibility of each of them . . . to implement this measure, in accordance with the accepted criteria and modalities."

At the end of April 1975 a Czech representative spoke of the threshold for notification in numerical terms for the first time—40,000 troops. (Descriptive terms such as division or army corps had proven to be vague, since the size of such units varies from country to country.) At this point the negotiation on parameters had become strictly numerical, thus vastly simplifying it. The NATO position favored a 12,000-man threshold, 700-kilometer border zone in the USSR, and seven weeks' notice; while the Warsaw Pact figures were 40,000 men, 100 kilometers, and ten days' notice.

In May the Soviets moved to 35,000 men and fourteen days; NATO moved to 15,000 men, 500 kilometers, and five weeks. At his meeting with Kissinger in Vienna May 19–20, Gromyko offered 30,000 men, 150 kilometers, and eighteen days (the "Vienna parameters"). In Washington in early June the Soviets fell back to 250 kilometers for the border zone. These "Washington parameters" satisfied Kissinger, but the European allies would not budge from their latest position of 22,000 men, 300 kilometers, and twenty-one days.

On June 20 the neutrals put forward compromise figures of 25,000 men, 300 kilometers, and twenty-one days, and on July 3 agreement was reached between the British, as NATO floor leader, and the USSR on 25,000 men, 250 kilometers, and twenty-one days, thus concluding the negotiation on parameters. The agreed confidence-building measure on notification of major maneuvers is contained in FA 107–113. Another confidence-building measure (FA 114–116) encourages—but does not require—notification of smaller-scale maneuvers.

The confidence-building measure on inviting observers to attend maneuvers was perhaps more significant than the agreement on notification of maneuvers. It constituted the first occasion on which the USSR formally agreed to permit qualified Western observers to attend military readiness activities in the Soviet Union, and reversed a long-standing Soviet position of principle opposed to observer activity. The confidence-building measure language on observers was initially agreed in July 1974, although its full scope was not evident until the parameters on notification of major maneuvers were agreed one year later, since these parameters also defined the maneuvers to which observers would be invited. In view of the date of basic Soviet concurrence in the observer concept, it appears that their decision to accept observers in the CSCE framework preceded by almost a year the Soviet decision to accept some verification procedures in the context of an agreement on peaceful nuclear explosions. The implications for other military negotiations—such as MBFR—where verification or inspection procedures are an issue may prove to be more important than was first realized.

Several other proposals of the confidence-building measure type were put forward during the Geneva negotiations, but only one obtained consensus. This was a Spanish proposal for exchanges of military personnel. Bilateral East-West exchanges of visits among military officers and units had, in fact, been fairly common in Europe for some time, and the Spanish proposal did little more than sanction and encourage an already existing practice. A clause in the original Spanish proposal on the "extension of facilities to military attaches for the better performance of their duties" appeared to suggest the facilitation of military espionage, and was dropped. The Spanish proposal, as agreed, appears in FA 127.

Sweden put forward an elaborate proposal on the publication of defense expenditures, similar to proposals made previously by the Swedes in the United Nations and the Geneva Conference of the Committee on Disarmament. The proposal, which was tabled on October 23, 1973, effectively died in July of 1974, after the Soviets made it clear they would not accept it.

Slightly more successful—although only slightly—was a Yugoslav suggestion that the CSCE states agree to refrain from certain types of military activities that could cause "anxiety," especially in frontier areas. The Yugoslav concept was significantly different from the Western concept of confidence-building measures in that it would have actually placed restrictions on military activities, whereas the Western idea was that there would be no restrictions on military activities, but that notification would be given and observers invited. The

Western approach even appeared to grant military readiness activities a certain legitimacy, while the Yugoslav idea identified such activities as undesirable. The Yugoslavs fell back considerably from their original proposal, and the only reflection of it in the Final Act is a phrase (FA 128) that commits states to "take into account and respect" the objective of confidence-building "when conducting their military activities."

The Yugoslavs also took the lead among the neutral and nonaligned countries in proposing some form of information link between the MBFR negotiations and the CSCE. The original Yugoslav proposal on this point stated: "All [CSCE] participating states should have a full opportunity of taking part in the consideration of [issues relating to reduction of forces and armaments in Europe]. They should, accordingly, be kept adequately informed of the progress of the negotiations on the reduction of armed forces and armaments in Europe, or on other disarmament measures, so that they may be able to secure their interests and offer their contribution to such negotiations."

The NATO countries participating in MBFR took the view that the neutrals could keep themselves adequately informed of the progress of the MBFR talks through normal bilateral diplomatic channels in Vienna. The NATO countries felt strongly that the neutrals should be granted no "right to be informed" on MBFR, which would have posed additional complications for the Vienna talks. The result was a carefully worded sentence (FA 137) recognizing "the importance that participants in negotiating fora see to it that information about relevant developments, progress and results is provided on an appropriate basis" to CSCE participants.

The concerns of several states (e.g., USSR, Turkey, Spain) about undertaking obligations toward neighboring states that were not CSCE participants resulted in an awkwardly worded exception to the area of applicability for the confidence-building measure on notification of major maneuvers, under which areas of CSCE participating states "contiguous" to "non-European nonparticipating" states are exempted (FA 111). The principal areas covered by this exception are those regions of Turkey and the USSR bordering on Syria, Iraq, and Iran.

A confidence-building measure on military movements could not be agreed. The USSR was opposed to it, and the United States had private hesitations. The Final Act language (FA 121–124) permits notification of major military movements (states "may, at their own discretion . . . notify") and indicates that "further consideration will be given" to this idea, presumably at the Belgrade follow-up meeting in 1977 and later such meetings.

25 The Many Fields
Economic and Related Issues in the CSCE

One of the best guarantees for lasting peace and security is reciprocal cooperation in as many fields as possible.

Anker Jorgensen Helsinki July 31, 1975

The notion that the CSCE should deal with economic, technical, and scientific cooperation was originally proposed by a Warsaw Pact foreign ministers' meeting in Prague in October of 1969. That meeting suggested a two-point agenda for the European conference: (1) security and (2) economic, technical, and scientific cooperation. A NATO declaration of the following December suggested a broader agenda item of economic, technical, and cultural exchanges, especially freer movement of people, ideas, and information, and the environment; and the NATO communique of May 1970 added science to this list. A subsequent Warsaw Pact statement, in Budapest in June 1970, accepted this enlarged agenda heading for the discussion of "cooperation" in a European conference.

During the Helsinki consultations, "Questions Relating to Security in Europe" were grouped in Basket I, while cooperation subjects were organized somewhat—but only somewhat—more logically into two baskets. Basket II was to cover "Cooperation in the Field of Economics, of Science and Technology, and of the Environment" and Basket III, "Cooperation in Humanitarian and Other Fields."

These titles were only general indications of what the baskets contained. Basket II was divided into five subsections, each of which became a subcommittee during the Geneva negotiations: (1) commercial exchanges, (2) industrial cooperation and projects of common interest, (3) science and technology, (4) environment, and (5) cooperation in other areas.

The first two subheadings and the fourth subheading were fairly clear. However, science and technology overlapped with the science topic included in the Basket III mandate for discussion of educational cooperation (HR 51). This problem was resolved by developing an informal rule of thumb that science as technology would be treated under Basket II and science as an area of education under Basket III. The fifth subheading, other areas, also had an overlap: the tourism subject contained in its agenda overlapped with the human contacts mandate (HR 46b). Here again, a simple dividing line was fixed: tourism as a freer movement issue would be dealt with in Basket III; tourism as an economic subject, in Basket II.

Eventually, even these subgroupings proved inadequate, and the Final Act set up a somewhat different organization for Basket II. This was because it was found that many provisions negotiated in the first or second subcommittee, or both, were equally applicable to commercial exchanges and industrial cooperation. These provisions were grouped together under an additional subheading, "Provisions Concerning Trade and Industrial Cooperation" (FA 244–260), for which there is no direct source in the Helsinki Recommendations.

From the beginning of the negotiations, Basket II faced special problems. First, the USSR and its allies, who should logically have assumed the role of demandeur, at least in the areas of trade, industrial cooperation, and science and technology, refused to do so. They apparently had identified their other objectives in the Conference (e.g., the principles and the summit-level conclusion) as of overriding importance. Thus, they were unwilling to overload their efforts with desiderata that, at least in the CSCE, were of secondary importance. Their general approach, here as elsewhere in the Conference, was to keep everything as simple and as general as possible, in order to bring the CSCE to a satisfactory conclusion quickly.

In addition, there was little of real substantive importance the CSCE could do in the major economic areas. Trade and industrial cooperation had long been leading areas of East-West cooperation, and bilateral agreements existed between many of the participating states. Such agreements were by definition more specific than a multilateral agreement could be, and the most the CSCE could hope to do in general was to fill in behind these bilateral agreements by identifying their common elements and by seeking to give these subject areas a kind of multilateral framework. This effort did have some importance as a point of reference for future trade relations, especially for smaller countries that did not have bilateral trade agreements. But the economic field is different from, for example, the cultural field, in that progress can come only in the form of mutually profitable deals between specific partners, and the CSCE could, of course, not arrange such deals.

The Basket II discussions revealed two main axes of negotiation: that between free market and state trading systems, and that between industrialized and developing countries. The first of these, most obvious in such an East-West conference, was central to the debate, both ideologically and from the viewpoint of national self-interest. While there was broad agreement that the Conference should aim to eliminate obstacles to trade, the communist countries saw this mainly as a matter of eliminating tariff barriers and granting Most Favored Nation (MFN) trading status to all the participating states. The Western countries were more concerned with other obstacles to trade inherent in the centralized state control of trade, and insisted that any reductions in trade barriers should be accomplished with full effective reciprocity of benefits, since simple mutual elimination of tariffs would give disproportionate advantages to the communist countries. This particular relationship was reflected in one of the most complicated sets of texts in the Final Act: the need for reciprocity is mentioned in the preamble to Basket II (FA 144); a phrase at the beginning of the commercial exchanges section (FA 154) states that "the provisions of the above preamble apply in particular to this sector"; further on, there is a clause recognizing "the beneficial effects which can result for the development of trade from the application of most favoured nation treatment" (FA 157). Thus, the granting of MFN is identified as something desirable rather than as an obligation, and the provision of reciprocity also applies to it.

Another feature of the East-West axis of negotiation was the "freer movement" aspect of Basket II. The freer movement concept has been associated primarily with Basket III, but there were a number of Western freer movement proposals in Basket II, as well. These related primarily to three fields. The first of these was the general heading of working conditions for businessmen, where Western efforts were aimed at improving the circumstances (often very rudimentary) under which company representatives conduct their business in the USSR and Eastern Europe. This effort included proposals for better office and residential accommodation, favorable consideration of applications to open offices, facilitated visa procedures, and contacts with prospective clients. A second major freer movement area in Basket II was an effort to obtain a commitment to publication of more complete and timely information and statistics of interest to businessmen. The third major effort was in the field of direct contacts and communication between people; in Basket II the people in question were businessmen, who should have the possibility of direct contact with the end-users of their products; scientists, who need direct contact and communication with their counterparts; environmental specialists, etc.

The second axis of negotiation was a less obvious one and generally aligned the northern tier of industrialized European countries (and the United States and Canada) against the southern tier of less-developed European countries, stretching from Portugal to Turkey and including Spain, Italy, Yugoslavia, Greece, Romania, and even, at times, Bulgaria. The southern tier of countries had a number of special interests in common in the general provisions of the Basket II preamble and certain specific subjects. Their efforts to have their interests reflected were usually resisted by the industrialized states, either on the grounds that they would distort the basic East-West nature of the Conference or on the simple basis of national self-interest. Compromises were not easily found, as the tortured language of FA 145, in the Basket II preamble, bears witness.

Two subsections under the Other Areas heading were of special interest to the southern tier of countries: "Promotion of Tourism" and "Economic and Social Aspects of Migrant Labor." The developing southern countries of

Europe are all more dependent on the tourism industry than their northern neighbors, and they wished to give special emphasis to this subject. The northern countries had little interest in singling out tourism as an industry in the Final Act, despite the fact that, at the same time, the Western countries were pressing for Basket III language that would support tourism as a means for enlarging direct contacts between people. While they were not directly opposed to the southern efforts in Basket II, the northern countries were unenthusiastic and saw the southerners as undercutting their own initiatives in Basket III.

The migrant labor subject came even closer to national interests. Virtually all the southern European countries export labor to northern Europe (this is true even among the communist bloc Council for Mutual Economic Assistance countries). It was of major political importance for these countries to obtain language in the Final Act supporting improvements in the status of their migrant workers. It was equally important for the northern countries, pressed by economic problems and unemployment, to avoid far-reaching commitments in this area. The United States wished to avoid any language that would suggest that commitments under this heading applied outside of Europe; obviously, such commitments could have been read as applying to the Mexican illegal immigrant problem.

The clearest example of the north-south conflict of interest was the position of Switzerland, for whom the presence of foreign laborers is both an economic necessity and a highly sensitive political issue (the Swiss had a national referendum on the question during the CSCE). The Swiss, who were giving firm support to the Western proposal on family reunification, opposed a Basket II provision that would have recognized the right of migrant workers to have their families with them; this was something Swiss law did not permit. A qualified commitment on this point was nevertheless included in the Final Act (FA 390).

The sections of Basket II on science and technology and the environment have a rather special organization in view of the disparity in size and technological capacities among the participating states and the existence of numerous bilateral and multilateral activities in these fields. The only format that seemed appropriate for these subjects was a simple listing of possible areas and forms of cooperation. These sections also make a number of references to ongoing work in existing international bodies, a tacit recognition that the CSCE was breaking little new ground here. Interestingly, the USSR after the Conference put forward a major proposal for three high-level meetings, all on relatively less-known Basket II issues: transportation, energy, and the environment.

Another feature of negotiations in Basket II was the role of the European Community. Unlike EC-Nine coordination on other CSCE subjects, which was based on the more informal framework of political cooperation, the positions of the Nine on most Basket II subjects were formally the same. This was because the subjects of Basket II largely coincided with the subjects for which the community has negotiating responsibility on behalf of the member states, deriving from the Treaty of Rome. The delegation of the EC-Nine presidency country had a special role in Basket II. It included representatives of the Commission of the European Communities, and it was the presidency delegation's responsibility to enunciate community positions whenever they were applicable. The representatives of the commission sometimes spoke in committee meetings on behalf of the community, and the provisions agreed were considered by the EC-Nine to be engagements entered into by the community as such. In his speech at the Helsinki Summit, Aldo Moro, then president-in-office of the community, confirmed this: "The conclusions of this Conference will be applied by the Communities in all matters which are within their competence, or may come within their competence in the future." Moro signed the Final Act both as Italian prime minister and as president of the EC-Nine.

U.S. interests in Basket II were limited. Our trade relations with the Soviet Union had already reached an important level, and the question of granting MFN status to the USSR was something of an embarrassment to the administration (which had negotiated a bilateral U.S.-Soviet trade agreement, only to see it unilaterally denounced by Moscow when the U.S. Congress added the Jackson-Vanik amendment requiring progress on Soviet emigration). In addition, Washington and Moscow had already reached agreement on bilateral exchanges in science and technology, environment, and a number of specific fields covered under these general headings, such as cooperation in space, health, peaceful uses of atomic energy, agriculture, oceanography, and transportation. There seemed little that Basket II of the CSCE could add that would be of major interest to the United States. Nevertheless, it was thought for a number of reasons that the U.S. delegation should make some positive contributions to the work in Basket II, as well as other areas of the Conference. Thus, the United States coauthored, with members of the EC-Nine, papers on business contacts and science and technology, and submitted U.S. proposals on arbitration of disputes in the commercial and industrial cooperation fields (this proposal resulted in the section on arbitration, FA 251–256), and on a study of techniques for predicting environmental consequences (which was accepted as FA 339).

Basket II was the only subject area of the CSCE for which there was an appropriate existing international organization ready to assure follow-up. The Economic Commission for Europe (ECE), a Geneva-based UN regional organization with sprawling interests, has virtually the same membership as the CSCE (a few of the ministates that participated in the CSCE are not members of the ECE, but otherwise membership is identical, including the United States and Canada). The ECE's mandate covers almost all of the Basket II subjects. Though the ECE has a special role as a point of continuing multilateral East-West contact on economic and related issues, its history has not been marked by political dynamism. The existence of the ECE probably had the effect of dampening some contries; enthusiasm for Basket II. In fact, many delegates to the CSCE's committees on Basket II matters were permanently assigned in Geneva as members of their national delegations to the ECE and saw the CSCE as unnecessarily duplicative. In any case, it was widely acknowledged from the outset that the ECE would be the agent for whatever follow-up was required for Basket II, and this was eventually formalized in the follow-up chapter of the Final Act (FA 664). By confiding a follow-up mandate to the ECE, the CSCE gave that organization a significant political boost.

26 And Finally, History
Agreeing on the Dates for
Helsinki, July 1–14, 1975

Our history unites us, in spite of everything.
Aldo Moro Helsinki July 30, 1975

The Conference moved into July with no agreement in sight on a date for Stage III. By now the pressure had become intense. The Coordinating Committee was meeting daily in an effort to work out a formula that would give the Finns some basis for going ahead with arrangements for a Stage III at the end of July. The lobbies of the old International Labor Organization Building, where the Conference was meeting, were jammed with journalists and cameramen, and the number of private meetings and bilateral consultations had multiplied to the point where it was difficult to keep track of them.

The focus was still on the Swedish proposal to begin Stage III on July 28, but during the first days of July the Finns revealed very privately to key delegations that in asking for a minimum of four weeks' notice for convening the Summit, they had actually left themselves one week's leeway. They now indicated that the Summit could be arranged with only three weeks' notice, but insisted that this was a firm deadline with no further flexibility. This meant that a Summit beginning on July 28 would have to be decided by July 7.

The problem at this point became clearer. It was evident that the final work of the Conference would not be finished by July 7, but it was equally recognized that the main substantive issues would probably be resolved by that date, leaving only cleanup work to follow. It was widely felt that in these circumstances agreement on a date for Stage III would be expedient, especially since it could be risky to complete substantive work and then allow a long interval before convening Stage III.

As more Western delegations became convinced by this logic, Conference delegates began to think in terms of a "two-tiered" decision on timing: agreement on a date for the Summit, provided substantive work was completed by another agreed date somewhat earlier than the Summit. Such an arrangement would protect the positions of those whose pet projects had not yet been adopted, give the Finns the go-ahead for planning purposes, create pressure for completion, and imply that the participating states would take financial responsibility for losses suffered by the Finns in the event the Summit did not materialize. This last point was important for the Finns, but was difficult to state clearly because the systems of some countries for the appropriation of funds for international conferences would not permit a commitment to pay for a conference that might not be held.

The delegates feverishly tried to fit these various factors together in a workable way during the first week of July, with several delegations, particularly the French, Swiss, Canadian, and FRG, taking a leading role. A Coordinating Committee meeting on July 1 produced only further acrimonious debate. Another meeting on July 2 was even more bitter, with several delegation heads trading personal criticisms.

The evening of July 2 had been reserved for some time for an excursion by train to the Chateau d'Oron, where the Swiss government had invited all delegation heads for dinner. The train trip was a perfect format for corridor work, and the many private contacts among delegation heads served to focus thinking on the two-tiered device for agreement on timing.

The meeting of the Coordinating Committee on the morning of July 3 adjourned until 9:00 P.M. in the hope that substantive progress during the day would create a better atmosphere that evening.

During the course of July 3, agreement was reached between the Soviets and the British as NATO floor leader for military subjects, on the parameters for notification of major military maneuvers: 25,000-man threshold, twenty-one days' advance notification, and a geographic area of applicability of "all of Europe," with an exception for the USSR, where only a 250-kilometer border zone would be covered. This agreement meant that virtually all delegations would agree to the compromise except Turkey, which was seeking an even broader geographic exception for itself. The Soviets also proposed language to conclude consideration of the Western proposal for prior notification of major military movements, by which this question would be subject to further consideration at a later date, bearing in mind experience gained with the confidence-building measure on notification of maneuvers. (This concept is reflected in FA 124.)

The agreement on maneuvers was an important step forward, but not enough, and the Coordinating Committee that evening made no further progress toward agreement on a date for the Summit.

The July 4 meeting of the Coordinating Committee also had no result. The East-West questions that remained unresolved—agreement on a saving clause for quadripartite rights and responsibilities in Berlin and Germany, registration of the sentence on peaceful changes of frontiers, agreement on Conference follow-up, and the "all of Europe" clause intended to ensure that the benefits of CSCE would apply to Berlin—made several key Western delegations unwilling to accept even a two-tiered decision on Stage III timing. On the same day the subcommittee on the principles reviewed the French-proposed language for a quadripartite rights saving clause, with the neutrals and several Western allies expressing sharp objections to it. As a result, the delegations of the four powers with postwar rights and responsibilities in Berlin and Germany met in the Soviet mission on the evening of July 4 to discuss how to proceed. In view of the situation, the four delegations agreed that a dramatic effort was required to demonstrate the importance of a quadripartite rights saving clause and to obtain early consensus of the full CSCE on its formulation. It was decided that the four powers would make an all-out effort to reach agreement the following day.

On July 5 the four powers proposed that the subcommittee on the principles go into informal session to consider the quadripartite rights phraseology, and a marathon negotiating session began, under British chairmanship, in a cramped upstairs meeting room. The session lasted all day, but the end result was agreement on a saving clause to be included in the final clauses of the declaration of principles (FA 72), with only a minor reservation by Romania on one part of the formulation. Following this success the U.S. delegation asked for the registration of the peaceful change formulation, but this was blocked by Romania, which was still not ready to accept it.

In another key development, the informal working group under Swedish chairmanship reached agreement late on July 5 on the main elements of a compromise on Conference follow-up. Although the language needed further refinement, the political compromise had been found.

By the evening of July 5 there had also been considerable progress in other areas of the Conference. The compromise language dealing with the Swiss proposal on peaceful settlement of disputes (FA 86–92) was registered. Most of the Basket II preamble (FA 139–149) was agreed (with the important exceptions of language on Most Favored Nation status and on the need for reciprocity in trade relationships), and the Basket II section on migrant labor in Europe (FA 376–391) was completed. All four sections of Basket III were finally registered, thus completing Basket III entirely. And agreement was reached on a disclaimer clause on the nonlegal nature of the Final Act (FA 672), as well as on the text of a letter to be sent by the government of Finland, as host for Stage III, forwarding the Final Act to the secretary general of the United Nations and specifically stating that the Final Act is neither a treaty nor an agreement. (The text of this letter appears in Appendix II, following the text of the Final Act.)

The French delegation was sufficiently convinced by the day's progress that at the evening meeting of the Coordinating Committee they made the first formal two-tiered proposal for acceptance of a Stage III date. Presenting their proposal without specific dates, the French suggested that the holding of Stage III by the end of July be agreed, on condition that all Stage II work be completed by a certain date, with the proviso that, if work should not be completed, delegations could reconsider their agreement on the July date. In the meanwhile, the Finnish government would be asked to begin preparations for the Stage III meeting, on the understanding that Finland would be reimbursed for any expenses incurred by simply adding these costs to each country's share of the costs for Stage III, whenever it might eventually be held.

The French proposal was an important new element giving substance to the ideas for a two-tiered agreement, which had been floating for some time. Nevertheless, the British and FRG delegations received instructions on July 5 not to agree to the French suggestion until all important East-West issues had been resolved. The Romanian blockage of the peaceful change language clearly meant that all East-West issues had not yet been resolved, and thus the British, FRG, and U.S. delegations, as well as several other NATO allies, stated at the Coordinating Committee on the evening of July 5 only that they would study the French proposal. There were also several delegations whose special interests had not yet been satisfied and who would not agree on Stage III timing. These were Turkey, which wanted an area exception for itself for prior notification of maneuvers; Romania, whose paper on nonuse of force had not yet been registered; and Malta, which was giving out ominous signals that much more far-reaching language would be required in the Mediterranean declaration. In addition, the Netherlands and Belgium were generally unhappy with the speed of movement toward the Summit and were reluctant to accept early agreement on a date.

At an evening meeting of the Coordinating Committee on July 7, Finnish Ambassador Iloniemi, after a phone consultation with Helsinki, announced that it was no longer possible for Stage III to be convened on July 28, since fewer than twenty-one days remained prior to that date. Iloniemi explained that, from then on, each day that passed without a decision on timing would eliminate another possible day for the opening of the Summit gathering. The earliest the Summit could now be convened was July 29. We reported this news by "flash" cable to Washington.

On July 8, we received urgent instructions by telephone from Washington: Press hard for Stage III to begin on July 29. July 30 would also probably be acceptable. Following our report that July 28 was no longer possible for the Finns, the White House had focused on the timing of Stage III in connection with the president's planned travels. If the Summit was to be at the end of July, and was to fit in with visits to two Eastern European countries after Helsinki, it could not be much later than July 29, since the Summit meeting would last at least three days and the president was obliged to receive the Japanese prime minister in Washington on August 5.

July 8 appeared to be a propitious day for reaching agreement on Stage III timing. The Romanian proposal on nonuse of force (FA 76–85) was agreed and the Romanians lifted their reservation on the peaceful change language, which was accepted for registration in the first principle (FA 25). The Romanians also indicated that they would accept the quadripartite rights saving clause as it stood, but not until the document on Conference follow-up had been completed.

We informed the NATO caucus in mid-afternoon that we now favored a Helsinki Summit beginning on July 29, but this ran somewhat counter to the instructions the EC-Nine had received from their political directors that same day. The Nine, in a step backwards, now opposed conditional acceptance of a date for Stage III. The situation in the Coordinating Committee that evening was confused. The Nine announced that they could not accept even conditional agreement on timing until the substantive issues had been resolved. This position was out of step with the Conference as a whole, which had been focusing for a week on a conditional, two-tiered approach to setting a date. Kovalev responded angrily, accusing the Nine of a deliberate "provocation." After a brief recess Polish Ambassador Marian Dobrosielski proposed agreement without conditions to a Stage III opening date of July 29, which was equally unacceptable to many delegations, and the meeting adjourned with no result.

July 9 also appeared to be a promising day for agreement on timing. The preamble to the declaration on principles (FA 17–22) was completed and the texts on notification of other military maneuvers (FA 114–116) and of major military movements (FA 121–124) were agreed. The Soviets were, meanwhile, working hard to encourage the Nine political directors to accept a Summit in July.

At a Coordinating Committee meeting at noon Iloniemi announced that it was now no longer possible for Stage III to begin on July 29. However, Canadian Ambassador Tom Delworth informed the NATO caucus at 5:30 P.M. that he had received instructions, "direct from Prime Minister Trudeau," to take the lead in seeking agreement on a Summit before the end of July.

Delworth unveiled the Canadian proposal in the Coordinating Committee that evening. It was the same as the earlier French proposal, except that the specific dates had been filled in. The Summit was to begin on July 30, provided all substantive work was finished by July 15. The Canadian proposal was supported by the United States and about twelve other delegations, many of which had not yet spoken in favor of a Summit in July. This brought the total number of delegations openly favoring a late July Stage III to more than twenty-five, and demonstrated that it was the clear intention of the great majority of the participating states to have a Stage III Summit in July. Although agreement on the Canadian proposal was blocked for the time being, primarily by Malta, the Finnish government understood the signal that had been given, and decided to go ahead on faith with preparations for the Summit.

Early on July 10, it looked as though the Canadian proposal might be fully approved that day. A key Basket II text on safeguards against market disruption (FA 163) had been agreed, and two more paragraphs had been drafted for addition to the Mediterranean declaration (FA 412 and 413) in an attempt to meet Maltese objections. These paragraphs indicated that the CSCE states would maintain and amplify "the contacts and dialogue initiated by the CSCE with the nonparticipating states to include all the states of the Mediterranean, . . . in the framework of their multilateral efforts." Most delegates believed these clauses would satisfy Mintoff, but this estimate proved to be wrong.

By the time the Coordinating Committee convened at noon, it had become apparent that the Maltese would not accept the Canadian proposal. The Maltese were also blocking agreement on the follow-up document. The Romanians in turn would not lift their reservation on the quadripartite rights saving clause until the follow-up document was complete, and the FRG would not agree, even conditionally, to a Stage III date until the quadripartite rights clause had been agreed. A package deal was offered to the Maltese under which they would get the two additional paragraphs in the Mediterranean declaration and in return would agree to the follow-up document and the Canadian proposal for timing of Stage III.

In the midst of this complex negotiating tangle, Kissinger and Gromyko arrived in Geneva for one of their periodic bilateral meetings. The Secretary of State and his Soviet counterpart were informed on arrival of the current situation, and that the Conference was now awaiting Mintoff's reply to the package offer.

Around 10:30 P.M. the special Maltese envoy Mintoff had sent to handle this problem announced that there would be no reply from Valletta until 11:00 A.M. the following day. Kovalev exploded with rage, grabbed Sherer by the arm, and pressed him to go directly to the Soviet mission, where Kissinger and Gromyko were dining together. The two delegation heads arrived while dinner was still in progress, and Kovalev burst into the dining room. Standing behind Gromyko's chair, Kovalev made a speech. Mintoff was humiliating the Conference, he said, and Malta should be isolated. The other delegations should either inform the Finns directly that they would go to Helsinki regardless of the Maltese, or should meet in "another room," minus the Maltese, to agree on a Stage III date. Kissinger then asked Sherer for his views. Sherer said he agreed the other delegations were being humiliated by the Maltese but did not agree with Kovalev's proposed solutions. The consensus rule was too strong in the CSCE, he continued, and an attempt to cut the Maltese out would lead other delegations to support them. In this situation the only agreement possible between the U.S. and Soviet sides was to support the Canadian proposal on timing and await Mintoff's reply.

On July 11 Mintoff, through his negotiators, indicated that he could accept the package as it had been offered, provided the phrase, "reducing armed forces in the region," was added as an additional objective of the future contacts and dialogue with the nonparticipating Mediterranean states (see FA 412). This was a bitter pill for many delegations to swallow, especially the U.S. and USSR, since it derived from the earlier Maltese formulation on gradual withdrawal of the U.S. and Soviet fleets from the Mediterranean. But Mintoff had the Conference over a barrel, and, in addition, the tenuous formulation of the phrase made it clear that there was no specific agreement to reduce arms in the Mediterranean, only that this should be an aim of further discussions. Kissinger decided that he could live with the phrase. The Soviets, though bitter, also swallowed it. On the following day the NATO caucus agreed to accept it.

July 14 was a banner day for the CSCE. The Maltese proposal was accepted, and the Mediterranean declaration (FA 398–413) registered. The Maltese then lifted their reservation on the follow-up document (FA 655–669), thus permitting it to be agreed. The Romanians thereupon withdrew their objections to the quadripartite rights saving clause, and this sentence, along with the other final clauses of the declaration on principles (FA 70–74), was accepted. And in the evening, with television cameras invited into the meeting room, the Coordinating Committee approved the Canadian proposal that Stage III begin in Helsinki on July 30, provided substantive work was completed by July 15. The delegates jammed into the meeting room greeted this decision with a delirious and prolonged standing ovation.

27 The Other Dimension

The Issue of the Nonparticipating Mediterranean States

Together with the East-West dimension, there exists another whose coordinates go from North to South; . . . the proper definition of the relations between the participating States should take both these axes into account.

Arias Navarro Helsinki July 31, 1975

"Europe," said Jacques Andreani, "has no southern frontier." Andreani, a chain-smoking Frenchman with a Corsican background, was one of the intellectual lights of the CSCE. He was perpetually disheveled, in rumpled tweeds, and conveyed the aura of a junior professor in a Left Bank cafe. But his understanding of the Conference was among the most perceptive of any of the delegates involved in the negotiations, and when he gave this analysis of the Mediterranean problem in the CSCE, he could not have been more correct. For the superpowers, Europe can be seen in the simplistic terms of East-West relations, but for the countries along Europe's southern coastline, the pattern of relationships between states is more complex—and always has been.

The CSCE was conceived by governments whose primary interest was in the East-West relationship, but once a conference opened that was intended to cover security and cooperation among the states present, it was not possible for the southern European participants to ignore their relations with the nations on the other side of the Mediterranean. And once the question of the relationship with these non-European states had been broached, the other West Europeans could not refuse to consider their views; they were trying to build better relations with the oil-producing Arab states, and most of the non-European Mediterranean countries are Arab.

The basic conflict on the Mediterranean issue within the CSCE was between those countries that wished to keep the Conference as simple as possible by maintaining the focus on East-West relations, and those that felt Europe's relationship with the other Mediterranean countries was also important—and thus should also be reflected in the CSCE. The former group, including most of the northern, industrialized countries of East and West Europe, the USSR, and the North Americans, considered that a discussion of Mediterranean issues would lead inexorably to a divisive discussion of the Middle East problem, with the prospect of Arab and Israeli participation or representation by proxy. Such a debate would change the focus and character of CSCE completely, and render it useless as a device for improving East-West relations.

Those nations that wished to open a discussion of Mediterranean issues— primarily Malta, Spain, and Yugoslavia, but also including in some degree virtually all Mediterranean littoral states—argued that there could be no European security or cooperation without security and cooperation in the Mediterranean. Their view was that the greatest threat to peace in the European region was no longer the East-West confrontation, but the Israeli-Arab conflict, and that therefore a discussion of European security that ignored this problem would be a farce.

It should be noted that the Cyprus problem, in the CSCE context, is not a "Mediterranean" problem but a "European" one, since all the parties to the conflict are participating states and the CSCE's provisions thus apply fully to them (though the CSCE principles have obviously not been applied in Cyprus).

Two non-European states—Algeria and Tunisia—circulated diplomatic notes to the Conference participants in Helsinki in 1972 expressing their desire to be associated with the Conference. Several participating states, notably Malta, Yugoslavia, and Spain, took up their cause, and a number of other delegations, including the French and Italians, were sympathetic. These delegations argued that the two Maghreb states, which had strong historical and cultural ties to Europe, were manifesting a "European vocation," which should not be spurned. They likened this vocation to that of Turkey under Ataturk, when the Turks decided that their future lay with Europe rather than the Arab world.

The argument was a forceful one, but there was an equally forceful counter-argument: if these countries were admitted it would be difficult to deny other nations expressing a European vocation an equal presence at the CSCE, and the process could expand the number of non-European participants indefinitely. Also, the two Maghreb states had to be considered Arab spokesmen, and their admission—without giving Israel a similar status—would make the Conference appear to be taking sides in the Arab-Israeli dispute, and would permit Arab statements to be made within the CSCE without an Israeli reply.

The Israelis themselves were not eager to enter the CSCE; they had a certain interest in advancement of some of the subjects to be treated, such as reunification of families, and had no reason to upset the East-West character of the negotiation. In addition, they did not want the Mideast situation to be the topic of discussion in another multilateral gathering. However, they were adamant that if any Arab state were given a voice in CSCE, they wanted equal status.

Most CSCE participants understood this set of problems, and thought the easiest way to avoid them was simply to exclude all non-European Mediterranean states from having any voice whatsoever in the Conference. But the interested states, with Malta the most insistent, stubbornly maintained their position that Algeria and Tunisia should be linked to the CSCE in some way. The advocates of Algeria and Tunisia made their position more difficult for others to accept by insisting that Israeli interest in a similar link should not be considered. This aspect raised a question of principle on which several delegations, notably the Dutch, Danes, and Canadians, would not yield. They maintained steadfastly that Israel had to receive equal treatment.

The issue was not resolved during the preparatory talks in Helsinki, nor during the first stage of the Conference itself, despite Prime Minister Mintoff's energetic parliamentary maneuvers. When the Coordinating Committee met in Geneva at the end of August 1973, the question of Mediterranean participation could no longer be avoided, since the actual schedule of meetings had to be agreed at that time. The basis of the final compromise was equal treatment for all interested nonparticipating Mediterranean states. Once this principle was accepted by the supporters of a special status for Algeria and Tunisia, it was relatively easy to agree on a formula under which nonparticipating states would make "contributions" on the "relevant" subjects (i.e., Baskets I and II, but not Basket III). These contributions were to be in the form of oral and written presentations in the committees responsible for the subject being treated. At Soviet insistence (for the Soviets wished to minimize this diversion and prevent it from complicating the work of the Conference), it was agreed that the contributions of the Mediterranean states would simply be "taken into account" by the relevant working bodies of the Conference.

Thus it was arranged for each interested Mediterranean state to appear on a given day before the appropriate bodies. The appearances were discreetly separated by several days so that Israelis and Arabs would not cross paths in the lobby. Six Mediterranean countries expressed a desire to make contributions: Morocco, Algeria, Tunisia, Egypt, Israel, and Syria (Libya and Lebanon did not respond to the Conference's invitation), and these six countries throughout the CSCE comprised the "nonparticipating Mediterranean States" referred to in Conference documents.

The arrangement worked well, and there were no incidents. All presentations were moderately worded, and touched only tangentially on the Arab-Israeli dispute. Under a gentlemen's agreement to avoid opening up disputes, there were no questions or discussions. The somewhat voluminous documents circulated were transmitted to foreign ministries in capitals for study, and that might have been the end of it. But this was the Mediterranean, and it is difficult for anything to be concluded so neatly in that part of the world.

The first slippage was when the Maltese and other Mediterranean participants suggested that a single appearance was not enough. They argued that if the contributions that had been made were to be taken seriously it was really necessary, after studying them, to invite the Mediterranean countries back for a second appearance, during which there could be questions and discussion. This idea was at first resisted, since it meant altering an agreement that had been reached only with difficulty and that, once abridged, would lose its finality. But a second appearance seemed harmless enough, and so the Mediterranean countries were invited back for a second round. This proved to be more awkward than the first series of appearances because the delegations of the participating states could, by their questions, reflect political preferences, and they did so. Those whose governments were favorable to the Arab states asked elaborate and friendly questions, while the Israelis got a highly embarrassing silent treatment (even those who were friendly to the Israelis remained silent for fear of provoking openly hostile remarks).

Following this second round of appearances, the Italian delegation began to sound out other Western delegates on the idea that the CSCE might produce a "declaration on the Mediterranean." The Italian idea was to have a document whose content would be meaningless, but whose title, along with the fact of its existence, would demonstrate the political importance that the CSCE attached to the Mediterranean. This was an idea that many Western delegations, including the United States, found difficult to swallow. First, it would once again reopen the Mediterranean issue, which they thought had been resolved; second, it would distort the central East-West emphasis of the Conference; third, once negotiations began on such a document it was very difficult to foresee how its wording would eventually come out; and fourth, a special section on the Mediterranean in the Final Act would permanently inscribe the subject on the CSCE's agenda.

The argument among the Western delegations on the desirability of a Mediterranean declaration went on for several months. Apart from the Mediterranean states, there was little enthusiasm for such a document. But the situation had changed sharply since the dispute about Mediterranean contributions at the opening of the CSCE. Israel had been granted equal status within the CSCE, and the Europeans had lived through the oil embargo following the October War. Those countries that had stood up strongly for Israel's rights in the summer of 1973 were unwilling one year later to take positions that could be construed as downgrading the importance of relations with the Arabs. Eventually, the United States was the only delegation within the NATO caucus opposing the Italian idea, and this opposition was reversed when FRG Foreign Minister Genscher, representing the EC-Nine, made a personal appeal to Kissinger not to block what the Nine considered an important initiative.

With U.S. opposition withdrawn, the Mediterranean declaration, sponsored by the Nine, entered negotiation in a special working group. An even more elaborate draft was submitted by Cyprus, Malta, and Yugoslavia. The declaration took shape relatively painlessly until the last few weeks of Stage II, when Mintoff tied the Conference in knots by insisting that the Mediterranean declaration include language on reducing the U.S. and Soviet Mediterranean fleets. The Conference refused this suggestion, but the Stage III Summit became possible only when the participating states, hostage to their own decision to go to Helsinki, accepted Mintoff's final demand for a phrase that made "reducing armed forces in the region" (see FA 412) one of their joint aims in the Mediterranean.

In this case, the original U.S. apprehensions about including a Mediterranean declaration in the Final Act proved to be justified, for the document became the vehicle for Mintoff's exaggerated demands, produced a generally useless follow-up meeting on the Mediterranean in Malta, and continues to distort the central issues of the CSCE.

28 The Best and the Worst
Cleaning Up the Last Issues, July 15–21, 1975

This conference has been—as all must clearly know—
an enormous talking exercise in which each country
has contributed the best and the worst, enthusiasm and
prudence, rigidity and willingness to maneuver, long-
range views and impulsiveness, diplomatic perplexity and
intricate legal arguments, and hours and hours of
meetings, and heaps of paper which only the specialists
would be able to explain—if they still had the taste
and the talent to do so—through all of which runs the
thread which leads to security and cooperation.

Michel Jobert Helsinki July 4, 1973

The negotiations were not over; several important problems remained unresolved, but these fell rapidly into place.

The subcommittee on principles reached final agreement and registered the full declaration on principles (FA 16–74) on July 19.

In the military subcommittee, the Turkish area problem remained difficult. In order to persuade the Turks to accept the same 250-kilometer border zone as applied to the USSR (the Turks were reluctant because such a zone covered virtually all of Turkey and thus left them with very little exempted territory), an additional sentence was agreed suggesting that notification of "combined" maneuvers should be considered even below the 25,000-troop threshold if "significant" numbers of amphibious and airborne troops were involved (last sentence of FA 109). The Turks also insisted on an exception from the maneuver notification provisions for areas bordering nonparticipating, non-European states (e.g., the area of their frontiers with Syria, Iraq, and Iran). Agreement on these elements was reached following a marathon negotiation in the early morning hours of July 19.

The last remaining issue in Basket II was resolved when the Soviets accepted a phrase (FA 154) indicating that the concept of reciprocity (FA 144) should apply to the granting of Most Favored Nation treatment (FA 157).

By July 18, completion of the opening phrases of the Final Act was held up solely by Soviet insistence on a reference to the "irreversibility" of detente. This Soviet desire was stoutly resisted by the Western and neutral delegations, but the Soviets were evidently under strict instructions to pursue it, and would not agree to an "all of Europe" formulation ensuring that the benefits of the CSCE would apply to Berlin without it. Shortly after midnight on July 19, Kovalev telephoned Moscow for permission to fall back. The Soviet delegation then accepted the substitution of "continuing and lasting" for "irreversible," together with a "throughout Europe" phrase (FA 5), and the Final Act was complete.

These steps made it possible for the Conference to confirm the July 30 opening date of Stage III. Although this confirmation was not made until July 19, no one seemed to object to the fact that the July 15 deadline established by the Canadian proposal on timing had slipped four days. In fact, a sense of relief and elation spread throughout the Conference as the cleanup work continued rapidly. Ambassador Sherer had departed from Geneva to become the deputy U.S. permanent representative to the UN, leaving me in charge of the delegation.

A procedure was agreed whereby each signatory to the Final Act would simply notify the secretariat of the title to be printed under his name. This permitted the Italian prime minister to inform the secretariat that his title as president-in-office of the European Community should also be printed under his signature. It also made it possible for other delegations, such as the USSR, to avoid having to object to inclusion of this title.

The many questions relating to Stage III were settled and a paper on the Stage III scenario was agreed. Lots were drawn for places on the Summit speakers' list. It was agreed that there would be no communique. Even the typeface to be used in printing the Final Act was negotiated, with agreement on the prominence and style to be given to titles and subtitles.

An important remaining point was the site of the 1977 follow-up meetings. The Yugoslavs had offered Belgrade, but the Finns were also interested. The Romanians were adamantly opposed to a return to Helsinki because they wished to establish firmly the principle of rotation. The Finns, feeling their position weakening, suggested splitting the two 1977 meetings, with the preparatory session to be held in Helsinki and the main substantive event in Belgrade. But the Yugoslavs refused this offer. Since Finland had already played host to the preparatory talks and Stages I and III, and since the Yugoslav candidacy was presented first, pressure built for the Finns to withdraw. They did this in the early morning hours of July 21, and Belgrade was agreed as the 1977 meeting site.

This was the last issue to be settled in the CSCE, but before the Geneva phase of the Conference adjourned, the delegates witnessed a strange spectacle. It was two o'clock in the morning of July 21. The Soviet delegation had taken the chairmanship of the Coordinating Committee in its regular turn at midnight, but Kovalev had already returned to Moscow. Kovalev's senior deputy, Dubinin, substituted for him, but was clearly competing with the number-three man in the delegation, Mendelevich, who sat next to him and kept asking for the floor. Romanian Ambassador Valentin Lipatti, meanwhile, was pressing for Conference approval of an innocuous resolution of appreciation to the Finnish and Swiss governments for being hosts to the Conference. The Soviets were adamantly opposed, and a bitter wrangle between Lipatti and both Dubinin and Mendelevich ensued. Simultaneously, the Turkish delegation sought to record its last-minute reservations about the Cypriot delegation, to which the Cypriots and Greeks gave stinging rebuttals.

In the midst of these sour and entirely superfluous attacks and counter-attacks, a Vatican envoy, sent specifically to Geneva by the pope to pronounce a benediction on the final session of the negotiations, asked for the floor. His speech gave thanks for the "peace and joy" the CSCE could bring to Europe, but was lost in the continuing Romanian-Soviet and Turkish-Cypriot-Greek squabbles.

At four o'clock in the morning, with delegates of all political persuasions begging him to end the session, the Soviet chairman mercifully brought down his gavel and adjourned Stage II of the CSCE.

I stumbled out of the building into the gloomy night without even shaking hands or bidding my colleagues farewell. At the United States mission, I sent a two-sentence telegram to Washington: "Stage II of CSCE completed its work and adjourned at 4:00 A.M. on July 21. Amen."

29 Whether Different or Opposed
The Signing at Helsinki, August 1, 1975

*True peace . . . presupposes a just, equitable and wise
regulation of the rights and legitimate interests of the
parties concerned, whether they be different or opposed.*

Cardinal Casaroli Helsinki August 1, 1975

The crowd returned to the room when the signing table had been arranged.
The signers themselves—presidents, prime ministers, communist leaders, special envoys—made their way to the stage, many surrounded by their bodyguards. They took their seats at the long shallow curve of the table, which was
absolutely bare except for thirty-five pens, one for each state represented. The
agitation in the lofty concert hall grew in anticipation of the final event. On the
stage, seated in a jovial, smiling row, were the chiefs of state and heads of
government who had gathered together for three days. The names conveyed
the power and rank of the assembled group: Schmidt, Ford, Trudeau, Giscard
d'Estaing, Wilson, Moro, Gierek, Brezhnev, Ceausescu, Tito. . . . Opposite
them, in the sharply banked rows of seats of Finlandia Hall, were their advisers
and assistants: foreign ministers, ambassadors, civil servants, and diplomats.
Above, in the balconies, the press.

The president of the Republic of Finland, Urho Kekkonen, intoned flatly:
"In accordance with the agreed program for the third stage, we shall now
proceed to the signing of the Final Act." The executive secretary of the meeting
stepped forward with a fat green leather-bound volume.

"I shall now request the executive secretary to present the Final Act for
signature," said Kekkonen. The official mounted the steps and gave a slight
bow to the chairman. The doors to the hall were opened and the picture-taking
press was admitted. They rushed down the aisles with their equipment and
spread out three-deep before the stage, with security men keeping them in
order. A murmur went through the gathering as the executive secretary leaned
over the shoulder of the first signer, Helmut Schmidt, chancellor of the Federal
Republic of Germany, and held the page for Schmidt's pen. The next to sign
was Erich Honecker of the German Democratic Republic. Two halves of the
divided nation that had been the enemy, thirty years before. The signing was

repeated thirty-five times, a new page being turned for each successive signature. Flashbulbs popped and motion picture cameras ground on with their bright spotlights trained on the group. Never had so many chiefs of state and government gathered at the same table to sign the same document.

The last to sign was Josip Broz Tito, president of Yugoslavia. There was a pause, and then the crowded room broke into prolonged applause. As the noise receded, Kekkonen again took the microphone.

"The signing ceremony is hereby completed. Today," he said, "our nations, who have had to live through so much tragedy, can at last turn their backs to the past and look forward to a better future. We know how fragile peace can be, and that progress will be achieved only step by step. The situation in Europe, much improved as it is in recent years, is complex; the road we have now designed for ourselves is long, and shortcuts do not exist. But our confidence rests on a firm basis, for the Final Act which we have adopted today constitutes a serious attempt to lay foundations on which we and the coming generations can build a world better than the one we have to live in. This was achieved by following the advice of an ancient Finnish proverb: Know your own stand and give the others their due."

The delegates drank a hurried glass of champagne together in the crowded lobby, for they were anxious to catch their planes, to return to their capitals and the many pressing problems their countries faced. After a few minutes, as required by protocol, they descended the great white marble steps, followed by their entourages of assistants, ministers, diplomats, and bodyguards, pausing occasionally to sign autographs, shake hands, or speak to newsmen.

Outside, the warm Helsinki summer day was marred by clouds and occasional showers. The limousines rushed through the streets with police escorts and sirens screaming. There were no cannons, no formal salutes, no honors rendered. The people of Helsinki stood in curious patient groups at street corners along the main routes, watching the dignitaries leave. The roads were lined with security forces and soldiers, and throughout the nearby countryside heavily armed troops guarded the intersections.

The Conference, which had begun two years earlier in this same hall, was over, but there were no celebrations, no parades, no dancing in the streets. Only the flat gray buildings of Helsinki, the security forces, the dull routine of diplomatic procedure, and, somewhere in a vault in the Finnish capital, a heavy green leather-bound book containing thirty-five signatures.

That evening many of the diplomats who had negotiated the document gathered for a farewell dinner in an eighteenth-century manor house deep in the Finnish forest. They had spent two years together in difficult, some-times bitter, discussions. The night was warm and the mood of the group philosophical.

"Well, they signed it," said one.

"And now it will be buried and forgotten," said another.

"No," replied a third, "you are wrong. We have started something."

A silence fell on the group as each man reflected on what had passed and what might come. Outside the open windows were the sounds of the forest, the smell of the dark pines, the heavy, humid air of an August night in the far north of Europe. There was no way to know what the effect of the Conference—their Conference—would be, for only the unfolding future his-tory of Europe would determine that.

Part VI
The Helsinki Process

30   The Process We Have Created
The Evolution of Attitudes
toward Conference Follow-up

*The present Conference does not mark the end but the
beginning of a process. . . . We must not fail to take
advantage of the opportunities we have created with
considerable effort. That is our great responsibility which
we have to face jointly.*

Josip Broz Tito Helsinki July 31, 1975

It is clear now, ten years after the Helsinki Summit, that the Final Act would
have had little lasting significance had it not included follow-up provisions of
some kind. The Final Act as written is not self-implementing; rather, it sets out
commitments that are subject to later implementation "unilaterally, bilaterally, and multilaterally." The need for a continuing dynamic is especially strong
in the freer movement subject areas, since only full implementation of these
provisions over time can balance the confirmation of the European status quo
obtained by the USSR at the Helsinki Summit. Follow-up is an indispensable
device for encouraging implementation. But the desirability of follow-up was
not always as evident as it is now, and there was a significant evolution of
attitudes toward the follow-up concept during, and after, the Conference.

Prior to the beginning of negotiations, it was the USSR that, with its allies,
was most interested in establishing the CSCE as a kind of permanent concert of
European nations. The Soviets picked up a proposal apparently tossed out
without much thought by the British for a "permanent organ" to be established by the CSCE. This idea was formally included in the Warsaw Pact communique of June 1970 as a proposed agenda item for the Conference. The
Western countries were in varying degrees suspicious of this idea, which they
saw as giving the Soviet Union a permanent droit de regard over the affairs of
Western Europe. The neutrals were somewhere in between the positions of
East and West. They understood Western hesitations, but were intrigued by the
possibility of being able to participate permanently in a multilateral European
consultative forum.

These attitudes began to evolve shortly after the negotiations opened. For
the Soviets, the realization that human rights and freer movement issues would

be an important element of the Conference was enough to sour them on establishment of a permanent forum where such discussions could be continued. They began a slow retreat from their own proposals, until at the end of the Conference their position had two principal elements: They were opposed to establishment of a permanent forum, or to any agreed regular periodicity of CSCE meetings. In fact, they preferred to avoid a specific commitment to even one future CSCE meeting. At the same time, they wished to retain the possibility of convening another CSCE at some future date when conditions were favorable, and on the basis of a future agreement among the participating states. The formal Warsaw Pact position was set out in a Czech proposal for an "advisory committee," which would meet "whenever its members consider this advisable." This arrangement would have given the Soviets a veto over whether future CSCE meetings would be convened, which they could have used to block meetings at any juncture they considered unfavorable to their interests.

The USSR's Warsaw Pact allies, with the exception of Romania, gave the Soviet position nuanced support. There were many indications in informal conversations during the Conference that several Warsaw Pact delegations were more favorable to the follow-up concept than the Soviets. Such an attitude was easily understandable. The Eastern European countries found significant advantages in the multilateral CSCE situation, both in leverage with the Soviets and in additional room for contacts with Western countries. Despite what probably were their own inclinations, however, the Eastern Europeans (except Romania) were officially committed to the Soviet and Warsaw Pact position.

The Romanians were another story. They were satisfied with the Warsaw Pact's attitude at the outset of the Conference, but as the negotiations progressed and the Soviets grew more and more negative on follow-up, the Romanian position became increasingly independent. Romanian delegation leader Lipatti emerged as one of the most ferocious advocates of follow-up in the Conference, on a level with the Yugoslavs and Finns.

In the Romanian conception, Europe's multilateral diplomatic future should be in the shape of a pyramid, with a wide variety of CSCE experts' meetings on specialized subjects taking place at various times and places, capped by regular, periodic meetings of the CSCE states at a plenipotentiary level, to receive reports from the specialized groups and give them guidance for their future work. What the Romanians were after was a structure that would reinforce their possibilities for asserting an independent foreign policy, as well as additional insurance against military intervention by the Soviet Union.

The neutrals, through a process of the appetite growing as one eats, and through exchanges of ideas among themselves, became increasingly convinced that follow-up was in their interests and those of Europe as a whole. A Yugoslav submission of March 1974, which had the support of most of the neutrals, proposed establishment of a "continuing committee," composed of all CSCE participants, to meet "at least once a year." Like the Romanians and, on a pro forma basis at least, the Warsaw Pact, the Yugoslav proposal mandated the continuing committee with responsibility for coordinating other CSCE follow-up activity, such as convening of experts' groups.

The NATO allies remained the most reluctant about follow-up. But as the negotiations advanced, some allies (notably Denmark and Norway) began to see broad advantages in follow-up, while others became less adamantly opposed to it. A Danish proposal of April 1974, worked out within the NATO and EC-Nine caucuses, was carefully nuanced to strike a balance among these differing views. It stressed the concept of implementation of the results of the Conference as the main element of follow-up, and advanced the idea of a single future CSCE meeting to assess "how the decisions taken by the CSCE have been carried out," and to receive proposals on "measures to pursue the aims" of the Conference, possibly including convening of experts' meetings or a new CSCE.

Real negotiations on follow-up did not begin until fairly late in the Conference, since many countries were reluctant to discuss what would happen after the CSCE until the results of the negotiations themselves began to take form. By the time follow-up negotiations were engaged, there was broad agreement on two general points: (1) There would be some form of follow-up activity, including the possibility of one or more meetings of plenipotentiaries and some experts' meetings. (2) The meeting(s) of plenipotentiaries would have a "coordinating" (that is, controlling) relationship toward whatever experts' meetings were agreed.

This left several major questions for negotiation: the periodicity and precise mandate of the plenipotentiary meetings, and the number and subject matter of experts' meetings. In June of 1974 the Finns attempted a compromise paper, which was intended to synthesize earlier proposals. It picked up the Western stress on implementation as well as the notion of a review function for future plenipotentiary meetings. In recognition of the reluctance by both the Warsaw Pact and the NATO groups to agree on regular periodic meetings, the Finnish paper proposed only one agreed future plenipotentiary meeting. But it also made clear that there would be further meetings by referring to this single future meeting as "the first meeting" of the "committee on the follow-up." The Finnish idea was that the implication in their text that there would be periodic meetings would constitute a commitment that each meeting of the committee would set the date for the subsequent meeting.

In the end, the Finnish proposal was not far off the mark. A single plenipotentiary meeting was agreed for Belgrade in 1977, with a mandate (FA 666) to exchange views both on implementation and on the possible "deepening of their mutual relations, the improvement of security and the development of co-operation in Europe, and the development of the process of detente in the future." (In other words, the meeting would consider new substantive proposals relating to the CSCE agenda.)

The Finnish idea that each plenipotentiary meeting should agree on the date and place of the subsequent meeting was not formally accepted until the preparatory meeting for the Belgrade conference. That meeting, in the summer of 1977, agreed on the following procedural rule for the Belgrade conference (and thus established a precedent for future Belgrade-type meetings): "The Meeting will, in accordance with the Agenda, end in any case by adopting its concluding document and by fixing the date and place of the next similar meeting." This key clause complemented the follow-up provisions of the Final Act and provided something of a guideline that there would be periodic follow-up meetings.

As for meetings of experts' groups, most of the subjects that might have been candidates for such meetings lost momentum toward the end of the CSCE, and only two specific meetings were agreed in the Final Act: one in Bonn on the elaboration of a "Scientific Forum," and another in Switzerland for further consideration of the Swiss proposal for a system for peaceful settlement of disputes in Europe. The door was nevertheless left open for the convening of other experts' meetings in the future, and it was clear that it was within the powers of the CSCE plenipotentiary sessions to decide on such meetings. This was done for the first time by the Belgrade meeting, which agreed to hold an experts' meeting on the Mediterranean in Malta in 1979.

While the Belgrade follow-up meeting did not produce agreed substantive results, it did provide for the thorough review of implementation that the West desired, and overturned the unwritten rule that specific human rights cases should not be cited in public. A number of new proposals were put forward, which were then left on the CSCE table. The preparatory session produced agreed procedures for the Belgrade conference, which included useful precedents for subsequent review meetings. The main Belgrade meeting agreed that a similar meeting would be convened in Madrid in 1980, thus fixing the precedent of periodic review conferences.

Moreover, the Belgrade meeting served to confirm the evolution of attitudes toward CSCE follow-up. In particular, it demonstrated broad Western agreement on the utility—even the necessity—for maintaining the continuity of the process begun by the CSCE itself.

31 Hopes and Desires
After Helsinki

. . . These are the hopes, these are the desires, We
formulate in the name of God, in the light of Our deep
concern for peace and reconciliation between all peoples,
whose cause We have at heart.

Pope Paul VI Message to Stage III August 1, 1975

The detente "window" available for the Helsinki Summit turned out to be very small. The fall of Saigon left America in a bitter and confused mood. During the summer of 1975 Portugal teetered on the brink of a communist takeover. In October the U.S. administration became preoccupied with Soviet intentions in Angola. By November, when Angola became independent, the Cuban presence there, supported by the USSR, soured the whole detente relationship. Faced with the events in Portugal and Angola, American political leaders of both parties, reflecting public opinion, questioned the very basis of U.S.-Soviet relations. Had the CSCE not been completed by the summer of 1975, it is doubtful that the Summit would have been politically possible during the remainder of the Ford administration, especially since the president's latitude for independent initiatives had grown extremely narrow following Watergate. Given President Carter's emphasis on human rights, one has to wonder whether Helsinki could have taken place at all after his election. The Soviets probably would not have gone to a summit meeting that Carter could have used as part of his human rights crusade.

In fact, after 1975 detente began to unravel with increasing speed. Leakage in April 1976 of the record of a high-level discussion of policy toward the communist bloc gave the impression that the Ford administration tacitly accepted Soviet domination of Eastern Europe. This so-called "Sonnenfeldt Doctrine" was an erroneous interpretation of remarks taken out of context, but nonetheless caused resentment and became an issue in the 1976 presidential campaign. (Helmut Sonnenfeldt, one of Kissinger's key advisers on Soviet affairs, was the speaker whose remarks were reported. Sonnenfeldt is known as something of a hard-liner toward the USSR; his comments were obviously misinterpreted, but this did not prevent his name from becoming a code word for acceptance of Soviet domination in Eastern Europe.)

The country was becoming so hostile to the notion of detente that President Ford concluded it was a political liability and formally excluded the word from his campaign vocabulary. His television debate with Carter put Ford in the position of awkwardly defending a badly misunderstood and increasingly unpopular policy against an opponent who projected himself as a champion of human rights. Carter thus came through the campaign looking like the candidate most likely to stand up to the Soviets, despite the common assumption that Republicans are more hawkish than Democrats. Carter's election victory may have benefitted from this image.

Public concern over Soviet and communist advances grew steadily. The attempt by the Portuguese communist party to seize power set off a flurry of interest among American intellectuals in the ephemeral notion of Eurocommunism. The idea that West European communist parties might enter governments in Italy, Spain, and France gained a certain credence and provoked puzzlement and concern. Though the concept of a broad communist wave in Western Europe faded fairly quickly, it added to American suspicions about where detente might be leading.

Despite the fact that Carter appeared during the campaign to be willing to take a tougher line with the Soviets, and his appointment of a reputed hardliner, Zbigniew Brzezinski, as his national security adviser, the new administration's defense and disarmament policies seemed a leftover from the earlier days of detente. Carter pursued an ambitious series of arms control negotiations and signed the SALT II Treaty with Brezhnev in Vienna in June of 1979. But these initiatives did not have strong backing in the United States, and the SALT II Treaty was left unratified by a Congress that had become broadly hostile to detente.

The Carter administration also reduced U.S. defense spending and made a series of negative decisions on new weapons systems, principally against production of the B-1 bomber and an enhanced radiation weapon, popularly called the neutron bomb.

In October of 1977 West German Chancellor Schmidt sounded the alarm about the continuing Soviet military buildup and an emerging gap in the credibility of the American will to defend Europe. Schmidt's speech before the International Institute of Strategic Studies in London called attention to the steady increase in Soviet arms in Eastern Europe, and particularly to a new class of missiles—the SS-20—which could, because of their accuracy and multiple warheads, destroy all major military targets in Western Europe without threatening the United States. Schmidt warned that unless this new imbalance was corrected, European confidence in the readiness of the United States to respond to a Soviet attack in Europe would crumble. Schmidt's speech eventually led to the NATO decision of December 1979 to install Pershing II and cruise missiles in several allied countries. It reflected the widespread feeling in Europe that the Soviets were succeeding in their effort to tip the military balance in their favor, thus making it easier for them to bring their influence to bear in Western Europe.

Any lingering inclinations toward pursuit of detente were caught up short by the Soviet invasion of Afghanistan in December 1979, which revealed a previously undemonstrated Soviet willingness to engage the Red Army directly outside the frontiers of the USSR. The invasion of Afghanistan, coupled with the Soviet-supported military takeover in Poland in December of 1981, effectively ended the detente era of the 1970s.

Washington attitudes toward the Helsinki Final Act evolved with the overall deterioration of detente. Immediately after the Helsinki Summit, no one was interested in the CSCE. Administration policy officials thought of it as an event that had provoked a hostile domestic reaction and was best forgotten. This attitude infected the entire bureaucracy, though a thorough working-level effort was made to monitor compliance with the Helsinki commitments.

But public attitudes toward Helsinki underwent a slow evolution. Gradually, the Final Act came to be seen less as a Western confirmation of the status quo in Europe and more as a potentially useful weapon for supporting human rights in the communist countries. The CSCE increasingly appeared as a unique basis for raising human-rights-related issues with the USSR and the East European governments and a unique forum for discussion of these issues.

A few members of Congress sensed this change in the political winds. Congresswoman Millicent Fenwick had all along stubbornly maintained that the CSCE was important. She drafted a law intended to force the administration to monitor closely how the commitments in the Final Act were being carried out, and to involve Congress in this activity by establishing a special joint commission solely for the purpose. No one in the administration took Fenwick's bill very seriously, but it gained ground steadily, and President Ford was finally obliged to approve it, because of overwhelming congressional support and the political needs of his campaign for the Republican presidential nomination. He signed it into law in June of 1976, despite the belief of a number of administration officials that it unconstitutionally mixed executive and legislative responsibilities with regard to foreign affairs.

Creation of the joint CSCE Commission had a major effect on the U.S. attitude toward the CSCE. Energetically chaired by Congressman Dante Fascell, the Commission forced the administration to adopt a tough attitude toward Soviet and East European violations of their Helsinki commitments. The interest of the Commission was an important element in the formulation of the U.S. approach to the review meetings in Belgrade (1977–78), Madrid (1980–83), and Vienna (1986–87). As a result, the United States used these meetings to cite specific Soviet and East European human rights violations in an effort to encourage implementation of the Final Act.

The three review meetings served as barometers of the state of East-West relations in Europe. The first was dominated by the activist human rights policy of the Carter administration, represented by former Supreme Court Justice Arthur Goldberg. There was virtually no dialogue between the U.S. and Soviet delegates, and no agreed results, but the taboo on mentioning specific human rights violations was effectively overcome.

The second review meeting, in Madrid, lasted for three years, primarily because of Western unwillingness to reach political agreements with the USSR as long as the situations in Poland and Afghanistan remained unchanged. Once again, however, West European interest in demonstrating that positive relations with Moscow were possible slowly grew, until it made conclusion on the basis of several Western proposals inevitable. Delegation chief Max Kampelman, a Washington lawyer, was able to manage this difficult situation and to develop a U.S. position that successfully bridged the views of both the European governments and the U.S. public.

The Madrid meeting reached agreement on a number of significant provisions, which expanded on the Helsinki Final Act in the areas of human rights, trade union rights, religious liberty, and freer circulation of information, among others. Madrid also mandated additional specialized meetings on human rights, human contacts, military confidence and security-building measures, and peaceful settlement of disputes. Another review session was scheduled for Vienna in 1986. The Madrid forum concluded with a meeting at the foreign minister level. Western foreign ministers were frankly critical of the Soviet record of compliance with the Helsinki accord. As Secretary of State George Shultz said in Madrid on September 9, 1983: "There are governments in the East which have from the outset treated their commitments to human rights under the Final Act with open contempt. The Helsinki monitoring groups that citizens created to gauge their governments' performance have been systematically suppressed. Emigration, after an initial rise, has fallen dramatically. Dissidents have been subjected to ever more brutal treatment. And courageous men and women who dared to assert their human rights—or demonstrate for peace and arms control—are rotting in prison or condemned to mental hospitals."

Yet Shultz and his colleagues were positive about the CSCE and the Helsinki process, as another part of his speech reveals: "In the most profound sense, the Helsinki process represents an historic effort to erode the cruel divisions between East and West in Europe. It is an effort that must continue because it embodies the most basic interests, deepest convictions, and highest hopes of all the peoples of Europe. . . . The light of Freedom can never be extinguished and the aspiration to human dignity is basic to all peoples. That is what the Helsinki process is all about."

The Vienna meeting generally followed the more reasoned approach pursued in Madrid. Moreover, it benefited from improved prospects for arms control between the superpowers and the greater public flexibility of the Gorbachev regime.

The most poignant effect of the Final Act was its impact on dissident groups in the USSR and Eastern Europe. Several movements, such as the Charter '77 group in Czechoslovakia, were directly inspired by Helsinki; others, particularly the Solidarity labor movement in Poland, were based in part on rights approved in the Final Act. These and other similar groups cited the Final Act to justify their activities in favor of human rights. Leading Soviet dissidents, including the Sakharovs, Yuri Orlov, and Anatoli Scharansky, based their Helsinki monitoring activities on the need to ensure compliance with the provisions of the Final Act.

The increased dissident activities had two effects: they brought a sharp crackdown by the Soviet and East European regimes, and they obliged supporters in the West to continue to press Western governments to take an active stance in support of human rights in the communist world. This pressure in turn ensured the continued interest of Western governments in pursuit of the CSCE process and the commitments undertaken at Helsinki.

32   The Ersatz Peace
Helsinki, Ten Years Later

Ten years ago at Helsinki the sovereign states of Europe adopted a Final Act destined to institutionalize this ersatz peace we have come to call "detente."

Andre Fontaine *Le Monde* July 31, 1985

More than ten years later, the Conference on Security and Cooperation in Europe remains the broadest East-West watershed since the Second World War. The Final Act of Helsinki serves many functions, some tacit and some explicit. It is a surrogate for a World War II Peace Treaty. It sets guidelines for interstate behavior and an implicit framework for a continuing system of East-West contacts. It establishes a relationship between all the European countries and the East-West equation and brings together the many fields available for East-West negotiations. Like an essay, history has its punctuation points as well as its nouns and verbs, and Helsinki provided such a point in the postwar evolution of Europe.

It is clear now that the CSCE was both a product and a reflection of the detente era of the 1970s. The original Soviet idea for a European security conference gained ground in a dialogue of communiqués between NATO and the Warsaw Pact in the early 1970s as interest in detente rose. The Summit conclusion was held just as detente began to unravel and would not have been possible later.

The CSCE and its spin-off meetings continue to be unique in many respects: the thirty-five participating states technically participate on an equal footing, and agreements genuinely are based on consensus among all participants. The list of subjects is vast and makes it possible for CSCE discussions to touch on just about any subject of interest to Europe. Because of the number of participants and their widely varying national interests, there are also many "wheels within wheels" during CSCE negotiations—subissues of importance to only one or two participants, but which must be dealt with in some fashion.

The central East-West negotiation, however, that led to the signing of the Final Act concerned the postwar geopolitical situation in Europe—the extent to which it would become fixed and permanent and the extent to which it could, and should, evolve. This equation continues to underlie all CSCE activities and to invest them with all the political drama of Europe's ideological division.

The principal Soviet objective in the CSCE was to obtain the broadest possible international recognition of the European status quo resulting from the Second World War. The Soviets came very close to explaining this themselves in an interesting pamphlet published on the tenth anniversary of Helsinki called "Helsinki: Ten Years Later, Report of the Soviet Committee for Security and Cooperation in Europe" (Moscow: Editions du Progres, 1985). In this analysis the USSR affirms that in the Soviet view Helsinki was "the logical prolongation of Yalta and Potsdam." The absolute top priority was to render the division of Germany irreversible so that a united, hostile German nation could never again threaten the Soviet Union. This was to be done through agreement on the "immutability" of postwar frontiers. The Soviets made no bones about their main objective during the negotiation, referring privately to the permanent division of Germany as the "key to European security." It was also clear from the importance they attached to obtaining agreement on a "crystal-clear" principle of inviolability of frontiers, which they saw as ensuring Germany's division. Everything else in the Conference had a lesser priority.

In "Helsinki, Ten Years Later" the Soviets also reveal just how important this division of Germany continues to be for them: "To hear revanchist circles in the FRG proclaim that the 'German question' remains open, insist on the modification of the political map of Europe 'in a historical perspective,' and lay claim to the 1937 borders of the German Reich, one understands better the current relevance and the importance of the efforts of progressive opinion in Europe to guarantee the principle of inviolability of frontiers."

Equally important for the Soviets was to obtain final multilateral recognition of the communist regimes of Eastern Europe, their borders, and the expanded frontiers of the Soviet Union itself resulting from the wartime annexation of the Baltic states and parts of Finland, Poland, Czechoslovakia, and Romania. The Soviets also hoped to establish some kind of system or regime that would permit them to enhance their influence over Western Europe as well. These were major ambitions, touching the very existence of the USSR and its communist buffer states and their future security. It is not surprising that the Soviets were willing to trade to achieve what they wanted.

The Western side accurately perceived these Soviet ambitions, but in the context of a nascent detente Western governments tended to see them as offering opportunities to reach broad political understanding while advancing the West's own vision of Europe's future. Thus the Soviet desire to convene a CSCE was used to encourage the Kremlin to reach a four-power modus vivendi agreement on Berlin and to accept an opening date for MBFR negotiations.

Later, the Soviet desire to conclude the CSCE at a thirty-five-nation Summit was used to shape the Conference agenda and its results.

Within the scope of the CSCE itself, the West was prepared to accept the existing frontiers in Europe, provided the principle of possible peaceful change was preserved. These frontiers had in any case already been explicitly accepted in bilateral treaties between the states concerned. Other CSCE participants had recognized the postwar frontiers implicitly through the maintenance of normal diplomatic contacts; recognition of the two Germanies had occurred with the establishment of diplomatic relations and admission to the United Nations.

The Western countries also had to preserve the principle of self-determination of peoples, and they continued their nonrecognition of the forced Soviet absorption of the Baltic states. At the same time the West wished to improve the human rights situation in the Soviet Union and Eastern Europe and the availability of information to the peoples of those countries. The general belief was that freer circulation of people and ideas—the concept that eventually produced Basket III—was a worthy objective and could help to bring about a gradual evolution of the communist regimes. These regimes could not in any case be removed by force or fiat.

Leonid Brezhnev was from the first deeply and personally committed to bringing the CSCE to a successful conclusion. Under his leadership the European Conference had been made a key element of the so-called "peace program" of the Twenty-fourth Congress of the Communist party of the Soviet Union. He wanted to report success in this venture to the Twenty-fifth party congress, set for 1976, and to portray the Helsinki conclusion as the final culmination of the Soviet victory in the Second World War.

This ambition put the Soviets under some pressure to complete the negotiations in time to link them to the fortieth anniversary of the war's end. The Western side felt no such time pressure and sought to use Soviet haste for negotiating advantages. The tactic worked fairly well until Western political leaders themselves began to plan on attendance at the final Summit. Once such planning was under way it became extremely difficult to slow or stop the momentum.

During the negotiations there were many indications of Brezhnev's direct interest and involvement. His personal letters to Western leaders pressed them to agree to the Summit in Helsinki, and he raised the subject with every Western visitor. Foreign Minister Gromyko was similarly absorbed in the CSCE project. Soviet statements and propaganda consistently focused on the CSCE as the pivotal negotiation for European security.

By contrast, American interest in the CSCE, until 1975, could not have been lower. Since it was a Soviet proposal it was seen primarily as a concession that the United States could give the Soviets in exchange for something more concrete. President Nixon and Secretary Kissinger did not believe the CSCE would add anything to the bilateral treaties that had already accepted postwar frontiers. They did not think the very general declaratory language that would result from the CSCE would differ in any important respect from that of the UN Charter and other such documents. Nor did they believe it would be possible to change the situation in the USSR and Eastern Europe through such a public multilateral conference.

The CSCE was convened at the height of U.S.-Soviet detente, just after President Nixon's landmark 1972 visit to Moscow, which produced a shower of bilateral agreements. The primary objective of the U.S. administration was to reach agreement with the Soviets on the balance of strategic nuclear weapons, and other aspects of the U.S.-Soviet relationship were secondary. Although the U.S. delegation to NATO played an important role in allied preparations for the CSCE by suggesting many of the specific Western "freer movement" proposals, this was a relatively low-level effort, did not have real backing from the highest levels of the administration, and ended with the opening of negotiations.

Though the Nixon administration saw the CSCE primarily as a concession to the Soviets, this did not mean the American side was prepared to give away important concessions within the negotiations. Positions of principle were to be maintained, and the U.S. delegation, which was not under close instruction until 1975, stuck as closely as possible to the positions agreed upon within the NATO caucus. However, the lack of high-level support in the U.S. government led the U.S. delegation to take a relatively low profile throughout much of the Conference, permitting the West Europeans to form joint positions and to take the lead on many subjects. While some desiderata appeared as the Conference took shape, the United States did not have formal objectives at the beginning of the negotiations.

The U.S. attitude differed from that of the West Europeans and Canadians. Since they were not directly engaged in the American negotiations with the USSR on strategic weapons, the CSCE took a much more central place for them in their relations with Moscow. The United States was skeptical that anything of real significance could be gained in the CSCE and thought it was likely to raise public expectations about detente that could not be fulfilled. Washington thus wanted to conclude the Conference more quickly than the Europeans and saw little utility in arguing over what Henry Kissinger called "abstruse and esoteric" points of language. From the communiqué of the U.S.-Soviet Summit of 1973, which contained a thinly qualified agreement to attend a Summit-level conclusion to the CSCE, to the negotiations themselves, when Secretary Kissinger pressed the Allies to be more flexible in order to reach early agreement, there was a continuing tension between the United States and the West Europeans over the CSCE. The importance and potential of the Conference were seen differently on the two sides of the Atlantic, and the Allies believed the United States was undercutting Western negotiating leverage in its haste to complete the CSCE.

The U.S. attitude changed abruptly, however, following the fall of Saigon and the beginning of the unraveling of detente. As part of a general stiffening of the U.S. stance toward the USSR, American CSCE negotiators joined the West Europeans in a tough position that evoked a final series of Soviet concessions and made the Summit possible.

By the spring of 1975, when the Summit conclusion was clearly within reach and the Allied delegations in Geneva made an overall proposal to the Soviets to settle the remaining issues in Basket III and ensure completion of the Conference, the Soviets were so deeply engaged, and considered a successful conclusion to the CSCE so important, that they met the essential Western conditions.

When it was announced that President Ford was going to Helsinki to sign a major East-West agreement, the U.S. public was unprepared. Since the administration had intentionally downplayed the importance of the CSCE for several years, there was a legitimate question as to why it was suddenly so important as to warrant a presidential signature. There had been only perfunctory consultation with Congress and interested nongovernmental organizations. The fact that the Accord was to be neither a treaty nor an agreement, and thus was not subject to Senate ratification, raised additional suspicions and provoked congressional resentment. Americans with ties to the Baltic states were so hostile to the agreement that Ford felt obliged to issue a special statement on the eve of his departure for Helsinki, denying that signature of the Final Act would change the U.S. position of nonrecognition of the annexation of the Baltic states by the USSR. Even this did not fully satisfy Baltic ethnic groups.

The CSCE has always been a bazaar. Every participating state brings its desires to the negotiating table and tries to obtain what it can. Trade-offs are so intricate that it is hard to keep track of them. Even the major deals have entailed numerous subsidiary arrangements to ensure that any country that might object was satisfied. Most importantly, in exchange for agreeing to convene a CSCE the West ensured completion of the four-power agreement on Berlin, the fixing of a date for the beginning of MBFR, and a CSCE agenda that included the key human rights topics of freer movement of people and ideas. The United States may also have gotten a marginally more cooperative attitude in its bilateral relationship with Moscow. In return for these Soviet moves the Western countries agreed to participate in a Conference that would ultimately put an international stamp of approval on postwar European frontiers.

At the Conference itself the West obtained measured Soviet commitments on human rights and a number of specific freer movement issues, as well as very modest military confidence-building measures, primarily prior notification of major military maneuvers in Eastern Europe and areas near the USSR's western borders. The Soviets obtained a qualified recognition of existing frontiers and the Summit-level signing ceremony they wanted. But every clause in the CSCE's Final Act was so thoroughly hedged that the principal achievements on both sides were only meaningful in a political sense.

As a technical matter, the Final Act is not legally binding. While this fact does not detract from the moral and political obligation to carry out commitments publicly undertaken at the highest level, it does provide an ample loophole for avoiding those that are difficult to implement. More specifically, the language on frontiers speaks of "inviolability" rather than "immutability," which, taken with the text of this principle, suggests that only physical attacks on frontiers (i.e., using armed force) are excluded. In addition, the concept of inviolability of frontiers is offset by recognition that frontiers can nevertheless be changed peacefully.

Respect for human rights is clearly established as a principle of interstate relations, one of the main achievements of the CSCE. The seventh of the Final Act's ten "Principles Guiding Relations between Participating States" is the principle of "Respect for human rights and fundamental freedoms, including the freedom of thought, conscience, religion or belief." While from a Western point of view this principle is not ideal (it does not, for example, mention the familiar freedoms of speech and assembly), it reflects a mainly Western conception of human rights, including "the effective exercise of civil, political, economic, social, cultural and other rights and freedoms," the "freedom of the individual to profess and practice, alone or in community with others, religion or belief," and equality of minorities. The principle confirms "the right of the individual to know and act upon his rights" and states that the countries concerned will act in conformity with the Universal Declaration of Human Rights (FA 56).

The reference to the Universal Declaration is essential, for it recommits the participating states to the much more detailed iteration contained in that document. The Universal Declaration of Human Rights, adopted by the UN General Assembly on December 10, 1948, affirms, inter alia, the right to privacy (art. 12), freedom of opinion and expression (art. 19), the right of assembly (art. 20), the right to marry and found a family (art. 16), and the right to own property alone or together with others (art. 17). The Universal Declaration (art. 13) also states that "Everyone has the right to leave any country, including his own, and to return to his country." Soviet practices do not appear to conform to any of these provisions; for example, the treatment of Andrei Sakharov, Yelena Bonner, and all the thousands of refuseniks is in flagrant violation of Article 13. The USSR abstained when the Universal

Declaration of Human Rights was approved by the UN General Assembly in 1948, so its commitment to respect the Declaration when Brezhnev signed the Helsinki Accord in 1975 represented a significant new undertaking.

As a result of Helsinki, no one can argue that human rights in one state are the exclusive business of the people of that state, since they have been formally recognized as an element of each state's relations with others. After Helsinki the Soviets argued that the principle of nonintervention in internal affairs prohibited governments from criticizing human rights practices in other states, but more recently they have dropped that line of argument. The fact that human rights are established as a distinct principle makes it difficult to maintain such a line. The Soviets' acceptance at Madrid of a CSCE experts' meeting specifically focused on human rights appears to confirm their recognition that international discussion of human rights practices is not only admissible but is a major component of the CSCE.

Domestic considerations have played a major role in the approaches of both the Soviet and American sides to the Helsinki negotiations and their aftermath. For the Soviets the effects of the specific freer movement clauses, e.g., on family reunification and availability of foreign publications, were a major concern. The Soviet delegation included a senior KGB officer whose obvious role was to weigh this angle of any commitment the Soviets were asked to accept. Soviet fears appeared to be confirmed following the Conference when the Final Act inspired movements in several Warsaw Pact countries, including the Helsinki Watch Group in Moscow. The Soviets and their allies cracked down hard to stop the contagion.

In the United States domestic problems over the CSCE began with the failure to inform the public about the Helsinki negotiations, what they entailed, and that they might conclude at the Summit. This was partly because the U.S. administration did not believe the negotiations were intrinsically important and partly because there was a desire not to raise expectations unduly. But there was also a sense of apprehension that public discussion would open a Pandora's box of problems and opposition similar to that which produced the Jackson-Vanik amendment to the 1974 Trade Act linking granting of MFN to the Soviet Union with positive performance on Jewish emigration.

The result was a wave of public criticism when President Ford went to Helsinki to sign the Final Act. Those groups with an interest in Soviet and East European policy saw Helsinki as a sellout that recognized the Soviet hold on Eastern Europe but gained nothing in return. Congress was moved to set up its CSCE Commission largely because it wanted to ensure that the administration would use the CSCE framework to press actively for human rights improvements in the communist countries.

Another domestic factor was related to the rise and fall of detente. As the Nixon administration pursued detente with the Soviet Union, apparently successfully, the American public was focused on the improvement of relations with the USSR and maintained a generally positive attitude toward the overall concept of detente. But as the shortcomings of detente became more evident through public debate about trade and emigration, and particularly following the fall of Saigon, every aspect of the relationship with Moscow came under scrutiny and suspicion, especially those in which the immediate gains for the United States were unclear. This period coincided with the lead-up to the Helsinki Summit; public attention zeroed in on the CSCE for the first time, and many conclusions were negative. The *Wall Street Journal*'s "Jerry Don't Go!" summed up the opinion of many Americans about Ford's planned trip to Helsinki.

With this experience in mind, the Carter and Reagan administrations sought deliberately to build public support for their approaches to the CSCE follow-up meetings in Belgrade, Madrid, and Vienna. The U.S. approach to the Belgrade meeting was simplistic and consisted mainly of detailed public criticism of the Soviet human rights record. While it satisfied the American public's desire to call a spade a spade, it made real agreement impossible. The principal achievement in Belgrade was to give meaning to the notion that human rights are an aspect of interstate relations; the taboo on mentioning specific human rights cases was overcome.

The approach to the Madrid meeting was more subtle, complicated by the overall difficulty of East-West relations following Soviet actions in Poland and Afghanistan. The Western strategy was to hold the same kind of frank review of implementation of the Helsinki Final Act as had been conducted in Belgrade but also to engage the Soviets in real negotiations with a view to building on the Helsinki provisions and improving them. The idea was to try to make Helsinki into a truly dynamic process. A broad range of new proposals was put forward, and negotiations similar to those of 1973–75 were held.

Opinions in the West were strongly divided over whether the West should negotiate at all with the USSR in view of Afghanistan and Poland and whether it was correct to conclude the Madrid meeting at a high level, an event that was bound to suggest to Western publics that detente was alive and well and to appear inconsistent with the sanctions many Western countries had invoked against the Soviets because of their behavior on the international scene.

The divergent views of domestic interest groups and the European allies were reconciled, however, and the Madrid meeting was brought to a conclusion. Its Final Document, which was similar to the Helsinki Final Act in its scope and content, contained new provisions on combating terrorism, on refraining from support for activities directed toward the violent overthrow of other states' regimes, on ensuring religious freedom, and on the rights of workers to establish trade unions free to exercise their legitimate activities. Existing Helsinki provisions were reiterated or expanded in numerous areas. Once again, the principal Western effort was to obtain commitments that would, if implemented, improve the human rights practices of communist countries. But, like the provisions of the original Final Act, these obligations have been largely ignored. Western tactics at the Vienna meeting have followed a similar pattern, and a substantial concluding document seems likely.

Though in theory the CSCE negotiations were carried out among the thirty-five participating countries, some key issues were nonetheless negotiated directly between the United States and the Soviet Union. The question of the convening of the Conference was agreed upon between Kissinger and Gromyko in Moscow in September 1972 as part of a deal providing for the parallel opening of MBFR talks. The precise language on peaceful changes of frontiers was agreed between a series of American and Soviet negotiators on the basis of phraseology worked out by the United States and the FRG. The conclusion of negotiations on the Basket III human rights issues was made possible by the frank discussion between Kissinger and Gromyko at their 1975 meeting in Vienna. The timing of the Helsinki Summit itself was the subject of last-minute bargaining involving the United States and the Soviets, although it was held hostage to a long string of demands by individual countries that had to be satisfied before the Summit could finally be pinned down.

There were also a number of issues in the Conference on which U.S. and Soviet interests overlapped, or even coincided. Both of the superpowers had an interest in protecting their rights as wartime victors over Germany. For the United States, as well as for Great Britain and France, these rights constitute the basis for a continuing presence in Berlin, an essential element of that city's stability and viability. For the Soviets, the four-power rights are an important lever for exercising a special form of pressure on the FRG, and on the GDR as well. When the four powers with rights and responsibilities in Germany met and decided to press for language protecting those rights, it was an extraordinary example of superpower cooperation. Other participating states of all political leanings were wary of this language because, if it was not carefully formulated, it could carry other meanings. After a marathon negotiating session the four achieved what they wanted, leaving the negotiators from other countries breathless with this demonstration of what could be done through the cooperative efforts of all the major powers.

The United States and the USSR also shared an interest in limiting the arms control content of the CSCE. Since they were deeply involved in bilateral negotiations on strategic weapons systems and had initiated a NATO-Warsaw

Pact negotiation on troop reductions in Central Europe (MBFR), neither the United States nor the USSR was keen on treating central arms control issues in an all-European forum. Moreover, the presence of neutral and nonaligned participants made the CSCE a more freewheeling negotiation, and neither military grouping was confident of its ability to control the outcome in such circumstances. As a result, the military content of the CSCE was limited to a few modest confidence-building measures, designed to reduce the uncertainties stemming from large-scale military activities.

From this unpromising beginning the CSCE's responsibilities in the military area have grown. The Madrid review meeting reached agreement on a new negotiating forum, subsidiary to the CSCE, to consider Confidence and Security-Building Measures (CSBMs) in the area reaching from the Atlantic to the Urals. This forum, meeting in Stockholm as the Conference on Disarmament in Europe (CDE), concluded in the fall of 1986 with an accord providing for an expanded notification regime, accompanied by original verification provisions. While still relatively modest in terms of real military significance, the CDE remains available for further related arms control discussions and will almost certainly be reconvened after the Vienna review meeting. It seems likely, however, that negotiations on actual reductions in levels of forces in Europe will continue in a bloc-to-bloc format, building on the existing MBFR arrangements with modifications to permit expanded participation (especially by France) and use of the now-accepted Atlantic-to-the-Urals zone of application. The interests of the two military pacts in pursuing such negotiations between themselves appear to outweigh any possible gains that might be derived from participation by the neutral and nonaligned CSCE participants.

A third issue on which U.S. and Soviet views coincided was the need to keep "Mediterranean" issues out of the CSCE. For both the superpowers, discussion of the Mediterranean could only raise Middle East issues and add another complex, divisive subject to an already overloaded agenda. Also, the Mediterranean was not central to the East-West focus of the CSCE. Despite the superpowers' opposition, however, the Mediterranean became a major side issue because of the insistence of Malta, Yugoslavia, Cyprus, Spain, and Italy.

In each of these examples the parallel interests of Washington and Moscow emerged over time. There was no explicit coordination, except for the one occasion when the four Berlin powers sought language to protect their rights. That case was exceptional in that there was a preexisting forum and logic on which a coordinated effort could be based. In the other instances shared interests only became evident as pressures forced the two sides to take firm positions, and both Soviets and Americans were constantly wary of the other side seeking to profit from their positions.

More important than these isolated examples of shared concerns was the convergence in the early 1970s of U.S. and Soviet interest in a positive bilateral relationship. It was this convergence, of course, that produced the period of detente and that led to the easing of rigid positions on both sides. The CSCE could not have taken place without this brief convergence. And by 1976 the word "detente" had taken on such negative connotations that President Ford actually banned it from his campaign vocabulary.

33 Toward a Day Not Soon

Drawing Up a Balance

*The Helsinki Accord provided a standard toward which
to strive and against which to measure our behavior.
Perhaps we shall not soon see the day when all nations
meet that standard, but the effort, in and of itself, could
lead to a more secure peace, greater individual freedom,
and, thus, a greater fulfillment of Europe's vast potential.*

George Shultz Helsinki July 30, 1985

One of the features of the CSCE that has been most disconcerting for Western
public opinion is the fact that the effects of the Conference are unbalanced.
The principal Soviet gain, recognition of postwar European frontiers, took
effect with the signing of the Final Act, whereas the principal Western
achievement, a commitment to greater respect for human rights and freer
movement of people and ideas in the Soviet Union and Eastern Europe,
depended on actions by individual governments after the conclusion of the
Conference. Thus the Soviets could pocket what they had achieved, but the
Western countries still had to press for implementation in order to obtain
what they had sought in the Conference.

Beyond this oversimplified scheme, the balance between the gains of the
two sides is more subtle, and perhaps also somewhat ephemeral. The West,
in particular the United States, obtained a recognized, legitimate role with
respect to events in the Soviet Union and Eastern Europe. Such legitimacy is
sometimes taken for granted by Americans, but as a non-European country
U.S. influence in Europe previously had real legitimacy only within the
member states of the North Atlantic Alliance. Through the North Atlantic
Treaty those countries had recognized and accepted an active American presence. The Helsinki Final Act had a similar effect with respect to the rest of
Europe and thus legitimized U.S. interest in the area as a whole.

It should also be noted that the West has an important continuing interest
in providing the East European countries increased breathing space by whatever means can be devised. The Helsinki Final Act, by giving a Soviet blessing
to increased contacts and exchanges of virtually all kinds, has done just that.
East Europeans have been emphatic since Helsinki in reminding Westerners
of how important this aspect of the agreement has been to them.

The overall Conference trade-off was not generally perceived as unbalanced before or during the Conference. The CSCE had been justified as an important element of detente, and each Western country had an investment of its own in detente with the Soviet Union. Thus the perception was that both sides— the USSR and the West—would gain in roughly equal measure through the successful conclusion of the Conference. The total gains for each side included tangible and intangible elements, topped by the concept of a dynamic detente leading to a more open and stable Europe with commercial and human benefits accruing to all concerned. While this may appear naive in hindsight, it was not applied solely to the CSCE; on the contrary, it was the basic Western approach to detente.

But the Final Act also contains some fairly specific provisions that were meant to be implemented. Many of them can be implemented only unilaterally, such as the lowering of fees associated with family reunification (i.e., fees charged for exit visas for emigration). The Western view of follow-up meetings was that they would provide a forum for reviewing implementation and thereby serve as an encouragement to respecting the obligations contained in the Final Act. Thus it was agreed that follow-up meetings would entail "a thorough exchange of views" on "the implementation of the provisions of the Final Act and of the tasks defined by the Conference" (FA 666).

But since the Helsinki meeting disagreement over implementation of the Final Act has been profound. The Soviets have published long lists of actions they have taken in implementation of Helsinki and have proposed several grandiose conferences on such issues as the environment. The aim of these proposals has been to pad the international agenda with "cooperative" efforts in relatively uncontroversial areas as a way of demonstrating the "momentum" of detente while distracting public attention from the more difficult issues. But the reality is that they have avoided implementing the human rights-related provisions almost entirely and have openly flouted them by decimating the Soviet Helsinki Watch Group and sending its leaders to prison camp or exile. The Eastern European states have followed the Soviet lead to a greater or lesser degree, adapting Soviet techniques to the needs of their own situations.

These actions have ensured continuing Western interest in the human rights situation in the USSR and Eastern Europe and continuing criticism of the "deal" struck at Helsinki. Critics of Helsinki have argued that the overall trade-off of recognition of frontiers for promises on human rights was so unbalanced that it should never have been made. Under this thesis, positions of principle should not have been traded for unenforceable and ambiguous promises.

In response, defenders of the Helsinki Accord argue that while there was a multilateral recognition of frontiers at Helsinki, this added nothing to the recognition already accorded through previous Western treaties, agreements, and actions over the years. Moreover, the Helsinki Accord protects, rather than concedes, Western positions of principle on the existing European geopolitical situation (1) by acknowledging only that existing frontiers will not be violated (e.g., by force), while reaffirming the sovereign right of peoples to self-determination; (2) by establishing an entirely new international concept recognizing that peaceful changes of frontiers are permissible; and (3) by specifically asserting in the Final Act that military occupations are illegal and that "No such occupation or acquisition will be recognized as legal" (FA 36). This phrase protects in particular the long-standing American position of not recognizing the Soviet annexation of Latvia, Lithuania, and Estonia.

Western negotiators had to tread a thin line to avoid language that would appear to recognize, or even reinforce, the Brezhnev Doctrine that intervention by one state in the affairs of another to defend socialism is permissible. The dilemma for the West was to obtain language that would permit Western governments to press communist regimes for human rights improvements, while excluding the types of state intervention that were exemplified by Soviet repressions in Budapest and Prague. A more acute problem was posed for the wartime Allies who retain rights and responsibilities in Germany. These Allies had to find language that would reserve those rights (thus proportionately limiting the rights of the two Germanies) without suggesting that there were other situations in which states might have limited sovereignty.

The balance among these various pitfalls is reflected in the language of several CSCE principles: those of sovereign equality, inviolability of frontiers, territorial integrity of states, nonintervention in internal affairs, and equal rights and self-determination of peoples. From the Western view a correct balance was found, and the Brezhnev Doctrine was contradicted. But the Soviets obviously did not see it this way since only two months after the Final Act was approved their "Treaty of Friendship, Cooperation, and Mutual Assistance" with the German Democratic Republic (October 7, 1975) specifically reiterated the Brezhnev Doctrine.

Many Westerners, including some critics of the Helsinki agreement, see it as a useful yardstick for measuring Soviet and East European human rights behavior and as an indispensable instrument for pressing those countries to improve. The fact that the Helsinki Accord is neither "a treaty nor an international agreement" (see Finnish government letter to the UN at the end of Appendix II) and therefore has no legal effect is not really relevant since it is unquestionably a central moral and political document whose commitments were undertaken at the highest level. It therefore should carry the same weight for implementation as a treaty of similar scope. In any event, the Final Act would be no more enforceable if it were a treaty than it is in its actual form.

During the CSCE, and in the years following the Helsinki Summit, attitudes toward the Conference have evolved in important ways in both the Soviet Union and the West. The change has been most easily discernible in connection with the concept of follow-up to the Conference. Long-standing Soviet interest in a regularized European body suggests that one of the original Soviet objectives in the CSCE was to establish some form of permanent all-European mechanism. Such a device would provide the Kremlin with a framework within which it could exercise more influence over Western Europe as well as the East European satellites.

As Charles E. Bohlen records in his book *Witness to History, 1929–1969*, as early as the meeting of wartime leaders in Teheran in 1943 Stalin spoke of a "committee" to oversee the postwar affairs of Europe. From the Rapacki Plan of 1958, which suggested "control machinery," to the Budapest Appeal of 1969, which foresaw the European conference leading to "a durable system of European Security," the Soviets clearly had in mind a permanent European security mechanism of some kind. The Warsaw Pact communiqué of 1970 formally suggested that the question of setting up "an appropriate body" be added to the agenda of the Conference. Specifics on the form and functions of such a body were always vague.

But by the time negotiations actually began, the Soviets were backpedaling. They evidently already foresaw that follow-up meetings could be used to pressure them on human rights. At first they did not explain what they had in mind as a continuing CSCE mechanism. When the communist bloc finally did table its formal follow-up proposal it retained for the Soviets a veto power over any follow-up gatherings. Significantly, the Warsaw Pact proposal avoided commitment even to one follow-up meeting. As the Helsinki negotiations came to a conclusion, the Soviets fought hard to avoid a commitment to regularized follow-up meetings, as was desired by the neutrals.

The Soviets knew they were on the defensive in the CSCE at Belgrade, which surely confirmed their worst fears about how the follow-up mechanism could be used. However, since then they appear to have developed considerable tolerance for the follow-up meetings and the criticisms that are now routinely leveled against them for failure to fulfill their human rights obligations. This was shown by their agreement in Madrid to specialized CSCE meetings on human rights and human contacts, where they were sure to be the focus of critical comment on issues such as emigration. The Kremlin has apparently concluded that the avalanche of criticism falls of its own weight and is therefore tolerable. The Soviets have also taken up an increasingly aggressive policy of defending their own human rights policies (e.g., by stressing such "social rights" as the right to work and medical care), while criticizing Western treatment of minorities and other human rights shortcomings.

The evolution of the Soviet attitude on this point was confirmed again at the outset of the Vienna follow-up session when the USSR proposed that a CSCE meeting on human rights issues be convened in Moscow. The proposal immediately divided Western analysts; some favored accepting the Soviet proposal as a means to influence thinking in the USSR itself, while others opposed the idea, suspicious that the Kremlin would so limit the gathering as to make it meaningless. In any case, such a meeting in the Soviet capital would give a tacit stamp of approval to the communist state's human rights record and thus would represent a major Soviet gain.

The Soviets appear once again to see the CSCE as offering them a useful mechanism for influencing Western Europe and separating it from the United States. The decision of the Twenty-sixth Congress of the Soviet Communist party in 1981 to accept an enlarged zone of application for military measures to be negotiated at the CSCE spin-off Conference on Disarmament in Europe showed a renewed Soviet commitment to the CSCE process. And in the 1985 pamphlet "Helsinki: Ten Years Later," the Soviets cited the Helsinki Accord as the third step in the process leading toward European security, one that "constitutes a multilateral system of commitments and corresponding measures." The new Soviet leader, Mikhail Gorbachev, was quoted, adding his stamp of approval: "The political Bureau starts from the assumption that the interstate documents of the detente period, including the Helsinki Final Act, have lost none of their value. They are an example of the way in which international relations can be built. . . ."

Despite the Western view that the Soviets gained more from the Helsinki Accord, and have failed to live up to their commitments, we can expect the Soviets to seek to use the CSCE forum aggressively in the future to achieve further objectives, including reduction of military readiness in Western Europe, the creation of a pro-Soviet climate among large sectors of Western public opinion, and the encouragement of divisions between the United States and its allies.

The Western attitude toward follow-up has also evolved, almost in mirror image to that of the USSR. Western apprehension about increasing Soviet influence carried over into the beginning of the Conference itself but was then influenced by two factors: (1) the desire of the neutrals, who were largely Western-oriented, to fix a regular follow-up mechanism to ensure their continuing role in East-West relations; and (2) the growing Western realization that the human rights-related commitments undertaken by the Soviets would need to be pursued if there was to be any chance of their being carried out.

The two years between Helsinki and Belgrade, and the dismal Soviet record of compliance, convinced the Western countries that regular follow-up would indeed be required. Also, the rising interest of Western public opinion in the use of the Helsinki Accord as a human rights prod, and the defensiveness of the Soviets, made it seem clear that follow-up was in the Western, not the Soviet, interest. It was Western and neutral insistence, in the face of strong Soviet resistance, that led to the procedures agreed at the Belgrade preparatory meeting in 1977 to guarantee periodic follow-up meetings.

The experience of implementation has been so disappointing in the human rights field that there has been a recurring debate among Western opinion leaders about possible abrogation of the Helsinki Accord. The reasoning has been that if the Soviets are not prepared to carry out their end of the broad Helsinki bargain by improving freer movement of people and ideas and the status of human rights in the communist countries, the West should withdraw its part of the bargain by renouncing the recognition of postwar frontiers that the Final Act entailed. The counterargument is that such abrogation would have no effect on the myriad acts of recognition of frontiers that were already in the record before Helsinki, such as establishment of diplomatic relations, bilateral treaties and agreements, high-level visits, membership in the UN, etc. At the same time the possibility of using the Helsinki Accord to press for human rights would end. The concept of abrogation could nonetheless gain ground if the Soviets continue to flout their human rights commitments.

But there is no question that the Helsinki experience has brought into focus what is perhaps the most basic dilemma for the West in reaching agreements with the Soviet Union: how to bring such a government to carry out its obligations after agreements have been reached. This question bears on almost every aspect of American-Soviet relations.

In an open, democratic society there are numerous internal forces that encourage a government to respect its international obligations: opposition political parties, an outspoken press, lobbying groups, and pressures from interested allies. All of these forces are at work in pressing the U.S. government to respect the commitments contained in its bilateral agreements with the USSR.

But in the closed, totalitarian society of the USSR there are no opposition politicians, no free press, and no organized lobbies. Whatever pressure there may be from allies is private and muted. At the same time major internal forces are actively engaged in resisting implementation, such as the KGB, the army, and the bureaucracy of the Soviet state. Pressures from hostile foreign countries generate added resistance from these groups rather than compliance. Public Western criticisms of the policies of Western governments also tend to stiffen the internal Soviet forces that are resisting reforms since they are then encouraged to believe that Western policies may be changed.

The failure of the Soviets to carry out their Helsinki human rights commitments has been nothing less than flagrant. While no experienced Soviet observer expected them to implement every detail of every obligation overnight, it was not an unreasonable hope that the Kremlin would make some effort to demonstrate a respect at least for the spirit of Helsinki. But the Soviets' treatment of dissidents like the Sakharovs, Anatoli Scharansky, and Yuri Orlov, and their extraordinary continuing bestiality toward those who want to leave the USSR has reflected a determination to move in exactly the opposite direction: to clamp down and strangle any group or individual who aspires to the Helsinki concept of freer movement. Even the much publicized recent efforts by Gorbachev to make what would appear in the West as humanitarian gestures have not materially changed the general practices of the Soviet state; they are clearly exceptions to the rule rather than fundamental reforms.

The deep-seated Soviet and Russian preoccupation with internal security has tended to outweigh any inclination there may have been within the Soviet system to permit even measured liberalization. Recent actions should not mislead us; they are intended to suggest liberalization but should be seen for what they are—token symbolic exceptions to an overall system that has shown little movement toward civilized standards since the death of Stalin.

The Soviets' post-Helsinki behavior has once again posed the question of whether the West, particularly the United States, should seek further agreements with the USSR in fields where commitments cannot be enforced through some built-in leverage. Indeed, this public demonstration of Soviet bad faith raises questions about entering any agreement with Moscow.

Thus far, no one has found a clear answer to these dilemmas. At the same time, however, there is a basic political need for Western governments, especially the U.S. government, to show publicly that they are pressing the Soviet Union and the East European regimes on human rights. Thus, whether they are effective or not, Western governments will continue to exert pressures on Moscow to carry out its Helsinki commitments. This East-West dialogue will continue, even if it has yielded meager results thus far.

In his address at the commemoration of the tenth anniversary of Helsinki, Secretary of State George Shultz confirmed America's commitment to the Helsinki Accord. "My country," he said, "and most other countries represented here remain committed to the goal of putting the program of the Final Act into practice in all of its provisions. . . . We believe that the truest tests of political intentions are actual steps to improve cooperation among states, to enhance contacts among peoples, and to strengthen respect for individual rights."

The enduring debate as to whether or not Helsinki was in the U.S. interest is likely to continue for years to come. Measured against the clearest Western objective within the Conference—improvement in the human rights situation in the USSR and Eastern Europe—it has thus far been a dismal failure. Nonetheless, there is a large body of opinion, especially in Europe, that believes it is better to have an agreed yardstick for Soviet behavior than none at all. By this logic the post-Helsinki situation is an improvement, for it permits the West to insist on respect for human rights and puts Soviet behavior under Western scrutiny.

The impact of the launching of what is usually called the Helsinki "process" deserves careful analysis and can perhaps be measured only at some point in the distant future. The Helsinki process has spawned a broad range of follow-up meetings at the plenary and expert levels, including one important new negotiation, the Conference on Disarmament in Europe, and numerous agreed upon all-European documents. This process has, in fact, begun to resemble something of a "system" of European security with its own rules and taboos, geographic and political limitations, competencies, and shortcomings. Thus, while the CSCE has so far been a failure in achieving the West's principal substantive objective, it may have unexpectedly given birth to a European system whose overall implications have never been fully anticipated.

The continuing existence of this "process" or "system" is stimulated by the Europeans, especially the smaller European states, but it depends on the acquiescence of the two superpowers, each of which has thus far evidently seen the process as serving its national interests. It would not be possible for the "process" to continue if one or the other superpower firmly decided that continuation was undesirable. It is this overlapping of U.S. and Soviet interests in Helsinki that keeps the process going.

For the Soviets there is an institutional need to justify the effort they expended to obtain the Helsinki Accord and to laud it as a glorious Soviet achievement. More substantively, the Soviet interest in maintaining the existing geopolitical situation is best served by ensuring that Helsinki is a living document with an institutional existence. In addition, the Soviets have recently shown renewed interest in using the Helsinki forum to divide the West and exercise influence throughout Europe.

The United States, too, must justify its signature of the Helsinki document by being able to show that it has brought human rights improvements. Since these have not been forthcoming, the next best alternative is to continue the Helsinki process and the pressure it puts on the Soviet Union.

European interest in Helsinki, which has an important effect on the American attitude, is far broader. The Europeans think of Helsinki as enhancing the political stability of their continent by establishing agreed behavioral norms for interstate activity—even if these norms may be ambiguous. While the Europeans generally consider this element fundamental, it is difficult for Americans to think in terms of "political" stability, and the United States thus tends to discount its importance—or not count it at all. Americans emphasize "strategic" stability, often to the exclusion of other concepts. The desire for "political" stability is shared throughout Europe, East and West, and there is a widespread belief that the Helsinki process makes a positive contribution. Washington is influenced by the desires of its European allies, and this has been a continuing factor in the U.S. approach to Helsinki.

The Helsinki Accord has been fully satisfactory to no one. The Western debate about its value is public and well known; the Soviets make positive comments about it, but this is mainly because it was a Soviet initiative, and they are condemned to portray it as a success. Despite the fact that it has put them on the defensive, the Soviets have a great capacity for claiming victory and trying to use even a negative situation to best advantage. Whether we like it or not, the Helsinki system is here to stay, with a proliferating series of spin-off meetings and conferences, more lengthy agreed documents, and increasing recognition as a set of standards accepted by both the communist and capitalist worlds. The West, particularly the United States, cannot allow the ambiguities of Helsinki to distract us from the central political objectives that it sets, and that remain valid.

The Helsinki experience has taught us many things and may teach us more in the future. Two broad lessons have emerged, which parallel those of the detente era. First, Helsinki has shown that improvements in the human rights situations in the USSR and Eastern Europe can and must be pursued with patience and firmness as part of a visible, continuing effort to advance the Western view of the dignity of the individual. The American people, and probably the people of any Western democracy, will not long support a policy of peaceful cooperation with the USSR without this.

The second lesson must be drawn from the fact that, during the same period when Leonid Brezhnev was signing the Final Act, he was obviously also taking the necessary decisions to produce and deploy the ss-20 and other advanced weapons systems. While the Carter administration was following the spirit of restraint that inspired the Helsinki meeting by unilaterally cutting back on defense expenditures and pursuing an array of arms control initiatives, the Soviets were actually increasing arms production and preparing the invasion of Afghanistan and the military takeover in Poland. When Soviet and East European citizens sought to use the rights their governments had recognized in the Final Act, they were brutally repressed. These activities cannot be reconciled with the spirit or the commitments of Helsinki. They serve as reminders of the contrast between Moscow's verbal declarations and its actions, which remains the foremost obstacle to improved relations with the West.

No doubt there will in future be renewed interest in seeking more positive relations with the USSR in areas where mutual benefits are possible. When that time comes, Western leaders would do well to bear in mind the lessons of the detente era of the 1970s. The Soviets have had ample opportunity to demonstrate a good faith effort to carry out their Helsinki commitments, but no one could contend that they have made a serious effort in this direction.

There may be other possibilities for paper agreements in the years ahead, but their value must be judged in the light of this experience. To reach new agreements when previous accords have not yet been implemented can only be misleading and illusory for both sides.

The West must be clear-eyed about Soviet behavior and ambitions as they have been revealed in the past decade. And we must be realistic about the limits they impose on possibilities for meaningful agreement. The hopes and desires of the peoples of Europe and North America must be pursued with caution, or they will be betrayed. And our ability to defend our own interests must be maintained, or the Western world as we know it will risk being slowly overwhelmed by the weight of Soviet influence and military might. These are the principal lessons of Helsinki.

Appendix I
Final Recommendations of the
Helsinki Consultations   Helsinki 1973

1   The participants in the Helsinki Consultations on the question of the
    Conference on Security and Co-operation in Europe, representing the
    Governments of States listed in the annex, recommend to their Govern-
    ments that this Conference should be convened under the conditions
    specified below, concerning its organization, agenda and the related in-
    structions, participation, date, place, rules of procedure and financial
    arrangements.
2   The participants expressed their collective agreement to these Recom-
    mendations on 8 June, 1973.
3   Each State entitled to participate in the Conference will inform the Gov-
    ernment of Finland, within the time limits laid down in Chapter 3, of its
    decision to take part in this Conference, thereby indicating its intention
    to do so on the basis of the Final Recommendations of the Helsinki
    Consultations. The Government of Finland will inform all States entitled
    to participate of the communications received in this respect.
4   The Government of Finland will take the necessary measures, in accor-
    dance with the arrangements provided for in the Final Recommendations,
    to organize the first stage of the Conference.
5   Index of Recommendations (1) Organization of the Conference (2)
    Agenda and the Related Instructions (3) Participation, Contributions,
    Guests (4) Date (5) Place (6) Rules of Procedure (7) Financial Ar-
    rangements Annex: List of Participating Countries

1   Organization of the Conference on Security and Co-operation in Europe

6   The Conference on Security and Co-operation in Europe will take place
    in three stages:

(a) Stage I
7   The first stage will consist of a meeting of the Ministers for Foreign
    Affairs of the participating States. In accordance with the recommenda-
    tions of the Helsinki Consultations, the Ministers will adopt the rules of
    procedure, the agenda and the instructions of the working bodies of the

Conference, together with the other arrangements relating to the conduct of the Conference. The Ministers will state the views of their Governments on the problems relating to security and co-operation in Europe. Should they so wish they will put forward, for consideration in the course of the second stage, proposals relating to the various topics on the agenda.

(b)   Stage II

8   The second stage will comprise the work of the specialized committees and sub-committees whose instructions are defined in Chapter 2 of these recommendations (points I, II and III of the agenda). Within this framework and on the basis of the proposals submitted either by the Ministers for Foreign Affairs, or subsequently by the delegations of the participating States, the committees and sub-committees will prepare drafts of declarations, recommendations, resolutions or any other final documents. The participating States will be represented in these bodies by such delegates and experts as they shall designate for the purpose.

9   A Co-ordinating Committee, composed of representatives appointed by the Ministers for Foreign Affairs, will meet periodically during the second stage of the Conference. It will co-ordinate the activities of the committees and assemble the results of their work with a view to the final stage of the Conference. The Co-ordinating Committee shall also be entrusted with the execution of the tasks defined in point IV of the agenda, as stated in Chapter 2 of the present recommendations. It will, furthermore, submit to the participating Governments such recommendations as it may consider useful regarding the conduct of the Conference, especially the organization of its third stage.

(c)   Stage III

10   In the light of the recommendations drawn up by the Co-ordinating Committee, the Conference will meet for its third stage.

11   The level of representation at the third stage will be decided by the participating States during the Conference, before the end of the second stage.

12   The Conference will adopt its final documents, in formal session, at the close of this third stage.

2   Agenda and the Related Instructions

I   Questions Relating to Security in Europe

13   In carrying out the instructions set out below, the Committee will bear in mind the wider objective of promoting better relations among participating States and ensuring conditions in which their people can live in peace free from any threat to or attempt against their security.

14   In its work the Committee will proceed from the premise that the strengthening of security in Europe is not directed against any State or continent and should constitute an important contribution to world peace and security.

15   In considering questions relating to security in Europe, the Committee will bear in mind the broader context of world security and in particular the relationship which exists between security in Europe and in the Mediterranean area.

16   The Committee will be assisted in its tasks by the appropriate Sub-Committees.

1.

17   (a) The Committee/Sub-Committee is charged with the task of considering and stating in conformity with the purposes and principles of the United Nations those basic principles which each participating State is to respect and apply in its relations with all other participating States, irrespective of their political, economic or social systems, in order to ensure the peace and security of all participating States.

18   The principles to be stated shall be included in a document of appropriate form to be submitted by the Committee for adoption by the Conference. It shall express the determination of the participating States to respect and apply the principles equally and unreservedly in all aspects to their mutual relations and co-operation, in order to ensure to all participating States the benefits resulting from the application of these principles by all.

19   The reaffirmation, with such clarifications and additions as may be deemed desirable, and the precise statement, in conformity with the purposes and principles of the United Nations, of the following principles of primary significance guiding the mutual relations of the participating States, are deemed to be of particular importance:

sovereign equality, respect for the rights inherent in sovereignty;

refraining from the threat or use of force;

inviolability of frontiers;

territorial integrity of States;

peaceful settlement of disputes;

non-intervention in internal affairs;

respect for human rights and fundamental freedoms, including the freedom of thought, conscience, religion or belief;

equal rights and self-determination of peoples;

co-operation among States;

fulfilment in good faith of obligations under international law.

20   In discharging itself of these tasks, the Committee/Sub-Committee shall take into account in particular the Declaration on Principles of International Law concerning Friendly Relations and Co-operation among States in accordance with the Charter of the United Nations.

21   (b) The Committee/Sub-Committee shall give expression to the idea that respect for the above-listed principles will encourage the development of normal and friendly relations among the participating States as well as of their political contacts which in turn would contribute to the furthering of their co-operation. It shall also consider proposals designed to give effect to refraining from the threat or use of force. In this context, it shall study proposals for and undertake the elaboration of a method for the peaceful settlement of disputes among participating States.

2.

22   The Committee/Sub-Committee shall have regard to the fact that the participating States are desirous of eliminating any causes of tension that may exist among them and of contributing to the strengthening of peace and security in the world, bearing in mind the fact that efforts aimed at disarmament complement political détente and are essential elements in a process in which all participating States have a vital interest.

23   In order to strengthen confidence and to increase stability and security, the Committee/Sub-Committee shall submit to the Conference appropriate proposals on confidence-building measures such as the prior notification of major military manoeuvres on a basis to be specified by the Conference, and the exchange of observers by invitation at military manoeuvres under mutually acceptable conditions. The Committee/Sub-Committee will also study the question of prior notification of major military movements and submit its conclusions.

24   The Committee/Sub-Committee shall pay due attention to the views expressed by participating States on the various subjects mentioned in the preceding paragraphs, on the particular interest they attach thereto, especially from the point of view of their own security and of their desire to be informed about the relevant developments.

II Co-operation in the Fields of Economics, of Science and Technology and of the Environment

25   The Committee shall be responsible for drawing up a draft final document/documents containing guidelines and concrete recommendations which could stimulate common efforts for increased co-operation in the fields of economics, science and technology and environment, which

might guide the participating States in their mutual relations in these areas and which they might utilize in the conclusion of bilateral or multi-lateral agreements, as well as recommendations on specific measures for the development of co-operation which could be agreed by participating States.

26   The Committee will bear in mind the contribution which such co-opera-tion could make to the reinforcement of peace and security in Europe. It will also bear in mind the interests of developing countries and regions and the positive effects which the broadening of co-operation among participating States could have on world economic relations.

27   The Committee, having in mind the foregoing, shall study ways and means that would make it possible, by mutual agreement among partici-pating States, to facilitate, with due regard for the diversity of economic and social systems and under conditions of reciprocity of advantages and obligations, the development of trade and co-operation in the various fields of economic activity, science, technology and in the field of the environment. In this regard, it will in particular take account of the work of the United Nations Economic Commission for Europe.

28   In considering questions relating to co-operation in Europe covered by this mandate, the Committee will bear in mind the relationship which exists between such co-operation in Europe and in the Mediterranean area.

29   The Committee in its final draft/drafts will formulate relevant proposals, based on full respect for the principles guiding relations among the par-ticipating States enumerated in the terms of reference for the Committee on item 1 of the agenda.

30   The Committee, assisted by the appropriate Sub-Committees, will ex-amine the following questions:

1   Commercial Exchanges
31   The Committee/Sub-Committee will examine general provisions de-signed to promote trade and the exchange of services between partici-pating States. It could discuss general problems relating to most favoured nation treatment. It could also examine measures aiming at the reduction or progressive elimination of all kinds of obstacles to the development of trade.

32   The Committee/Sub-Committee will examine specific measures de-signed to facilitate commercial transactions and the exchange of services, such as measures aiming at the improvement of

business contacts and facilities

the exchange of information on commercial opportunities and specific trading conditions provisions for the settlement of commercial disputes including various forms of arbitration.

2   Industrial Co-operation and Projects of Common Interest

33   The Committee/Sub-Committee will study the forms and modalities of industrial co-operation and will examine the various measures by which participating States could encourage the development of this co-operation using, as appropriate, the framework of bilateral or multilateral intergovernmental agreements.

34   The Committee/Sub-Committee will examine, in particular, the measures which governments could take to create conditions favourable to this co-operation between competent organizations, firms and enterprises of participating States. It will bear in mind that the specific forms of such co-operation should be settled bilaterally unless otherwise agreed upon by the participants. This examination could bear on the various forms of co-operation, such as co-operation in production and sales, on the exchange of information concerning the possibilities of industrial co-operation, on the improvement of conditions for setting up projects, and on other measures which could develop and facilitate various forms of industrial co-operation.

35   The Committee/Sub-Committee will also examine the possibilities of encouraging projects of common interest and of working out, where relevant, recommendations in this respect.

36   This examination could bear on the possibilities of implementing projects of common interest in the fields of energy resources, exploitation of raw materials and, when appropriate, of transport and communications.

3   Science and Technology

37   The Committee/Sub-Committee shall consider proposals for the development of co-operation in the field of science and technology, taking into account already existing or planned co-operation in this field, with a view to facilitating, through such means as the improvement of contacts and information, access to new developments in science and technology, and to contributing to the most effective solution of problems of common interest and to the betterment of the conditions of human life.

38   These proposals, in particular, shall be concerned with the areas where there are the most favourable prerequisites for such co-operation, the forms and methods for its implementation, as well as with the obstacles that hinder such co-operation and measures for their removal. In the consideration of these questions, the Committee/Sub-Committee will seek to build on existing practices and take into account the possibilities and capabilities of relevant existing international organizations.

4   Environment

39   The Committee/Sub-Committee shall be responsible for discussing questions of environmental protection and improvement and in particular for determining the fields that are important for the participating States and can best lend themselves to the development of co-operation between them, such as: protection of the seas surrounding Europe, of the waters and of the atmosphere; improvement of environmental and living conditions, especially in towns; protection of nature and of its resources.

40   The Committee/Sub-Committee shall examine and put forward the most appropriate bilateral and multilateral forms and methods of co-operation, including co-operation on a regional and subregional basis, for the various fields that have been determined. In the consideration of these questions, the Committee/Sub-Committee will seek to build on existing practices and take into account the possibilities and capabilities of the relevant existing international organizations.

5   Co-operation in Other Areas

41   The Committee/Sub-Committee could examine the following questions:

problems relating to the development of transport and communications between participating States;

promotion of tourism by the exchange of information, techniques and the results of practical experience and by the study of appropriate measures;

economic and social aspects of migrant labour;

training of personnel in various fields of economic activity;

such other questions as may be decided by common agreement.

III   **Co-operation in Humanitarian and Other Fields**

42   With the aim of contributing to the strengthening of peace and understanding among the peoples of the participating States and to the spiritual enrichment of the human personality, without distinction as to race, sex, language or religion and irrespective of their political, economic and social systems, the Committee, assisted by the appropriate Sub-Committees, shall be charged with examining all possibilities of co-operation conducive to creating better conditions for increased cultural and educational exchanges, for broader dissemination of information, for contacts between people, and for the solution of humanitarian problems. In this connection, it shall not only draw upon existing forms of co-operation, but shall also work out new ways and means appropriate to these aims.

43   The Committee in its final document will formulate relevant proposals, based on full respect for the principles guiding relations among the par-

ticipating States enumerated in the terms of reference for the Committee on item I of the agenda.

44   The Committee shall also consider to what extent existing institutions could be used to achieve these aims.

1 Human Contacts

45   The Committee/Sub-Committee shall prepare proposals to facilitate freer movement and contacts, individually or collectively, privately or officially, among persons, institutions and organisations of the participating States.

46   With a view to contributing to the favourable examination and settlement of relevant matters by the States concerned under mutually acceptable conditions, it shall pay particular attention to: (a) contacts and regular meetings on a basis of family ties; reunification of families; marriage between nationals of different States; (b) travel for personal or professional reasons; improvement of conditions for tourism, on an individual or collective basis; (c) meetings among young people; expansion of contacts and competitions, particularly in the field of sport.

2 Information

47   The Committee/Sub-Committee shall prepare proposals to facilitate the freer and wider dissemination of information of all kinds. In doing so it shall pay particular attention to: (a) improving the circulation of, and access to, oral, printed, filmed and broadcast information and extending the exchange of information; (b) encouraging co-operation in these fields of information on a basis of short or long term agreements; (c) improving conditions under which journalists from one participating State exercise their profession in another participating State.

3 Co-operation and Exchanges in the Field of Culture

48   The Committee/Sub-Committee shall prepare proposals aimed at extending and improving co-operation and exchanges in the various fields of culture and shall indicate the components and objectives of a consistent long-term development of such exchanges. In its work, it shall bear in mind the results of the Intergovernmental Conference on Cultural Policies in Europe, Helsinki, June 1972 including the broader concept of culture outlined by that Conference.

49   The Committee/Sub-Committee shall consider in particular: (a) Extension of relations among competent government agencies and non-governmental bodies dealing with matters of culture; (b) Promotion of fuller mutual knowledge of and access to achievements in literature, art and other fields of cultural activity; (c) Improvement of facilities for contacts and exchanges in the above-mentioned spheres; (d) Extension of contacts

and co-operation among creative artists and people engaged in cultural activities; (e) Common search for new fields and forms of co-operation; co-operation in the investigation of the social aspects of culture; (f) Encouragement of such forms of cultural co-operation as: international events in the fields of art, film, theatre, music, folklore, etc.; book fairs and exhibitions; joint projects in the field of protection of monuments and sites; co-production and exchange of films and of radio and television programmes.

50   The Committee/Sub-Committee while considering the role of States in co-operation in the field of culture will bear in mind the contribution that national minorities or regional cultures could make to it within the framework of respect for principles referred to above.

4   *Co-operation and Exchanges in the Field of Education*

51   The Committee/Sub-Committee shall prepare proposals aimed at broadening co-operation and exchanges in the fields of education and science on a short or long-term basis. These proposals shall be carried out bilaterally and multilaterally as appropriate, between participating States and non-governmental bodies. The Committee/Sub-Committee shall consider in particular: (a) Expansion of links between State institutions and non-governmental bodies whose activities are concerned with questions of education and science. (b) Improved access, under mutually acceptable conditions, for students, teachers and scholars from the participating States to each other's educational, cultural and scientific institutions, and a more exact assessment of the problems of comparison and equivalence between academic degrees and diplomas. (c) Encouragement of the study of the languages and civilizations of other peoples for the purpose of creating favourable conditions for promoting wider acquaintance with the culture of each country. (d) Exchange of experience in teaching methods in various fields including those used in adult education and exchanges in the field of teaching materials.

52   The Committee/Sub-Committee while considering the role of States in co-operation in the field of education will bear in mind the contribution that national minorities or regional cultures could make to it within the framework of respect for principles referred to above.

IV   **Follow-up to the Conference**

53   The Co-ordinating Committee shall consider, on the basis of the progress made at the Conference such measures as may be required to give effect to the decisions of the Conference and to further the process of improving security and developing co-operation in Europe. Having considered proposals to this effect, including proposals of an organizational nature, it

shall make any recommendations which it deems necessary. In examining the follow-up of the Conference, the Committee shall also consider the contributions which it believes could be asked from existing international organizations.

3 Participation, Contributions, Guests

(a) Participation

54   All European States, the United States and Canada shall be entitled to take part in the Conference on Security and Co-operation in Europe. If any of these States wishes to attend as an observer it may do so. In that case, its representatives may attend all stages of the Conference and of its working bodies, but shall not participate in the taking of decisions. Such a State may decide later to accept these decisions or some of them under the conditions defined by the Conference.

55   States referred to in the first sentence of the paragraph above wishing to participate in the Conference or to attend as observers must so inform the Finnish Government at the latest on 25 June 1973.

(b) Contributions

56   The Conference and its working bodies will acquaint themselves, in such manner as they may determine, with the points of view held by non-participating States on the subject of the various agenda items.

57   States situated in regions adjacent to Europe and to whom reference is made in the provisions of Chapter 2, and in particular those of the Mediterranean States which have already expressed their interest in stating their views to the Conference, are especially envisaged by this Chapter.

58   The Co-ordinating Committee may decide, by consensus, the means by which the working bodies of the Conference may consult appropriate international organizations, on the subject of the various agenda items.

(c) Guests

59   The Secretary-General of the United Nations will be invited as guest of honour to the inaugural session of the Conference.

4 Date

60   1 The Conference on Security and Co-operation in Europe shall be opened on 3 July 1973 at 11:30 A.M.

61   2 The date of the opening of the second stage shall be determined by the Ministers during the first stage.

62   3 The date of the opening of the third stage shall be decided during the second stage by agreement among the participating States on the basis of the recommendations of the Co-ordinating Committee.

5   Place of the Conference

63   Taking into account with appreciation the invitation by the Government of Finland, having in view practical considerations and rotation, the first stage of the Conference on Security and Co-operation in Europe will be held in Helsinki; the second stage will be held in Geneva; the third stage will be held in Helsinki.

6   Rules of Procedure

64   The States participating in the Conference on Security and Co-operation in Europe shall conduct their work as follows:

65   1 All States participating in the Conference shall do so as sovereign and independent States and in conditions of full equality. The Conference shall take place outside military alliances.

66   2 The representation of the participating States at each stage of the Conference shall be determined in accordance with the provisions laid down in Chapter 1 of these Final Recommendations.

67   3 The working bodies of the Conference shall be the Co-ordinating Committee, the Committees and the Sub-Committees. These working bodies will function during the second stage of the Conference. However, the Co-ordinating Committee will meet at the site of the second stage before the opening of the second stage in order to settle questions relating to the organization of that stage.

68   The working bodies of the Conference may, if they so wish, set up such working groups as they may consider useful. The working bodies and working groups of the Conference shall be open to all participating States.

69   4 Decisions of the Conference shall be taken by consensus. Consensus shall be understood to mean the absence of any objection expressed by a Representative and submitted by him as constituting an obstacle to the taking of the decision in question.

    5   *Chairmanship*

70   A. The Chair at the inaugural and closing meetings of the first stage of the Conference shall be taken by the Minister for Foreign Affairs of the host country. The Chair at other meetings shall be taken on a basis of rotation, as follows: (a) The Chair at each meeting shall be taken by the Minister for Foreign Affairs of a different participating State, in an order established in accordance with a list selected by lot country by country before the end of the Helsinki Consultations; (b) If the Conference should meet both in the morning and in the afternoon of the same day, the two meetings shall be regarded as constituting two distinct meetings; (c) In the interval between meetings of the Conference, the functions of the Chair shall be exercised by that Minister for Foreign Affairs who presided

over the immediately preceding meeting of the Conference; (d) Should a Minister for Foreign Affairs be prevented from taking the Chair, it shall be taken by the Minister for Foreign Affairs of the country next in the order established.

71   B. The Chair at the inaugural meetings of the working bodies of the Conference shall be taken by the Representative of the host country. Thereafter, the office of Chairman shall be filled as follows: (a) The Chairman of the Co-ordinating Committee and the Chairmen of the Committees shall be designated on a basis of daily rotation, in French alphabetical order, starting from a letter drawn by lot; (b) The Chairmen of Sub-Committees and of other subsidiary bodies of the Conference shall be designated on a basis of rotation in accordance with practical arrangements to be established at the appropriate time by the bodies in question.

72   Where necessary, a rapporteur shall be designated by consensus.

73   C. The provisions laid down for the meetings of the first stage shall be applicable *mutatis mutandis* to the meetings of the third stage of the Conference. They may be further defined by the Co-ordinating Committee.

74   6 The Executive Secretary for technical matters at each stage of the Conference shall be a national of the corresponding host country. He is designated by the host country subject to agreement by the participating States.

75   In organizing the services, the Executive Secretary of each stage will be responsible for the recruitment of his staff and assured of the collaboration of the Secretariats of the other stages.

76   The Executive Secretaries will work under the authority of the Conference and report on their activities to the appropriate body of each stage of the Conference, especially on financial matters.

77   7 Official verbatim records shall be taken at the meetings of the first and third stages of the Conference.

78   Proposals on matters of substance and amendments thereto shall be submitted in writing to the Chairman and circulated to all participants. The proposals adopted shall be registered by the Executive Secretary and circulated among the participants.

79   Representatives of States participating in the Conference may ask for their formal reservations or interpretative statements concerning given decisions to be duly registered by the Executive Secretary and circulated to the participating States. Such statements must be submitted in writing to the Executive Secretary.

80   8 The inaugural and closing sessions of the first stage of the Conference will be open. Other sessions of the first stage may be open if the Ministers so decide. The Co-ordinating Committee, the Committees and the Sub-

Committees shall not, as a rule, meet in open sessions, unless the participants decide otherwise. Arrangements for the third stage will be similar to those for the first stage and may be further defined by the Coordinating Committee.

81   9 The working languages of the Conference and of its working bodies shall be: English, French, German, Italian, Russian and Spanish.

82   Speeches made in any of the working languages shall be interpreted into the other working languages.

83   10 Any Representative may make a statement in a language other than the working languages. In this case, he shall himself provide for interpretation into one of the working languages.

84   11 Records and decisions of the Conference shall be issued and circulated to participants in the working languages.

85   The participants shall decide by consensus whether it is desirable to make public, through the appropriate services of the Conference, certain documents or communiqués on the work of the Conference and if they decide in the affirmative shall specify the contents.

86   12 During the discussion of any matter, a Representative may raise a point of order and the Chairman shall give him the floor immediately. A Representative raising a point of order may not speak on the substance of the matter under discussion.

87   13 During the meeting the Chairman shall keep a list of speakers and may declare it closed with the consent of the meeting. He shall, however, accord the right of reply to any Representative if a speech after he has declared the list closed makes this desirable.

88   14 These procedural arrangements shall be adopted by consensus. Once adopted, they can only be altered by consensus.

7 Financial Arrangements

A Distribution of Expenses

89   The following scale of distribution has been agreed for the expenses of the Conference, subject to the reservation that the distribution in question concerns the Conference only and shall not be considered as a precedent which could be relied on in other circumstances:

90   France 8.80%
Federal Republic of Germany 8.80%
Italy 8.80%
Union of Soviet Socialist Republics 8.80%
United Kingdom 8.80%
United States of America 8.80%   52.80%

Distribution of Expenses (continued)

Canada	5.52%	5.52%
Belgium	3.48%	
German Democratic Republic	3.48%	
Netherlands	3.48%	
Poland	3.48%	
Spain	3.48%	
Sweden	3.48%	20.88%
Austria	2.00%	
Czechoslovakia	2.00%	
Denmark	2.00%	
Finland	2.00%	
Hungary	2.00%	
Norway	2.00%	
Switzerland	2.00%	14.00%
Greece	0.80%	
Romania	0.80%	
Turkey	0.80%	
Yugoslavia	0.80%	3.20%
Bulgaria	0.60%	
Ireland	0.60%	
Luxembourg	0.60%	
Portugal	0.60%	2.40%
Cyprus	0.20%	
Holy See	0.20%	
Iceland	0.20%	
Liechtenstein	0.20%	
Malta	0.20%	
San Marino	0.20%	1.20%
	100 %	100 %

91   Necessary alterations of the cost-sharing scale due to any possible modifications in the list of participating States above will be decided upon by consensus.

B   *System of Financing*

92   1 The monies needed to finance the Conference will be advanced by the host country of each stage subject to reimbursement out of the contributions of the participating States according to the agreed cost-sharing scale.

93   2 Payment of contributions by participating States shall be made to a special account of the Conference.

94   3 Payment shall be made in the currency of the host country.

95   4 Accounts will be rendered in respect of each stage or at intervals of three (3) months, as appropriate.

96   5 Accounts shall be expressed in the currency of the host country and shall be rendered as soon as technically possible after the termination of a billing period. They shall be payable within sixty (60) days of presentation.

The cost-sharing scale (paragraph 90) has been altered by the following decision of the Co-ordinating Committee, made in Geneva, 31st August 1973: "Decision No. 7   Monaco's share in the expenses of the Conference is fixed at 0.20%; this percentage will be deducted from Canada's share, which will thus amount to 5.32%."

Annex

Austria, Belgium, Bulgaria, Canada, Cyprus, Czechoslovakia, Denmark, Finland, France, German Democratic Republic, Federal Republic of Germany, Greece, Holy See, Hungary, Iceland, Ireland, Italy, Liechtenstein, Luxembourg, Malta, Netherlands, Norway, Poland, Portugal, Romania, San Marino, Spain, Sweden, Switzerland, Turkey, Union of Soviet Socialist Republics, United Kingdom, United States of America, Yugoslavia.

Communique on the First Stage of the Conference on Security and Co-operation in Europe

1   The first stage of the Conference on Security and Co-operation in Europe took place in Helsinki from 3 to 7 July 1973. In accordance with the agreement reached earlier, this stage of the Conference was held at Foreign Minister level.

2   The following States are participating in the Conference: Austria, Belgium, Bulgaria, Canada, Cyprus, Czechoslovakia, Denmark, Finland, France, German Democratic Republic, Federal Republic of Germany, Greece, Holy See, Hungary, Iceland, Ireland, Italy, Liechtenstein, Luxembourg, Malta, Monaco, Netherlands, Norway, Poland, Portugal, Romania, San Marino, Spain, Sweden, Switzerland, Turkey, Union of Soviet Socialist Republics, United Kingdom, United States of America, Yugoslavia.

3   At the inaugural session of the Conference Dr. Urho Kekkonen, President of the Republic of Finland made a speech of welcome. Dr. Kurt Waldheim, Secretary-General of the United Nations also addressed the Conference.

4   The Ministers adopted the Final Recommendations of the Helsinki Consultations which comprise the agenda and instructions of the working bodies of the Conference together with the rules of procedure and the other arrangements relating to the conduct of the Conference. The text of these Final Recommendations is available to the public.

5   The Ministers stated the views of their Governments on essential problems relating to security and co-operation in Europe, and on the further work of the Conference.

6   The Foreign Ministers of several States submitted proposals on various questions relating to the agenda. Others announced the intention to submit proposals during the second stage of the Conference.

7   The Ministers examined the manner in which the Conference would acquaint itself with points of view expressed by non-participating States on the subject of various agenda items. This matter was in particular considered in connection with the request of Malta and Spain in favour of Algeria and Tunisia. This matter was also considered in relation to other non-participating States bordering the Mediterranean. No consensus was reached for the time being.

8   The Ministers decided that the second stage of the Conference will meet in Geneva on 18 September 1973 in order to pursue the study of the questions on the agenda and in order to prepare drafts of declarations, recommendations, resolutions or any other final documents on the basis of the proposals submitted during the first stage as well as those to be submitted.

9   The Co-ordinating Committee made up of representatives of participating States will assemble for its first meeting in Geneva on 29 August 1973 in order to prepare the organization of the second stage.

10   The Ministers expressed the determination of their Governments to contribute to the success of the further work of the Conference.

11   The participants in the Conference expressed their profound gratitude to the Government of Finland for its hospitality and for the important contribution made by Finland to the preparation of the Conference on Security and Co-operation in Europe and to the conduct of the first stage.

Appendix II
Conference on Security and Co-operation
in Europe Final Act Helsinki 1975

1   The Conference on Security and Co-operation in Europe, which opened at Helsinki on 3 July 1973 and continued at Geneva from 18 September 1973 to 21 July 1975, was concluded at Helsinki on 1 August 1975 by the High Representatives of Austria, Belgium, Bulgaria, Canada, Cyprus, Czechoslovakia, Denmark, Finland, France, the German Democratic Republic, the Federal Republic of Germany, Greece, the Holy See, Hungary, Iceland, Ireland, Italy, Liechtenstein, Luxembourg, Malta, Monaco, the Netherlands, Norway, Poland, Portugal, Romania, San Marino, Spain, Sweden, Switzerland, Turkey, the Union of Soviet Socialist Republics, the United Kingdom, the United States of America and Yugoslavia.

2   During the opening and closing stages of the Conference the participants were addressed by the Secretary-General of the United Nations as their guest of honour. The Director-General of UNESCO and the Executive Secretary of the United Nations Economic Commission for Europe addressed the Conference during its second stage.

3   During the meetings of the second stage of the Conference, contributions were received, and statements heard, from the following non-participating Mediterranean States on various agenda items: the Democratic and Popular Republic of Algeria, the Arab Republic of Egypt, Israel, the Kingdom of Morocco, the Syrian Arab Republic, Tunisia.

4   Motivated by the political will, in the interest of peoples, to improve and intensify their relations and to contribute in Europe to peace, security, justice and co-operation as well as to rapprochement among themselves and with the other States of the world,

5   Determined, in consequence, to give full effect to the results of the Conference and to assure, among their States and throughout Europe, the benefits deriving from those results and thus to broaden, deepen and make continuing and lasting the process of détente,

6   The High Representatives of the participating States have solemnly adopted the following:

7   Questions Relating to Security in Europe

8   The States participating in the Conference on Security and Co-operation in Europe,

9   Reaffirming their objective of promoting better relations among themselves and ensuring conditions in which their people can live in true and lasting peace free from any threat to or attempt against their security;

10   Convinced of the need to exert efforts to make détente both a continuing and an increasingly viable and comprehensive process, universal in scope, and that the implementation of the results of the Conference on Security and Co-operation in Europe will be a major contribution to this process;

11   Considering that solidarity among peoples, as well as the common purpose of the participating States in achieving the aims as set forth by the Conference on Security and Co-operation in Europe, should lead to the development of better and closer relations among them in all fields and thus to overcoming the confrontation stemming from the character of their past relations, and to better mutual understanding;

12   Mindful of their common history and recognizing that the existence of elements common to their traditions and values can assist them in developing their relations, and desiring to search, fully taking into account the individuality and diversity of their positions and views, for possibilities of joining their efforts with a view to overcoming distrust and increasing confidence, solving the problems that separate them and co-operating in the interest of mankind;

13   Recognizing the indivisibility of security in Europe as well as their common interest in the development of co-operation throughout Europe and among themselves and expressing their intention to pursue efforts accordingly;

14   Recognizing the close link between peace and security in Europe and in the world as a whole and conscious of the need for each of them to make its contribution to the strengthening of world peace and security and to the promotion of fundamental rights, economic and social progress and well-being for all peoples;

15   Have adopted the following:

1.

16   (a)   Declaration on Principles Guiding Relations between Participating States

17   The participating States,

18   Reaffirming their commitment to peace, security and justice and the continuing development of friendly relations and co-operation;

19   Recognizing that this commitment, which reflects the interest and as-

pirations of peoples, constitutes for each participating State a present and future responsibility, heightened by experience of the past;

20   Reaffirming, in conformity with their membership in the United Nations and in accordance with the purposes and principles of the United Nations, their full and active support for the United Nations and for the enhancement of its role and effectiveness in strengthening international peace, security and justice, and in promoting the solution of international problems, as well as the development of friendly relations and co-operation among States;

21   Expressing their common adherence to the principles which are set forth below and are in conformity with the Charter of the United Nations, as well as their common will to act, in the application of these principles, in conformity with the purposes and principles of the Charter of the United Nations;

22   Declare their determination to respect and put into practice, each of them in its relations with all other participating States, irrespective of their political, economic or social systems as well as of their size, geographical location or level of economic development, the following principles, which all are of primary significance, guiding their mutual relations:

23   I   *Sovereign equality, respect for the rights inherent in sovereignty*

24   The participating States will respect each other's sovereign equality and individuality as well as all the rights inherent in and encompassed by its sovereignty, including in particular the right of every State to juridical equality, to territorial integrity and to freedom and political independence. They will also respect each other's right freely to choose and develop its political, social, economic and cultural systems as well as its right to determine its laws and regulations.

25   Within the framework of international law, all the participating States have equal rights and duties. They will respect each other's right to define and conduct as it wishes its relations with other States in accordance with international law and in the spirit of the present Declaration. They consider that their frontiers can be changed, in accordance with international law, by peaceful means and by agreement. They also have the right to belong or not to belong to international organizations, to be or not to be a party to bilateral or multilateral treaties including the right to be or not to be a party to treaties of alliance; they also have the right to neutrality.

26   II   *Refraining from the threat or use of force*

27   The participating States will refrain in their mutual relations, as well as in their international relations in general, from the threat or use of force against the territorial integrity or political independence of any State, or in any other manner inconsistent with the purposes of the United

Nations and with the present Declaration. No consideration may be invoked to serve to warrant resort to the threat or use of force in contravention of this principle.

28   Accordingly, the participating States will refrain from any acts constituting a threat of force or direct or indirect use of force against another participating State. Likewise they will refrain from any manifestation of force for the purpose of inducing another participating State to renounce the full exercise of its sovereign rights. Likewise they will also refrain in their mutual relations from any act of reprisal by force.

29   No such threat or use of force will be employed as a means of settling disputes, or questions likely to give rise to disputes, between them.

30   III   *Inviolability of frontiers*

31   The participating States regard as inviolable all one another's frontiers as well as the frontiers of all States in Europe and therefore they will refrain now and in the future from assaulting these frontiers.

32   Accordingly, they will also refrain from any demand for, or act of, seizure and usurpation of part or all of the territory of any participating State.

33   IV   *Territorial integrity of States*

34   The participating States will respect the territorial integrity of each of the participating States.

35   Accordingly, they will refrain from any action inconsistent with the purposes and principles of the Charter of the United Nations against the territorial integrity, political independence or the unity of any participating State, and in particular from any such action constituting a threat or use of force.

36   The participating States will likewise refrain from making each other's territory the object of military occupation or other direct or indirect measures of force in contravention of international law, or the object of acquisition by means of such measures or the threat of them. No such occupation or acquisition will be recognized as legal.

37   V   *Peaceful settlement of disputes*

38   The participating States will settle disputes among them by peaceful means in such a manner as not to endanger international peace and security, and justice.

39   They will endeavour in good faith and a spirit of cooperation to reach a rapid and equitable solution on the basis of international law.

40   For this purpose they will use such means as negotiation, enquiry, mediation, conciliation, arbitration, judicial settlement or other peaceful means of their own choice including any settlement procedure agreed to in advance of disputes to which they are parties.

41   In the event of failure to reach a solution by any of the above peaceful

means, the parties to a dispute will continue to seek a mutually agreed way to settle the dispute peacefully.

42 Participating States, parties to a dispute among them, as well as other participating States, will refrain from any action which might aggravate the situation to such a degree as to endanger the maintenance of international peace and security and thereby make a peaceful settlement of the dispute more difficult.

43 VI *Non-intervention in internal affairs*

44 The participating States will refrain from any intervention, direct or indirect, individual or collective, in the internal or external affairs falling within the domestic jurisdiction of another participating State, regardless of their mutual relations.

45 They will accordingly refrain from any form of armed intervention or threat of such intervention against another participating State.

46 They will likewise in all circumstances refrain from any other act of military, or of political, economic or other coercion designed to subordinate to their own interest the exercise by another participating State of the rights inherent in its sovereignty and thus to secure advantages of any kind.

47 Accordingly, they will, inter alia, refrain from direct or indirect assistance to terrorist activities, or to subversive or other activities directed towards the violent overthrow of the regime of another participating State.

48 VII *Respect for human rights and fundamental freedoms, including the freedom of thought, conscience, religion or belief*

49 The participating States will respect human rights and fundamental freedoms, including the freedom of thought, conscience, religion or belief, for all without distinction as to race, sex, language or religion.

50 They will promote and encourage the effective exercise of civil, political, economic, social, cultural and other rights and freedoms all of which derive from the inherent dignity of the human person and are essential for his free and full development.

51 Within this framework the participating States will recognize and respect the freedom of the individual to profess and practise, alone or in community with others, religion or belief acting in accordance with the dictates of his own conscience.

52 The participating States on whose territory national minorities exist will respect the right of persons belonging to such minorities to equality before the law, will afford them the full opportunity for the actual enjoyment of human rights and fundamental freedoms and will, in this manner, protect their legitimate interests in this sphere.

53 The participating States recognize the universal significance of human

rights and fundamental freedoms, respect for which is an essential factor for the peace, justice and well-being necessary to ensure the development of friendly relations and co-operation among themselves as among all States.

54   They will constantly respect these rights and freedoms in their mutual relations and will endeavour jointly and separately, including in co-operation with the United Nations, to promote universal and effective respect for them.

55   They confirm the right of the individual to know and act upon his rights and duties in this field.

56   In the field of human rights and fundamental freedoms, the participating States will act in conformity with the purposes and principles of the Charter of the United Nations and with the Universal Declaration of Human Rights. They will also fulfil their obligations as set forth in the international declarations and agreements in this field, including inter alia the International Covenants on Human Rights, by which they may be bound.

57   VIII   *Equal rights and self-determination of peoples*

58   The participating States will respect the equal rights of peoples and their right to self-determination, acting at all times in conformity with the purposes and principles of the Charter of the United Nations and with the relevant norms of international law, including those relating to territorial integrity of States.

59   By virtue of the principle of equal rights and self-determination of peoples, all peoples always have the right, in full freedom, to determine, when and as they wish, their internal and external political status, without external interference, and to pursue as they wish their political, economic, social and cultural development.

60   The participating States reaffirm the universal significance of respect for and effective exercise of equal rights and self-determination of peoples for the development of friendly relations among themselves as among all States; they also recall the importance of the elimination of any form of violation of this principle.

61   IX   *Co-operation among States*

62   The participating States will develop their co-operation with one another and with all States in all fields in accordance with the purposes and principles of the Charter of the United Nations. In developing their co-operation the participating States will place special emphasis on the fields as set forth within the framework of the Conference on Security and Co-operation in Europe, with each of them making its contribution in conditions of full equality.

63   They will endeavour, in developing their co-operation as equals, to promote mutual understanding and confidence, friendly and good-

neighbourly relations among themselves, international peace, security and justice. They will equally endeavour, in developing their co-operation, to improve the well-being of peoples and contribute to the fulfilment of their aspirations through, inter alia, the benefits resulting from increased mutual knowledge and from progress and achievement in the economic, scientific, technological, social, cultural and humanitarian fields. They will take steps to promote conditions favourable to making these benefits available to all; they will take into account the interest of all in the narrowing of differences in the levels of economic development, and in particular the interest of developing countries throughout the world.

64　They confirm that governments, institutions, organizations and persons have a relevant and positive role to play in contributing toward the achievement of these aims of their co-operation.

65　They will strive, in increasing their co-operation as set forth above, to develop closer relations among themselves on an improved and more enduring basis for the benefit of peoples.

66　x　*Fulfilment in good faith of obligations under international law*

67　The participating States will fulfil in good faith their obligations under international law, both those obligations arising from the generally recognized principles and rules of international law and those obligations arising from treaties or other agreements, in conformity with international law, to which they are parties.

68　In exercising their sovereign rights, including the right to determine their laws and regulations, they will conform with their legal obligations under international law; they will furthermore pay due regard to and implement the provisions in the Final Act of the Conference on Security and Co-operation in Europe.

69　The participating States confirm that in the event of a conflict between the obligations of the members of the United Nations under the Charter of the United Nations and their obligations under any treaty or other international agreement, their obligations under the Charter will prevail, in accordance with Article 103 of the Charter of the United nations.

70　All the principles set forth above are of primary significance and, accordingly, they will be equally and unreservedly applied, each of them being interpreted taking into account the others.

71　The participating States express their determination fully to respect and apply these principles, as set forth in the present Declaration, in all aspects, to their mutual relations and co-operation in order to ensure to each participating State the benefits resulting from the respect and application of these principles by all.

72　The participating States, paying due regard to the principles above and, in particular, to the first sentence of the tenth principle, "Fulfilment in good faith of obligations under international law," note that the present Declaration does not affect their rights and obligations, nor the corresponding treaties and other agreements and arrangements.

73   The participating States express the conviction that respect for these principles will encourage the development of normal and friendly relations and the progress of co-operation among them in all fields. They also express the conviction that respect for these principles will encourage the development of political contacts among them which in turn would contribute to better mutual understanding of their positions and views.

74   The participating States declare their intention to conduct their relations with all other States in the spirit of the principles contained in the present Declaration.

75   (b)   Matters related to giving effect to certain of the above Principles
76   (i) The participating States,
77   Reaffirming that they will respect and give effect to refraining from the threat or use of force and convinced of the necessity to make it an effective norm of international life,
78   Declare that they are resolved to respect and carry out, in their relations with one another, inter alia, the following provisions which are in conformity with the Declaration on Principles Guiding Relations between Participating States:
79   —To give effect and expression, by all the ways and forms which they consider appropriate, to the duty to refrain from the threat or use of force in their relations with one another.
80   —To refrain from any use of armed forces inconsistent with the purposes and principles of the Charter of the United Nations and the provisions of the Declaration on Principles Guiding Relations between Participating States, against another participating State, in particular from invasion of or attack on its territory.
81   —To refrain from any manifestation of force for the purpose of inducing another participating State to renounce the full exercise of its sovereign rights.
82   —To refrain from any act of economic coercion designed to subordinate to their own interest the exercise by another participating State of the rights inherent in its sovereignty and thus to secure advantages of any kind.
83   —To take effective measures which by their scope and by their nature constitute steps towards the ultimate achievement of general and complete disarmament under strict and effective international control.
84   —To promote, by all means which each of them considers appropriate,

a climate of confidence and respect among peoples consonant with their duty to refrain from propaganda for wars of aggression or for any threat or use of force inconsistent with the purposes of the United Nations and with the Declaration on Principles Guiding Relations between Participating States, against another participating State.

85 — To make every effort to settle exclusively by peaceful means any dispute between them, the continuance of which is likely to endanger the maintenance of international peace and security in Europe, and to seek, first of all, a solution through the peaceful means set forth in Article 33 of the United Nations Charter.

To refrain from any action which could hinder the peaceful settlement of disputes between the participating States.

86 (ii) The participating States,

87 Reaffirming their determination to settle their disputes as set forth in the Principle of Peaceful Settlement of Disputes;

88 Convinced that the peaceful settlement of disputes is a complement to refraining from the threat or use of force, both being essential though not exclusive factors for the maintenance and consolidation of peace and security;

89 Desiring to reinforce and to improve the methods at their disposal for the peaceful settlement of disputes;

90 1. Are resolved to pursue the examination and elaboration of a generally acceptable method for the peaceful settlement of disputes aimed at complementing existing methods, and to continue to this end to work upon the "Draft Convention on a European System for the Peaceful Settlement of Disputes" submitted by Switzerland during the second stage of the Conference on Security and Co-operation in Europe, as well as other proposals relating to it and directed towards the elaboration of such a method.

91 2. Decide that, on the invitation of Switzerland, a meeting of experts of all the participating States will be convoked in order to fulfil the mandate described in paragraph 1 above within the framework and under the procedures of the follow-up to the Conference laid down in the chapter "Follow-up to the Conference."

92 3. This meeting of experts will take place after the meeting of the representatives appointed by the Ministers of Foreign Affairs of the participating States, scheduled according to the chapter "Follow-up to the Conference" for 1977; the results of the work of this meeting of experts will be submitted to Governments.

2.

93 **Document on confidence-building measures and certain aspects of security and disarmament**

94   The participating States,

95   Desirous of eliminating the causes of tension that may exist among them and thus of contributing to the strengthening of peace and security in the world;

96   Determined to strengthen confidence among them and thus to contribute to increasing stability and security in Europe;

97   Determined further to refrain in their mutual relations, as well as in their international relations in general, from the threat or use of force against the territorial integrity or political independence of any State, or in any other manner inconsistent with the purposes of the United Nations and with the Declaration on Principles Guiding Relations between Participating States as adopted in this Final Act;

98   Recognizing the need to contribute to reducing the dangers of armed conflict and of misunderstanding or miscalculation of military activities which could give rise to apprehension, particularly in a situation where the participating States lack clear and timely information about the nature of such activities;

99   Taking into account considerations relevant to efforts aimed at lessening tension and promoting disarmament;

100   Recognizing that the exchange of observers by invitation at military manoeuvres will help to promote contacts and mutual understanding;

101   Having studied the question of prior notification of major military movements in the context of confidence-building;

102   Recognizing that there are other ways in which individual States can contribute further to their common objectives;

103   Convinced of the political importance of prior notification of major military manoeuvres for the promotion of mutual understanding and the strengthening of confidence, stability and security;

104   Accepting the responsibility of each of them to promote these objectives and to implement this measure, in accordance with the accepted criteria and modalities, as essentials for the realization of these objectives;

105   Recognizing that this measure deriving from political decision rests upon a voluntary basis;

106   Have adopted the following:

I

107   *Prior notification of major military manoeuvres*

108   They will notify their major military manoeuvres to all other participating States through usual diplomatic channels in accordance with the following provisions:

109   Notification will be given of major military manoeuvres exceeding a total of 25,000 troops, independently or combined with any possible air

or naval components (in this context the word "troops" includes amphibious and airborne troops). In the case of independent manoeuvres of amphibious or airborne troops, or of combined manoeuvres involving them, these troops will be included in this total. Furthermore, in the case of combined manoeuvres which do not reach the above total but which involve land forces together with significant numbers of either amphibious or airborne troops, or both, notification can also be given.

110   Notification will be given of major military manoeuvres which take place on the territory, in Europe, of any participating State as well as, if applicable, in the adjoining sea area and air space.

111   In the case of a participating State whose territory extends beyond Europe, prior notification need be given only of manoeuvres which take place in an area within 250 kilometres from its frontier facing or shared with any other European participating State; the participating State need not, however, give notification in cases in which that area is also contiguous to the participating State's frontier facing or shared with a non-European non-participating State.

112   Notification will be given 21 days or more in advance of the start of the manoeuvre or in the case of a manoeuvre arranged at shorter notice at the earliest possible opportunity prior to its starting date.

113   Notification will contain information of the designation, if any, the general purpose of and the States involved in the manoeuvre, the type or types and numerical strength of the forces engaged, the area and estimated time-frame of its conduct. The participating States will also, if possible, provide additional relevant information, particularly that related to the components of the forces engaged and the period of involvement of these forces.

114   *Prior notification of other military manoeuvres*

115   The participating States recognize that they can contribute further to strengthening confidence and increasing security and stability, and to this end may also notify smaller-scale military manoeuvres to other participating States, with special regard for those near the area of such manoeuvres.

116   To the same end, the participating States also recognize that they may notify other military manoeuvres conducted by them.

117   *Exchange of observers*

118   The participating States will invite other participating States, voluntarily and on a bilateral basis, in a spirit of reciprocity and goodwill towards all participating States, to send observers to attend military manoeuvres.

119   The inviting State will determine in each case the number of observers,

the procedures and conditions of their participation, and give other information which it may consider useful. It will provide appropriate facilities and hospitality.

120   The invitation will be given as far ahead as is conveniently possible through usual diplomatic channels.

121   *Prior notification of major military movements*

122   In accordance with the Final Recommendations of the Helsinki Consultations the participating States studied the question of prior notification of major military movements as a measure to strengthen confidence.

123   Accordingly, the participating States recognize that they may, at their own discretion and with a view to contributing to confidence-building, notify their major military movements.

124   In the same spirit, further consideration will be given by the States participating in the Conference on Security and Co-operation in Europe to the question of prior notification of major military movements, bearing in mind, in particular, the experience gained by the implementation of the measures which are set forth in this document.

125   *Other confidence-building measures*

126   The participating States recognize that there are other means by which their common objectives can be promoted.

127   In particular, they will, with due regard to reciprocity and with a view to better mutual understanding, promote exchanges by invitation among their military personnel, including visits by military delegations.

128   In order to make a fuller contribution to their common objective of confidence-building, the participating Staes, when conducting their military activities in the area covered by the provisions for the prior notification of major military manoeuvres, will duly take into account and respect this objective.

129   They also recognize that the experience gained by the implementation of the provisions set forth above, together with further efforts, could lead to developing and enlarging measures aimed at strengthening confidence.

II

130   *Questions relating to disarmament*

131   The participating States recognize the interest of all of them in efforts aimed at lessening military confrontation and promoting disarmament which are designed to complement political détente in Europe and to strengthen their security. They are convinced of the necessity to take effective measures in these fields which by their scope and by their nature constitute steps towards the ultimate achievement of general and complete disarmament under strict and effective international control, and which should result in strengthening peace and security throughout the world.

III

132 *General considerations*

133 Having considered the views expressed on various subjects related to the strengthening of security in Europe through joint efforts aimed at promoting détente and disarmament, the participating States, when engaged in such efforts, will, in this context, proceed, in particular, from the following essential considerations:

134 —The complementary nature of the political and military aspects of security;

135 —The interrelation between the security of each participating State and security in Europe as a whole and the relationship which exists, in the broader context of world security, between security in Europe and security in the Mediterranean area;

136 —Respect for the security interests of all States participating in the Conference on Security and Co-operation in Europe inherent in their sovereign equality;

137 —The importance that participants in negotiating fora see to it that information about relevant developments, progress and results is provided on an appropriate basis to other States participating in the Conference on Security and Co-operation in Europe and, in return, the justified interest of any of those States in having their views considered.

138 **Co-operation in the Field of Economics, of Science and Technology and of the Environment**

139 The participating States,

140 Convinced that their efforts to develop co-operation in the fields of trade, industry, science and technology, the environment and other areas of economic activity contribute to the reinforcement of peace and security in Europe and in the world as a whole,

141 Recognizing that co-operation in these fields would promote economic and social progress and the improvement of the conditions of life,

142 Aware of the diversity of their economic and social systems,

143 Reaffirming their will to intensify such co-operation between one another, irrespective of their systems,

144 Recognizing that such co-operation, with due regard for the different levels of economic development, can be developed, on the basis of equality and mutual satisfaction of the partners, and of reciprocity permitting, as a whole, an equitable distribution of advantages and obligations of comparable scale, with respect for bilateral and multilateral agreements,

145 Taking into account the interests of the developing countries throughout the world, including those among the participating countries as long as they are developing from the economic point of view; reaffirming their

will to co-operate for the achievement of the aims and objectives established by the appropriate bodies of the United Nations in the pertinent documents concerning development, it being understood that each participating State maintains the positions it has taken on them; giving special attention to the least developed countries,

146   Convinced that the growing world-wide economic interdependence calls for increasing common and effective efforts towards the solution of major world economic problems such as food, energy, commodities, monetary and financial problems, and therefore emphasizes the need for promoting stable and equitable international economic relations, thus contributing to the continuous and diversified economic development of all countries,

147   Having taken into account the work already undertaken by relevant international organizations and wishing to take advantage of the possibilities offered by these organizations, in particular by the United Nations Economic Commission for Europe, for giving effect to the provisions of the final documents of the Conference,

148   Considering that the guidelines and concrete recommendations contained in the following texts are aimed at promoting further development of their mutual economic relations, and convinced that their co-operation in this field should take place in full respect for the principles guiding relations among participating States as set forth in the relevant document,

149   Have adopted the following:

150   **1   Commercial Exchanges**
151   *General provisions*
152   The participating States,
153   Conscious of the growing role of international trade as one of the most important factors in economic growth and social progress,
154   Recognizing that trade represents an essential sector of their co-operation, and bearing in mind that the provisions contained in the above preamble apply in particular to this sector,
155   Considering that the volume and structure of trade among the participating States do not in all cases correspond to the possibilities created by the current level of their economic, scientific and technological development,
156   are resolved to promote, on the basis of the modalities of their economic co-operation, the expansion of their mutual trade in goods and services, and to ensure conditions favourable to such development;
157   recognize the beneficial effects which can result for the development of trade from the application of most favoured nation treatment;
158   will encourage the expansion of trade on as broad a multilateral basis as

possible, thereby endeavouring to utilize the various economic and commercial possibilities;

159   recognize the importance of bilateral and multilateral intergovernmental and other agreements for the long-term development of trade;

160   note the importance of monetary and financial questions for the development of international trade, and will endeavour to deal with them with a view to contributing to the continuous expansion of trade;

161   will endeavour to reduce or progressively eliminate all kinds of obstacles to the development of trade;

162   will foster a steady growth of trade while avoiding as far as possible abrupt fluctuations in their trade;

163   consider that their trade in various products should be conducted in such a way as not to cause or threaten to cause serious injury—and should the situation arise, market disruption—in domestic markets for these products and in particular to the detriment of domestic producers of like or directly competitive products; as regards the concept of market disruption, it is understood that it should not be invoked in a way inconsistent with the relevant provisions of their international agreements; if they resort to safeguard measures, they will do so in conformity with their commitments in this field arising from international agreements to which they are parties and will take account of the interests of the parties directly concerned;

164   will give due attention to measures for the promotion of trade and the diversification of its structure;

165   note that the growth and diversification of trade would contribute to widening the possibilities of choice of products;

166   consider it appropriate to create favourable conditions for the participation of firms, organizations and enterprises in the development of trade.

167   *Business contacts and facilities*

168   The participating States,

169   Conscious of the importance of the contribution which an improvement of business contacts, and the accompanying growth of confidence in business relationships, could make to the development of commercial and economic relations,

170   will take measures further to improve conditions for the expansion of contacts between representatives of official bodies, of the different organizations, enterprises, firms and banks concerned with foreign trade, in particular, where useful, between sellers and users of products and services, for the purpose of studying commercial possibilities, concluding contracts, ensuring their implementation and providing after-sales services;

171   will encourage organizations, enterprises and firms concerned with

foreign trade to take measures to accelerate the conduct of business negotiations;

172 will further take measures aimed at improving working conditions of representatives of foreign organizations, enterprises, firms and banks concerned with external trade, particularly as follows:

173 —by providing the necessary information, including information on legislation and procedures relating to the establishment and operation of permanent representation by the above mentioned bodies;

174 —by examining as favourably as possible requests for the establishment of permanent representation and of offices for this purpose, including, where appropriate, the opening of joint offices by two or more firms;

175 —by encouraging the provision, on conditions as favourable as possible and equal for all representatives of the above-mentioned bodies, of hotel accommodation, means of communication, and of other facilities normally required by them, as well as of suitable business and residential premises for purposes of permanent representation;

176 recognize the importance of such measures to encourage greater participation by small and medium sized firms in trade between participating States.

177 *Economic and commercial information*

178 The participating States,

179 Conscious of the growing role of economic and commercial information in the development of international trade,

180 Considering that economic information should be of such a nature as to allow adequate market analysis and to permit the preparation of medium and long term forecasts, thus contributing to the establishment of a continuing flow of trade and a better utilization of commercial possibilities,

181 Expressing their readiness to improve the quality and increase the quantity and supply of economic and relevant administrative information,

182 Considering that the value of statistical information on the international level depends to a considerable extent on the possibility of its comparability,

183 will promote the publication and dissemination of economic and commercial information at regular intervals and as quickly as possible, in particular:

184 —statistics concerning production, national income, budget, consumption and productivity;

185 —foreign trade statistics drawn up on the basis of comparable classification including breakdown by product with indication of volume and value, as well as country of origin or destination;

186 —laws and regulations concerning foreign trade;

187 —information allowing forecasts of development of the economy to assist in trade promotion, for example, information on the general orientation of national economic plans and programmes;

188 —other information to help businessmen in commercial contacts, for example, periodic directories, lists, and where possible, organizational charts of firms and organizations concerned with foreign trade;

189 will in addition to the above encourage the development of the exchange of economic and commercial information through, where appropriate, joint commissions for economic, scientific and technical co-operation, national and joint chambers of commerce, and other suitable bodies;

190 will support a study, in the framework of the United Nations Economic Commission for Europe, of the possibilities of creating a multilateral system of notification of laws and regulations concerning foreign trade and changes therein;

191 will encourage international work on the harmonization of statistical nomenclatures, notably in the United Nations Economic Commission for Europe.

192 *Marketing*

193 The participating States,

194 Recognizing the importance of adapting production to the requirements of foreign markets in order to ensure the expansion of international trade,

195 Conscious of the need of exporters to be as fully familiar as possible with and take account of the requirements of potential users,

196 will encourage organizations, enterprises and firms concerned with foreign trade to develop further the knowledge and techniques required for effective marketing;

197 will encourage the improvement of conditions for the implementation of measures to promote trade and to satisfy the needs of users in respect of imported products, in particular through market research and advertising measures as well as, where useful, the establishment of supply facilities, the furnishing of spare parts, the functioning of after sales services, and the training of the necessary local technical personnel;

198 will encourage international co-operation in the field of trade promotion, including marketing, and the work undertaken on these subjects within the international bodies, in particular the United Nations Economic Commission for Europe.

199 2   Industrial co-operation and projects of common interest

200 *Industrial co-operation*

201 The participating States,

202   Considering that industrial co-operation, being motivated by economic considerations, can

203   —create lasting ties thus strengthening long-term overall economic co-operation,

204   —contribute to economic growth as well as to the expansion and diversification of international trade and to a wider utilization of modern technology,

205   —lead to the mutually advantageous utilization of economic complementarities through better use of all factors of production, and

206   —accelerate the industrial development of all those who take part in such co-operation,

207   propose to encourage the development of industrial co-operation between the competent organizations, enterprises and firms of their countries;

208   consider that industrial co-operation may be facilitated by means of intergovernmental and other bilateral and multilateral agreements between the interested parties;

209   note that in promoting industrial co-operation they should bear in mind the economic structures and the development levels of their countries;

210   note that industrial co-operation is implemented by means of contracts concluded between competent organizations, enterprises and firms on the basis of economic considerations;

211   express their willingness to promote measures designed to create favourable conditions for industrial co-operation;

212   recognize that industrial co-operation covers a number of forms of economic relations going beyond the framework of conventional trade, and that in concluding contracts on industrial co-operation the partners will determine jointly the appropriate forms and conditions of co-operation; taking into account their mutual interests and capabilities;

213   recognize further that, if it is in their mutual interest, concrete forms such as the following may be useful for the development of industrial co-operation: joint production and sale, specialization in production and sale, construction, adaptation and modernization of industrial plants, co-operation for the setting up of complete industrial installations with a view to thus obtaining part of the resultant products, mixed companies, exchanges of "know-how," of technical information, of patents and of licences, and joint industrial research within the framework of specific co-operation projects;

214   recognize that new forms of industrial co-operation can be applied with a view to meeting specific needs;

215   note the importance of economic, commercial, technical and adminis-

trative information such as to ensure the development of industrial co-operation;

216   Consider it desirable:

217   to improve the quality and the quantity of information relevant to industrial co-operation, in particular the laws and regulations, including those relating to foreign exchange, general orientation of national economic plans and programmes as well as programme priorities and economic conditions of the market; and

218   to disseminate as quickly as possible published documentation thereon;

219   will encourage all forms of exchange of information and communication of experience relevant to industrial co-operation, including through contacts between potential partners and, where appropriate, through joint commissions for economic, industrial, scientific and technical co-operation, national and joint chambers of commerce, and other suitable bodies;

220   consider it desirable, with a view to expanding industrial co-operation, to encourage the exploration of co-operation possibilities and the implementation of co-operation projects and will take measures to this end, *inter alia*, by facilitating and increasing all forms of business contacts between competent organizations, enterprises and firms and between their respective qualified personnel;

221   note that the provisions adopted by the Conference relating to business contacts in the economic and commercial fields also apply to foreign organizations, enterprises and firms engaged in industrial co-operation, taking into account the specific conditions of this co-operation, and will endeavour to ensure, in particular, the existence of appropriate working conditions for personnel engaged in the implementation of co-operation projects;

222   consider it desirable that proposals for industrial co-operation projects should be sufficiently specific and should contain the necessary economic and technical data, in particular preliminary estimates of the cost of the project, information on the form of co-operation envisaged, and market possibilities, to enable potential partners to proceed with initial studies and to arrive at decisions in the shortest possible time;

223   will encourage the parties concerned with industrial co-operation to take measures to accelerate the conduct of negotiations for the conclusion of co-operation contracts;

224   recommend further the continued examination—for example within the framework of the United Nations Economic Commission for Europe—of means of improving the provision of information to those concerned on general conditions of industrial co-operation and guidance on the preparation of contracts in this field;

225   consider it desirable to further improve conditions for the implementation of industrial co-operation projects, in particular with respect to:

226   —the protection of the interests of the partners in industrial co-operation projects, including the legal protection of the various kinds of property involved;

227   —the consideration, in ways that are compatible with their economic systems, of the needs and possibilities of industrial co-operation within the framework of economic policy and particularly in national economic plans and programmes;

228   consider it desirable that the partners, when concluding industrial co-operation contracts, should devote due attention to provisions concerning the extension of the necessary mutual assistance and the provision of the necessary information during the implementation of these contracts, in particular with a view to attaining the required technical level and quality of the products resulting from such co-operation;

229   recognize the usefulness of an increased participation of small and medium sized firms in industrial co-operation projects.

230   *Projects of common interest*

231   The participating States,

232   Considering that their economic potential and their natural resources permit, through common efforts, long-term co-operation in the implementation, including at the regional or sub-regional level, of major projects of common interest, and that these may contribute to the speeding-up of the economic development of the countries participating therein,

233   Considering it desirable that the competent organizations, enterprises and firms of all countries should be given the possibility of indicating their interest in participating in such projects, and, in case of agreement, of taking part in their implementation,

234   Noting that the provisions adopted by the Conference relating to industrial co-operation are also applicable to projects of common interest,

235   regard it as necessary to encourage, where appropriate, the investigation by competent and interested organizations, enterprises and firms of the possibilities for the carrying out of projects of common interest in the fields of energy resources and of the exploitation of raw materials, as well as of transport and communications;

236   regard it as desirable that organizations, enterprises and firms exploring the possibilities of taking part in projects of common interest exchange with their potential partners, through the appropriate channels, the requisite economic, legal, financial and technical information pertaining to these projects;

237   consider that the fields of energy resources, in particular, petroleum, natural gas and coal, and the extraction and processing of mineral raw

materials, in particular, iron ore and bauxite, are suitable ones for strengthening long-term economic co-operation and for the development of trade which could result;

238 consider that possibilities for projects of common interest with a view to long-term economic co-operation also exist in the following fields:

239 —exchanges of electrical energy within Europe with a view to utilizing the capacity of the electrical power stations as rationally as possible;

240 —co-operation in research for new sources of energy and, in particular, in the field of nuclear energy;

241 —development of road networks and co-operation aimed at establishing a coherent navigable network in Europe;

242 —co-operation in research and the perfecting of equipment for multimodal transport operations and for the handling of containers;

243 recommend that the States interested in projects of common interest should consider under what conditions it would be possible to establish them, and if they so desire, create the necessary conditions for their actual implementation.

244 **3 Provisions concerning trade and industrial co-operation**

245 *Harmonization of standards*

246 The participating States,

247 Recognizing the development of international harmonization of standards and technical regulations and of international co-operation in the field of certification as an important means of eliminating technical obstacles to international trade and industrial co-operation, thereby facilitating their development and increasing productivity,

248 reaffirm their interest to achieve the widest possible international harmonization of standards and technical regulations;

249 express their readiness to promote international agreements and other appropriate arrangements on acceptance of certificates of conformity with standards and technical regulations;

250 consider it desirable to increase international co-operation on standardization, in particular by supporting the activities of intergovernmental and other appropriate organizations in this field.

251 *Arbitration*

252 The participating States,

253 Considering that the prompt and equitable settlement of disputes which may arise from commercial transactions relating to goods and services and contracts for industrial co-operation would contribute to expanding and facilitating trade and co-operation,

254 Considering that arbitration is an appropriate means of settling such disputes,

255 recommend, where appropriate, to organizations, enterprises and firms

in their countries, to include arbitration clauses in commercial contracts and industrial co-operation contracts, or in special agreements;

256 recommend that the provisions on arbitration should provide for arbitration under a mutually acceptable set of arbitration rules, and permit arbitration in a third country, taking into account existing intergovernmental and other agreements in this field.

257 *Specific bilateral arrangements*

258 The participating States,

259 Conscious of the need to facilitate trade and to promote the application of new forms of industrial co-operation,

260 will consider favourably the conclusion, in appropriate cases, of specific bilateral agreements concerning various problems of mutual interest in the fields of commercial exchanges and industrial co-operation, in particular with a view to avoiding double taxation and to facilitating the transfer of profits and the return of the value of the assets invested.

261 **4 Science and technology**

262 The participating States,

263 Convinced that scientific and technological co-operation constitutes an important contribution to the strengthening of security and co-operation among them, in that it assists the effective solution of problems of common interest and the improvement of the conditions of human life,

264 Considering that in developing such co-operation, it is important to promote the sharing of information and experience, facilitating the study and transfer of scientific and technological achievements, as well as the access to such achievements on a mutually advantageous basis and in fields of co-operation agreed between interested parties,

265 Considering that it is for the potential partners, i.e. the competent organizations, institutions, enterprises, scientists and technologists of the participating States to determine the opportunities for mutually beneficial co-operation and to develop its details,

266 Affirming that such co-operation can be developed and implemented bilaterally and multilaterally at the governmental and non-governmental levels, for example, through intergovernmental and other agreements, international programmes, co-operative projects and commercial channels, while utilizing also various forms of contacts, including direct and individual contacts,

267 Aware of the need to take measures further to improve scientific and technological co-operation between them,

268 *Possibilities for improving co-operation*

269 Recognize that possibilities exist for further improving scientific and

technological co-operation, and to this end, express their intention to remove obstacles to such co-operation, in particular through:

270   —the improvement of opportunities for the exchange and dissemination of scientific and technological information among the parties interested in scientific and technological research and co-operation including information related to the organization and implementation of such co-operation;

271   —the expeditious implementation and improvement in organization, including programmes, of international visits of scientists and specialists in connexion with exchanges, conferences and co-operation;

272   —the wider use of commercial channels and activities for applied scientific and technological research and for the transfer of achievements obtained in this field while providing information on and protection of intellectual and industrial property rights;

273   *Fields of co-operation*

274   Consider that possibilities to expand co-operation exist within the areas given below as examples, noting that it is for potential partners in the participating countries to identify and develop projects and arrangements of mutual interest and benefit:

275   *Agriculture*   Research into new methods and technologies for increasing the productivity of crop cultivation and animal husbandry; the application of chemistry to agriculture; the design, construction and utilization of agricultural machinery; technologies of irrigation and other agricultural land improvement works;

276   *Energy*   New technologies of production, transport and distribution of energy aimed at improving the use of existing fuels and sources of hydroenergy, as well as research in the field of new energy sources, including nuclear, solar and geothermal energy;

277   *New technologies, rational use of resources*   Research on new technologies and equipment designed in particular to reduce energy consumption and to minimize or eliminate waste;

278   *Transport technology*   Research on the means of transport and the technology applied to the development and operation of international, national and urban transport networks including container transport as well as transport safety;

279   *Physics*   Study of problems in high energy physics and plasma physics; research in the field of theoretical and experimental nuclear physics;

280   *Chemistry*   Research on problems in electrochemistry and the chemistry of polymers, of natural products, and of metals and alloys, as well as the development of improved chemical technology, especially materials processing; practical application of the latest achievements of chemistry to industry, construction and other sectors of the economy;

281   *Meteorology and hydrology*   Meteorological and hydrological research, including methods of collection, evaluation and transmission of data and their utilization for weather forecasting and hydrology forecasting;

282   *Oceanography*   Oceanographic research, including the study of air/sea interactions;

283   *Seismological research*   Study and forecasting of earthquakes and associated geological changes; development and research of technology of seism-resisting constructions;

284   *Research on glaciology, permafrost and problems of life under conditions of cold*   Research on glaciology and permafrost; transportation and construction technologies; human adaptation to climatic extremes and changes in the living conditions of indigenous populations;

285   *Computer, communication and information technologies*   Development of computers as well as of telecommunications and information systems; technology associated with computers and telecommunications, including their use for management systems, for production processes, for automation, for the study of economic problems, in scientific research and for the collection, processing and dissemination of information;

286   *Space research*   Space exploration and the study of the earth's natural resources and the natural environment by remote sensing in particular with the assistance of satellites and rocket-probes;

287   *Medicine and public health*   Research on cardiovascular, tumour and virus diseases, molecular biology, neurophysiology; development and testing of new drugs; study of contemporary problems of pediatrics, gerontology and the organization and techniques of medical services;

289   *Environmental research*   Research on specific scientific and technological problems related to human environment.

289   *Forms and methods of co-operation*

290   Express their view that scientific and technological co-operation should, in particular, employ the following forms and methods:

291   —exchange and circulation of books, periodicals and other scientific and technological publications and papers among interested organizations, scientific and technological institutions, enterprises and scientists and technologists, as well as participation in international programmes for the abstracting and indexing of publications;

292   —exchanges and visits as well as other direct contacts and communications among scientists and technologists, on the basis of mutual agreement and other arrangements, for such purposes as consultations, lecturing and conducting research, including the use of laboratories, scientific libraries, and other documentation centres in connexion therewith;

293   —holding of international and national conferences, symposia, semi-

nars, courses and other meetings of a scientific and technological character, which would include the participation of foreign scientists and technologists;

294   —joint preparation and implementation of programmes and projects of mutual interest on the basis of consultation and agreement among all parties concerned, including, where possible and appropriate, exchanges of experience and research results, and correlation of research programmes, between scientific and technological research institutions and organizations;

295   —use of commercial channels and methods for identifying and transferring technological and scientific developments, including the conclusion of mutually beneficial co-operation arrangements between firms and enterprises in fields agreed upon between them and for carrying out, where appropriate, joint research and development programmes and projects;

296   consider it desirable that periodic exchanges of views and information take place on scientific policy, in particular on general problems of orientation and administration of research and the question of a better use of large-scale scientific and experimental equipment on a co-operative basis;

297   recommend that, in developing co-operation in the field of science and technology, full use be made of existing practices of bilateral and multilateral co-operation, including that of a regional or sub-regional character, together with the forms and methods of co-operation described in this document;

298   recommend further that more effective utilization be made of the possibilities and capabilities of existing international organizations, intergovernmental and non-governmental, concerned with science and technology, for improving exchanges of information and experience, as well as for developing other forms of co-operation in fields of common interest, for example:

299   —in the United Nations Economic Commission for Europe, study of possibilities for expanding multilateral co-operation, taking into account models for projects and research used in various international organizations; and for sponsoring conferences, symposia, and study and working groups such as those which would bring together younger scientists and technologists with eminent specialists in their field;

300   —through their participation in particular international scientific and technological co-operation programmes, including those of UNESCO and other international organizations, pursuit of continuing progress towards the objectives of such programmes, notably those of UNISIST with particular respect to information policy guidance, technical advice, information contributions and data processing.

301   **5   Environment**
302   The participating States,
303   Affirming that the protection and improvement of the environment, as well as the protection of nature and the rational utilization of its resources in the interests of present and future generations, is one of the tasks of major importance to the well-being of peoples and the economic development of all countries and that many environmental problems, particularly in Europe, can be solved effectively only through close international co-operation,
304   Acknowledging that each of the participating States, in accordance with the principles of international law, ought to ensure, in a spirit of co-operation, that activities carried out on its territory do not cause degradation of the environment in another State or in areas lying beyond the limits of national jurisdiction,
305   Considering that the success of any environmental policy presupposes that all population groups and social forces, aware of their responsibilities, help to protect and improve the environment, which necessitates continued and thorough educative action, particularly with regard to youth,
306   Affirming that experience has shown that economic development and technological progress must be compatible with the protection of the environment and the preservation of historical and cultural values; that damage to the environment is best avoided by preventive measures; and that the ecological balance must be preserved in the exploitation and management of natural resources,
307   *Aims of co-operation*
308   Agree to the following aims of co-operation, in particular:
309   —to study, with a view to their solution, those environmental problems which, by their nature, are of a multilateral, bilateral, regional or sub-regional dimension; as well as to encourage the development of an interdisciplinary approach to environmental problems;
310   —to increase the effectiveness of national and international measures for the protection of the environment, by the comparison and, if appropriate, the harmonization of methods of gathering and analyzing facts, by improving the knowledge of pollution phenomena and rational utilization of natural resources, by the exchange of information, by the harmonization of definitions and the adoption, as far as possible, of a common terminology in the field of the environment:
311   —to take the necessary measures to bring environmental policies closer together and, where appropriate and possible, to harmonize them;
312   —to encourage, where possible and appropriate, national and international efforts by their interested organizations, enterprises and firms

in the development, production and improvement of equipment designed for monitoring, protecting and enhancing the environment.

313   *Fields of co-operation*

314   To attain these aims, the participating States will make use of every suitable opportunity to co-operate in the field of environment and, in particular, within the areas described below as examples:

315   *Control of air pollution*   Desulphurization of fossil fuels and exhaust gases; pollution control of heavy metals, particles, aerosols, nitrogen oxides, in particular those emitted by transport, power stations, and other industrial plants; systems and methods of observation and control of air pollution and its effects, including long-range transport of air pollutants;

316   *Water pollution control and fresh water utilization*   Prevention and control of water pollution, in particular of transboundary rivers and international lakes; techniques for the improvement of the quality of water and further development of ways and means for industrial and municipal sewage effluent purification; methods of assessment of fresh water resources and the improvement of their utilization, in particular by developing methods of production which are less polluting and lead to less consumption of fresh water;

317   *Protection of the marine environment*   Protection of the marine environment of participating States, and especially the Mediterranean Sea, from pollutants emanating from land-based sources and those from ships and other vessels, notably the harmful substances listed in Annexes i and ii to the London Convention on the Prevention of Marine Pollution by the Dumping of Wastes and Other Matters; problems of maintaining marine ecological balances and food chains, in particular such problems as may arise from the exploration and exploitation of biological and mineral resources of the seas and the sea-bed;

318   *Land utilization and soils*   Problems associated with more effective use of lands, including land amelioration, reclamation and recultivation; control of soil pollution, water and air erosion, as well as other forms of soil degradation; maintaining and increasing the productivity of soils with due regard for the possible negative effects of the application of chemical fertilizers and pesticides;

319   *Nature conservation and nature reserves*   Protection of nature and nature reserves; conservation and maintenance of existing genetic resources, especially rare animal and plant species; conservation of natural ecological systems; establishment of nature reserves and other protected landscapes and areas, including their use for research, tourism, recreation and other purposes;

320   *Improvement of environmental conditions in areas of human settle-*

ment   Environmental conditions associated with transport, housing, working areas, urban development and planning, water supply and sewage disposal systems; assessment of harmful effects of noise, and noise control methods; collection, treatment and utilization of wastes, including the recovery and recycling of materials; research on substitutes for non-biodegradable substances;

321   *Fundamental research, monitoring, forecasting and assessment of environmental changes*   Study of changes in climate, landscapes and ecological balances under the impact of both natural factors and human activities; forecasting of possible genetic changes in flora and fauna as a result of environmental pollution; harmonization of statistical data, development of scientific concepts and systems of monitoring networks, standardized methods of observation, measurement and assessment of changes in the biosphere; assessment of the effects of environmental pollution levels and degradation of the environment upon human health; study and development of criteria and standards for various environmental pollutants and regulation regarding production and use of various products;

322   *Legal and administrative measures*   Legal and administrative measures for the protection of the environment including procedures for establishing environmental impact assessments.

323   *Forms and methods of co-operation*

324   The participating States declare that problems relating to the protection and improvement of the environment will be solved on both a bilateral and a multilateral, including regional and sub-regional, basis, making full use of existing patterns and forms of co-operation. They will develop co-operation in the field of the environment in particular by taking into consideration the Stockholm Declaration on the Human Environment, relevant resolutions of the United Nations General Assembly and the United Nations Economic Commission for Europe Prague symposium on environmental problems.

325   The participating States are resolved that co-operation in the field of the environment will be implemented in particular through:

326   —exchanges of scientific and technical information, documentation and research results, including information on the means of determining the possible effects on the environment of technical and economic activities;

327   —organization of conferences, symposia and meetings of experts;

328   —exchanges of scientists, specialists and trainees;

329   —joint preparation and implementation of programmes and projects for the study and solution of various problems of environmental protection;

330   —harmonization, where appropriate and necessary, of environmental

protection standards and norms, in particular with the object of avoiding possible difficulties in trade which may arise from efforts to resolve ecological problems of production processes and which relate to the achievement of certain environmental qualities in manufactured products;

331   —consultations on various aspects of environmental protection, as agreed upon among countries concerned, especially in connexion with problems which could have international consequences.

332   The participating States will further develop such co-operation by:

333   —promoting the progressive development, codification and implementation of international law as one means of preserving and enhancing the human environment, including principles and practices, as accepted by them, relating to pollution and other environmental damage caused by activities within the jurisdiction or control of their States affecting other countries and regions;

334   —supporting and promoting the implementation of relevant international Conventions to which they are parties, in particular those designed to prevent and combat marine and fresh water pollution, recommending States to ratify Conventions which have already been signed, as well as considering possibilities of accepting other appropriate Conventions to which they are not parties at present;

335   —advocating the inclusion, where appropriate and possible, of the various areas of co-operation into the programmes of work of the United Nations Economic Commission for Europe, supporting such co-operation within the framework of the Commission and of the United Nations Environment Programme, and taking into account the work of other competent international organizations of which they are members;

336   —making wider use, in all types of co-operation, of information already available from national and international sources, including internationally agreed criteria, and utilizing the possibilities and capabilities of various competent international organizations.

337   The participating States agree on the following recommendations on specific measures:

338   —to develop through international co-operation an extensive programme for the monitoring and evaluation of the long-range transport of air pollutants, starting with sulphur dioxide and with possible extension to other pollutants, and to this end to take into account basic elements of a co-operation programme which were identified by the experts who met in Oslo in December 1974 at the invitation of the Norwegian Institute of Air Research;

339   —to advocate that within the framework of the United Nations Economic Commission for Europe a study be carried out of procedures and relevant experience relating to the activities of Governments in

developing the capabilities of their countries to predict adequately environmental consequences of economic activities and technological development.

340 **6 Co-operation in other areas**
341 *Development of transport*
342 The participating States,
343 Considering that the improvement of the conditions of transport constitutes one of the factors essential to the development of co-operation among them,
344 Considering that it is necessary to encourage the development of transport and the solution of existing problems by employing appropriate national and international means,
345 Taking into account the work being carried out on these subjects by existing international organizations, especially by the Inland Transport Committee of the United Nations Economic Commission for Europe,
346 note that the speed of technical progress in the various fields of transport makes desirable a development of co-operation and an increase in exchanges of information among them;
347 declare themselves in favour of a simplification and a harmonization of administrative formalities in the field of international transport, in particular at frontiers;
348 consider it desirable to promote, while allowing for their particular national circumstances in this sector, the harmonization of administrative and technical provisions concerning safety in road, rail, river, air and sea transport;
349 express their intention to encourage the development of international inland transport of passengers and goods as well as the possibilities of adequate participation in such transport on the basis of reciprocal advantage;
350 declare themselves in favour, with due respect for their rights and international commitments, of the elimination of disparities arising from the legal provisions applied to traffic on inland waterways which are subject to international conventions and, in particular, of the disparity in the application of those provisions; and to this end invite the member States of the Central Commission for the Navigation of the Rhine, of the Danube Commission and of other bodies to develop the work and studies now being carried out, in particular within the United Nations Economic Commission for Europe;
351 express their willingness, with a view to improving international rail transport and with due respect for their rights and international commitments, to work towards the elimination of difficulties arising from disparities in existing international legal provisions governing the recip-

rocal railway transport of passengers and goods between their territories;

352 express the desire for intensification of the work being carried out by existing international organizations in the field of transport, especially that of the Inland Transport Committee of the United Nations Economic Commission for Europe, and express their intention to contribute thereto by their efforts;

353 consider that examination by the participating States of the possibility of their accession to the different conventions or to membership of international organizations specializing in transport matters, as well as their efforts to implement conventions when ratified, could contribute to the strengthening of their co-operation in this field.

354 *Promotion of tourism*

355 The participating States,

356 Aware of the contribution made by international tourism to the development of mutual understanding among peoples, to increased knowledge of other countries' achievements in various fields, as well as to economic, social and cultural progress,

357 Recognizing the interrelationship between the development of tourism and measures taken in other areas of economic activity,

358 express their intention to encourage increased tourism on both an individual and group basis in particular by:

359 —encouraging the improvement of the tourist infrastructure and co-operation in this field;

360 —encouraging the carrying out of joint tourist projects including technical co-operation, particularly where this is suggested by territorial proximity and the convergence of tourist interests;

361 —encouraging the exchange of information, including relevant laws and regulations, studies, data and documentation relating to tourism, and by improving statistics with a view to facilitating their comparability;

362 —dealing in a positive spirit with questions connected with the allocation of financial means for tourist travel abroad, having regard to their economic possibilities, as well as with those connected with the formalities required for such travel, taking into account other provisions on tourism adopted by the Conference;

363 —facilitating the activities of foreign travel agencies and passenger transport companies in the promotion of international tourism;

364 —encouraging tourism outside the high season;

365 —examining the possibilities of exchanging specialists and students in the field of tourism, with a view to improving their qualifications;

366 —promoting conferences and symposia on the planning and development of tourism;

367 consider it desirable to carry out in the appropriate international

framework, and with the co-operation of the relevant national bodies, detailed studies on tourism, in particular:

368   —a comparative study on the status and activities of travel agencies as well as on ways and means of achieving better co-operation among them;

369   —a study of the problems raised by the seasonal concentration of vacations, with the ultimate objective of encouraging tourism outside peak periods;

370   —studies of the problems arising in areas where tourism has injured the environment;

371   consider also that interested parties might wish to study the following questions:

372   —uniformity of hotel classification; and

373   —tourist routes comprising two or more countries;

374   will endeavour, where possible, to ensure that the development of tourism does not injure the environment and the artistic, historic and cultural heritage in their respective countries;

375   will pursue their co-operation in the field of tourism bilaterally and multilaterally with a view to attaining the above objectives.

376   *Economic and social aspects of migrant labour*

377   The participating States,

378   Considering that the movements of migrant workers in Europe have reached substantial proportions, and that they constitute an important economic, social and human factor for host countries as well as for countries of origin,

379   Recognizing that workers' migrations have also given rise to a number of economic, social, human and other problems in both the receiving countries and the countries of origin,

380   Taking due account of the activities of the competent international organizations, more particularly the International Labour Organisation, in this area,

381   are of the opinion that the problems arising bilaterally from the migration of workers in Europe as well as between the participating States should be dealt with by the parties directly concerned, in order to resolve these problems in their mutual interest, in the light of the concern of each State involved to take due account of the requirements resulting from its socio-economic situation, having regard to the obligation of each State to comply with the bilateral and multilateral agreements to which it is party, and with the following aims in view:

382   to encourage the efforts of the countries of origin directed towards increasing the possibilities of employment for their nationals in their own territories, in particular by developing economic co-operation ap-

propriate for this purpose and suitable for the host countries and the countries of origin concerned;

383   to ensure, through collaboration between the host country and the country of origin, the conditions under which the orderly movement of workers might take place, while at the same time protecting their personal and social welfare and, if appropriate, to organize the recruitment of migrant workers and the provision of elementary language and vocational training;

384   to ensure equality of rights between migrant workers and nationals of the host countries with regard to conditions of employment and work and to social security, and to endeavour to ensure that migrant workers may enjoy satisfactory living conditions, especially housing conditions;

385   to endeavour to ensure, as far as possible, that migrant workers may enjoy the same opportunities as nationals of the host countries of finding other suitable employment in the event of unemployment;

386   to regard with favour the provision of vocational training to migrant workers and, as far as possible, free instruction in the language of the host country, in the framework of their employment;

387   to confirm the right of migrant workers to receive, as far as possible, regular information in their own language, covering both their country of origin and the host country;

388   to ensure that the children of migrant workers established in the host country have access to the education usually given there, under the same conditions as the children of that country and, furthermore, to permit them to receive supplementary education in their own language, national culture, history and geography;

389   to bear in mind that migrant workers, particularly those who have acquired qualifications, can by returning to their countries after a certain period of time help to remedy any deficiency of skilled labour in their country of origin;

390   to facilitate, as far as possible, the reuniting of migrant workers with their families;

391   to regard with favour the efforts of the countries of origin to attract the savings of migrant workers, with a view to increasing, within the framework of their economic development, appropriate opportunities for employment, thereby facilitating the reintegration of these workers on their return home.

392   *Training of personnel*

393   The participating States,

394   Conscious of the importance of the training and advanced training of professional staff and technicians for the economic development of every country,

395   declare themselves willing to encourage co-operation in this field notably by promoting exchange of information on the subject of institutions,
programmes and methods of training and advanced training open to
professional staff and technicians in the various sectors of economic
activity and especially in those of management, public planning, agriculture and commercial and banking techniques;

396   consider that it is desirable to develop, under mutually acceptable
conditions, exchanges of professional staff and technicians, particularly
through training activities, of which it would be left to the competent
and interested bodies in the participating States to discuss the modalities
—duration, financing, education and qualification levels of potential
participants;

397   declare themselves in favour of examining, through appropriate channels, the possibilities of co-operating on the organization and carrying
out of vocational training on the job, more particularly in professions
involving modern techniques.

398   Questions relating to Security and Co-operation in the Mediterranean
399   The participating States,
400   Conscious of the geographical, historical, cultural, economic and political aspects of their relationship with the non-participating Mediterranean States,
401   Convinced that security in Europe is to be considered in the broader
context of world security and is closely linked with security in the
Mediterranean area as a whole, and that accordingly the process of
improving security should not be confined to Europe but should extend
to other parts of the world, and in particular to the Mediterranean area,
402   Believing that the strengthening of security and the intensification of co-
operation in Europe would stimulate positive processes in the Mediterranean region, and expressing their intention to contribute towards
peace, security and justice in the region, in which ends the participating
States and the non-participating Mediterranean States have a common
interest,
403   Recognizing the importance of their mutual economic relations with
the non-participating Mediterranean States, and conscious of their common interest in the further development of co-operation,
404   Noting with appreciation the interest expressed by the non-participating
Mediterranean States in the Conference since its inception, and having
duly taken their contributions into account,
405   Declare their intention:
406   —to promote the development of good-neighbourly relations with the
non-participating Mediterranean States in conformity with the purposes
and principles of the Charter of the United Nations, on which their

relations are based, and with the United Nations Declaration on Principles of International Law concerning Friendly Relations and Cooperation among States and accordingly, in this context, to conduct their relations with the non-participating Mediterranean States in the spirit of the principles set forth in the Declaration on Principles Guiding Relations between Participating States;

407 —to seek, by further improving their relations with the non-participating Mediterranean States, to increase mutual confidence, so as to promote security and stability in the Mediterranean area as a whole;

408 —to encourage with the non-participating Mediterranean States the development of mutually beneficial co-operation in the various fields of economic activity, especially by expanding commercial exchanges, on the basis of a common awareness of the necessity for stability and progress in trade relations, of their mutual economic interests, and of differences in the levels of economic development, thereby promoting their economic advancement and well-being;

409 —to contribute to a diversified development of the economies of the non-participating Mediterranean countries, whilst taking due account of their national development objectives, and to co-operate with them, especially in the sectors of industry, science and technology, in their efforts to achieve a better utilization of their resources, thus promoting a more harmonious development of economic relations;

410 —to intensify their efforts and their co-operation on a bilateral and multilateral basis with the non-participating Mediterranean States directed towards the improvement of the environment of the Mediterranean, especially the safeguarding of the biological resources and ecological balance of the sea by appropriate measures including the prevention and control of pollution; to this end, and in view of the present situation, to co-operate through competent international organizations and in particular within the United Nations Environment Programme (UNEP);

412 —to promote further contacts and co-operation with the non-participating Mediterranean States in other relevant fields.

412 In order to advance the objectives set forth above, the participating States also declare their intention of maintaining and amplifying the contacts and dialogue as initiated by the CSCE with the non-participating Mediterranean States to include all the States of the Mediterranean, with the purpose of contributing to peace, reducing armed forces in the region, strengthening security, lessening tensions in the region, and widening the scope of co-operation, ends in which all share a common interest, as well as with the purpose of defining further common objectives.

413 The participating States would seek, in the framework of their multi-

lateral efforts, to encourage progress and appropriate initiatives and to proceed to an exchange of views on the attainment of the above purposes.

414   Co-operation in Humanitarian and Other Fields

415   The participating States,

416   Desiring to contribute to the strengthening of peace and understanding among peoples and to the spiritual enrichment of the human personality without distinction as to race, sex, language or religion,

417   Conscious that increased cultural and educational exchanges, broader dissemination of information, contacts between people, and the solution of humanitarian problems will contribute to the attainment of these aims,

418   Determined therefore to co-operate among themselves, irrespective of their political, economic and social systems, in order to create better conditions in the above fields, to develop and strengthen existing forms of co-operation and to work out new ways and means appropriate to these aims,

419   Convinced that this co-operation should take place in full respect for the principles guiding relations among participating States as set forth in the relevant document,

420   Have adopted the following:

421   1   Human Contacts

422   The participating States,

423   Considering the development of contacts to be an important element in the strengthening of friendly relations and trust among peoples,

424   Affirming, in relation to their present effort to improve conditions in this area, the importance they attach to humanitarian considerations,

425   Desiring in this spirit to develop, with the continuance of détente, further efforts to achieve continuing progress in this field

426   And conscious that the questions relevant hereto must be settled by the States concerned under mutually acceptable conditions,

427   Make it their aim to facilitate freer movement and contacts, individually and collectively, whether privately or officially, among persons, institutions and organizations of the participating States, and to contribute to the solution of the humanitarian problems that arise in that connexion,

428   Declare their readiness to these ends to take measures which they consider appropriate and to conclude agreements or arrangements among themselves, as may be needed, and

429   Express their intention now to proceed to the implementation of the following:

430   *(a) Contacts and Regular Meetings on the Basis of Family Ties*

431   In order to promote further development of contacts on the basis of family ties the participating States will favourably consider applications for travel with the purpose of allowing persons to enter or leave their territory temporarily, and on a regular basis if desired, in order to visit members of their families.

432   Applications for temporary visits to meet members of their families will be dealt with without distinction as to the country of origin or destination; existing requirements for travel documents and visas will be applied in this spirit. The preparation and issue of such documents and visas will be effected within reasonable time limits; cases of urgent necessity—such as serious illness or death—will be given priority treatment. They will take such steps as may be necessary to ensure that the fees for official travel documents and visas are acceptable.

433   They confirm that the presentation of an application concerning contacts on the basis of family ties will not modify the rights and obligations of the applicant or of members of his family.

434   *(b) Reunification of Families*

435   The participating States will deal in a positive and humanitarian spirit with the applications of persons who wish to be reunited with members of their family, with special attention being given to requests of an urgent character—such as requests submitted by persons who are ill or old.

436   They will deal with applications in this field as expeditiously as possible.

437   They will lower where necessary the fees charged in connexion with these applications to ensure that they are at a moderate level.

438   Applications for the purpose of family reunification which are not granted may be renewed at the appropriate level and will be reconsidered at reasonably short intervals by the authorities of the country of residence or destination, whichever is concerned; under such circumstances fees will be charged only when applications are granted.

439   Persons whose applications for family reunification are granted may bring with them or ship their household and personal effects; to this end the participating States will use all possibilities provided by existing regulations.

440   Until members of the same family are reunited meetings and contacts between them may take place in accordance with the modalities for contacts on the basis of family ties.

441   The participating States will support the efforts of Red Cross and Red Crescent Societies concerned with the problems of family reunification.

442   They confirm that the presentation of an application concerning family reunification will not modify the rights and obligations of the applicant or of members of his family.

443   The receiving participating State will take appropriate care with regard to employment for persons from other participating States who take up

permanent residence in that State in connexion with family reunification with its citizens and see that they are afforded opportunities equal to those enjoyed by its own citizens for education, medical assistance and social security.

444   *(c) Marriage between Citizens of Different States*

445   The participating States will examine favourably and on the basis of humanitarian considerations requests for exit or entry permits from persons who have decided to marry a citizen from another participating State.

446   The processing and issuing of the documents required for the above purposes and for the marriage will be in accordance with the provisions accepted for family reunification.

447   In dealing with requests from couples from different participating States, once married, to enable them and the minor children of their marriage to transfer their permanent residence to a State in which either one is normally a resident, the participating States will also apply the provisions accepted for family reunification.

448   *(d) Travel for Personal or Professional Reasons*

449   The participating States intend to facilitate wider travel by their citizens for personal or professional reasons and to this end they intend in particular:

450   —gradually to simplify and to administer flexibly the procedures for exit and entry;

451   —to ease regulations concerning movement of citizens from the other participating States in their territory, with due regard to security requirements.

452   They will endeavour gradually to lower, where necessary, the fees for visas and official travel documents.

453   They intend to consider, as necessary, means—including, in so far as appropriate, the conclusion of multilateral or bilateral consular conventions or other relevant agreements or understandings—for the improvement of arrangements to provide consular services, including legal and consular assistance.

.   .   .   .   .

454   They confirm that religious faiths, institutions and organizations, practising within the constitutional framework of the participating States, and their representatives can, in the field of their activities, have contacts and meetings among themselves and exchange information.

455   *(e) Improvement of Conditions for Tourism on an Individual or Collective Basis*

456   The participating States consider that tourism contributes to a fuller

knowledge of the life, culture and history of other countries, to the growth of understanding among peoples, to the improvement of contacts and to the broader use of leisure. They intend to promote the development of tourism, on an individual or collective basis, and, in particular, they intend:

457 — to promote visits to their respective countries by encouraging the provision of appropriate facilities and the simplification and expediting of necessary formalities relating to such visits;

458 — to increase, on the basis of appropriate agreements or arrangements where necessary, co-operation in the development of tourism, in particular by considering bilaterally possible ways to increase information relating to travel to other countries and to the reception and service of tourists, and other related questions of mutual interest.

459 *(f) Meetings among Young People*

460 The participating States intend to further the development of contacts and exchanges among young people by encouraging:

461 — increased exchanges and contacts on a short or long term basis among young people working, training or undergoing education through bilateral or multilateral agreements or regular programmes in all cases where it is possible;

462 — study by their youth organizations of the question of possible agreements relating to frameworks of multilateral youth co-operation;

463 — agreements or regular programmes relating to the organization of exchanges of students, of international youth seminars, of courses of professional training and foreign language study;

464 — the further development of youth tourism and the provision to this end of appropriate facilities;

465 — the development, where possible, of exchanges, contacts and co-operation on a bilateral or multilateral basis between their organizations which represent wide circles of young people working, training or undergoing education;

466 — awareness among youth of the importance of developing mutual understanding and of strengthening friendly relations and confidence among peoples.

467 *(g) Sport*

468 In order to expand existing links and co-operation in the field of sport the participating States will encourage contacts and exchanges of this kind, including sports meetings and competitions of all sorts, on the basis of the established international rules, regulations and practice.

469 *(h) Expansion of Contacts*

470 By way of further developing contacts among governmental institutions and non-governmental organizations and associations, including

women's organizations, the participating States will facilitate the convening of meetings as well as travel by delegations, groups and individuals.

471   **2   Information**
472   The participating States,
473   Conscious of the need for an ever wider knowledge and understanding of the various aspects of life in other participating States,
474   Acknowledging the contribution of this process to the growth of confidence between peoples,
475   Desiring, with the development of mutual understanding between the participating States and with the further improvement of their relations, to continue further efforts towards progress in this field,
476   Recognizing the importance of the dissemination of information from the other participating States and of a better acquaintance with such information,
477   Emphasizing therefore the essential and influential role of the press, radio, television, cinema and news agencies and of the journalists working in these fields,
478   Make it their aim to facilitate the freer and wider dissemination of information of all kinds, to encourage co-operation in the field of information and the exchange of information with other countries, and to improve the conditions under which journalists from one participating State exercise their profession in another participating State, and
479   Express their intention in particular:
480   *(a) Improvement of the Circulation of, Access to, and Exchange of Information*
481   *(i) Oral Information*
482   — To facilitate the dissemination of oral information through the encouragement of lectures and lecture tours by personalities and specialists from the other participating States, as well as exchanges of opinions at round table meetings, seminars, symposia, summer schools, congresses and other bilateral and multilateral meetings.
483   *(ii) Printed Information*
484   — To facilitate the improvement of the dissemination, on their territory, of newspapers and printed publications, periodical and non-periodical, from the other participating States. For this purpose:
485   they will encourage their competent firms and organizations to conclude agreements and contracts designed gradually to increase the quantities and the number of titles of newspapers and publications imported from the other participating States. These agreements and contracts should in particular mention the speediest conditions of delivery and the use of

the normal channels existing in each country for the distribution of its own publications and newspapers, as well as forms and means of payment agreed between the parties making it possible to achieve the objectives aimed at by these agreements and contracts;

486   where necessary, they will take appropriate measures to achieve the above objectives and to implement the provisions contained in the agreements and contracts.

487   — To contribute to the improvement of access by the public to periodical and non-periodical printed publications imported on the bases indicated above. In particular:

488   they will encourage an increase in the number of places where these publications are on sale;

489   they will facilitate the availability of these periodical publications during congresses, conferences, official visits and other international events and to tourists during the season;

490   they will develop the possibilities for taking out subscriptions according to the modalities particular to each country;

491   they will improve the opportunities for reading and borrowing these publications in large public libraries and their reading rooms as well as in university libraries.

492   They intend to improve the possibilities for acquaintance with bulletins of official information issued by diplomatic missions and distributed by those missions on the basis of arrangements acceptable to the interested parties.

493   *(iii) Filmed and Broadcast Information*

494   — To promote the improvement of the dissemination of filmed and broadcast information. To this end:

495   they will encourage the wider showing and broadcasting of a greater variety of recorded and filmed information from the other participating States, illustrating the various aspects of life in their countries and received on the basis of such agreements or arrangements as may be necessary between the organizations and firms directly concerned;

496   they will facilitate the import by competent organizations and firms of recorded audio-visual material from the other participating States.

497   The participating States note the expansion in the dissemination of information broadcast by radio, and express the hope for the continuation of this process, so as to meet the interest of mutual understanding among peoples and the aims set forth by this Conference.

498   *(b) Co-operation in the Field of Information*

499   — To encourage co-operation in the field of information on the basis of short or long term agreements or arrangements. In particular:

500   they will favour increased co-operation among mass media organiza-

tions, including press agencies, as well as among publishing houses and organizations;

501   they will favour co-operation among public or private, national or international radio and television organizations, in particular through the exchange of both live and recorded radio and television programmes, and through the joint production and the broadcasting and distribution of such programmes;

502   they will encourage meetings and contacts both between journalists' organizations and between journalists from the participating States;

503   they will view favourably the possibilities of arrangements between periodical publications as well as between newspapers from the participating States, for the purpose of exchanging and publishing articles;

504   they will encourage the exchange of technical information as well as the organization of joint research and meetings devoted to the exchange of experience and views between experts in the field of the press, radio and television.

505   *(c) Improvement of Working Conditions for Journalists*

506   The participating States, desiring to improve the conditions under which journalists from one participating State exercise their profession in another participating State, intend in particular to:

507   —examine in a favourable spirit and within a suitable and reasonable time scale requests from journalists for visas;

508   —grant to permanently accredited journalists of the participating States, on the basis of arrangements, multiple entry and exit visas for specified periods;

509   —facilitate the issue to accredited journalists of the participating States of permits for stay in their country of temporary residence and, if and when these are necessary, of other official papers which it is appropriate for them to have;

510   —ease, on a basis of reciprocity, procedures for arranging travel by journalists of the participating States in the country where they are exercising their profession, and to provide progressively greater opportunities for such travel, subject to the observance of regulations relating to the existence of areas closed for security reasons;

511   —ensure that requests by such journalists for such travel receive, in so far as possible, an expeditious response, taking into account the time scale of the request;

512   —increase the opportunities for journalists of the participating States to communicate personally with their sources, including organizations and official institutions;

513   —grant to journalists of the participating States the right to import, subject only to its being taken out again, the technical equipment

(photographic, cinematographic, tape recorder, radio and television) necessary for the exercise of their profession;*

514   —enable journalists of the other participating States, whether permanently or temporarily accredited, to transmit completely, normally and rapidly by means recognized by the participating States to the information organs which they represent, the results of their professional activity, including tape recordings and undeveloped film, for the purpose of publication or of broadcasting on the radio or television.

515   The participating States reaffirm that the legitimate pursuit of their professional activity will neither render journalists liable to expulsion nor otherwise penalize them. If an accredited journalist is expelled, he will be informed of the reasons for this act and may submit an application for re-examination of his case.

516   3   Co-operation and Exchanges in the Field of Culture
517   The participating States,
518   Considering that cultural exchanges and co-operation contribute to a better comprehension among people and among peoples, and thus promote a lasting understanding among States,
519   Confirming the conclusions already formulated in this field at the multilateral level, particularly at the Intergovernmental Conference on Cultural Policies in Europe, organized by UNESCO in Helsinki in June 1972, where interest was manifested in the active participation of the broadest possible social groups in an increasingly diversified cultural life,
520   Desiring, with the development of mutual confidence and the further improvement of relations between the participating States, to continue further efforts toward progress in this field,
521   Disposed in this spirit to increase substantially their cultural exchanges, with regard both to persons and to cultural works, and to develop among them an active co-operation, both at the bilateral and the multilateral level, in all the fields of culture,
522   Convinced that such a development of their mutual relations will contribute to the enrichment of the respective cultures, while respecting the originality of each, as well as to the reinforcement among them of a consciousness of common values, while continuing to develop cultural co-operation with other countries of the world,

---

* While recognizing that appropriate local personnel are employed by foreign journalists in many instances, the participating States note that the above provisions would be applied, subject to the observance of the appropriate rules, to persons from the other participating States, who are regularly and professionally engaged as technicians, photographers or cameramen of the press, radio, television or cinema.

523   Declare that they jointly set themselves the following objectives:

524   (a) to develop the mutual exchange of information with a view to a better knowledge of respective cultural achievements,

525   (b) to improve the facilities for the exchange and for the dissemination of cultural property,

526   (c) to promote access by all to respective cultural achievements,

527   (d) to develop contacts and co-operation among persons active in the field of culture,

528   (e) to seek new fields and forms of cultural co-operation,

529   Thus give expression to their common will to take progressive, coherent and long-term action in order to achieve the objectives of the present declaration; and

530   Express their intention now to proceed to the implementation of the following:

531   *Extension of Relations*

532   To expand and improve at the various levels co-operation and links in the field of culture, in particular by:

533   —concluding, where appropriate, agreements on a bilateral or multilateral basis, providing for the extension of relations among competent State institutions and non-governmental organizations in the field of culture, as well as among people engaged in cultural activities, taking into account the need both for flexibility and the fullest possible use of existing agreements, and bearing in mind that agreements and also other arrangements constitute important means of developing cultural co-operation and exchanges;

534   —contributing to the development of direct communication and co-operation among relevant State institutions and non-governmental organizations, including, where necessary, such communication and co-operation carried out on the basis of special agreements and arrangements;

535   —encouraging direct contacts and communications among persons engaged in cultural activities, including, where necessary, such contacts and communications carried out on the basis of special agreements and arrangements.

536   *Mutual Knowledge*

537   Within their competence to adopt, on a bilateral and multilateral level, appropriate measures which would give their peoples a more comprehensive and complete mutual knowledge of their achievements in the various fields of culture, and among them:

538   —to examine jointly, if necessary with the assistance of appropriate international organizations, the possible creation in Europe and the structure of a bank of cultural data, which would collect information from the participating countries and make it available to its correspon-

dents on their request, and to convene for this purpose a meeting of experts from interested States;

539   —to consider, if necessary in conjunction with appropriate international organizations, ways of compiling in Europe an inventory of documentary films of a cultural or scientific nature from the participating States;

540   —to encourage more frequent book exhibitions and to examine the possibility of organizing periodically in Europe a large-scale exhibition of books from the participating States;

541   —to promote the systematic exchange, between the institutions concerned and publishing houses, of catalogues of available books as well as of pre-publication material which will include, as far as possible, all forthcoming publications; and also to promote the exchange of material between firms publishing encyclopaedias, with a view to improving the presentation of each country;

542   —to examine jointly questions of expanding and improving exchanges of information in the various fields of culture, such as theatre, music, library work as well as the conservation and restoration of cultural property.

543   *Exchanges and Dissemination*

544   To contribute to the improvement of facilities for exchanges and the dissemination of cultural property, by appropriate means, in particular by:

545   —studying the possibilities for harmonizing and reducing the charges relating to international commercial exchanges of books and other cultural materials; and also for new means of insuring works of art in foreign exhibitions and for reducing the risks of damage or loss to which these works are exposed by their movement;

546   —facilitating the formalities of customs clearance, in good time for programmes of artistic events, of the works of art, materials and accessories appearing on lists agreed upon by the organizers of these events;

547   —encouraging meetings among representatives of competent organizations and relevant firms to examine measures within their field of activity—such as the simplification of orders, time limits for sending supplies and modalities of payment—which might facilitate international commercial exchanges of books;

548   —promoting the loan and exchange of films among their film institutes and film libraries;

549   —encouraging the exchange of information among interested parties concerning events of a cultural character foreseen in the participating States, in fields where this is most appropriate, such as music, theatre and the plastic and graphic arts, with a view to contributing to the compilation and publication of a calendar of such events, with the

assistance, where necessary, of the appropriate international organizations;

550   —encouraging a study of the impact which the foreseeable development, and a possible harmonization among interested parties, of the technical means used for the dissemination of culture might have on the development of cultural co-operation and exchanges, while keeping in view the preservation of the diversity and originality of their respective cultures;

551   —encouraging, in the way they deem appropriate, within their cultural policies, the further development of interest in the cultural heritage of the other participating States, conscious of the merits and the value of each culture;

552   —endeavouring to ensure the full and effective application of the international agreements and conventions on copyrights and on circulation of cultural property to which they are party or to which they may decide in the future to become party.

553   *Access*

554   To promote fuller mutual access by all to the achievements—works, experiences and performing arts—in the various fields of culture of their countries, and to that end to make the best possible efforts, in accordance with their competence, more particularly:

555   —to promote wider dissemination of books and artistic works, in particular by such means as:

556   facilitating, while taking full account of the international copyright conventions to which they are party, international contacts and communications between authors and publishing houses as well as other cultural institutions, with a view to a more complete mutual access to cultural achievements;

557   recommending that, in determining the size of editions, publishing houses take into account also the demand from the other participating States, and that rights of sale in other participating States be granted, where possible, to several sales organizations of the importing countries, by agreement between interested partners;

558   encouraging competent organizations and relevant firms to conclude agreements and contracts and contributing, by this means, to a gradual increase in the number and diversity of works by authors from the other participating States available in the original and in translation in their libraries and bookshops;

559   promoting, where deemed appropriate, an increase in the number of sales outlets where books by authors from the other participating States, imported in the original on the basis of agreements and contracts, and in translation, are for sale;

560   promoting, on a wider scale, the translation of works in the sphere of

literature and other fields of cultural activity, produced in the languages of the other participating States, especially from the less widely-spoken languages, and the publication and dissemination of the translated works by such measures as:

561 encouraging more regular contacts between interested publishing houses;

562 developing their efforts in the basic and advanced training of translators;

563 encouraging, by appropriate means, the publishing houses of their countries to publish translations;

564 facilitating the exchange between publishers and interested institutions of lists of books which might be translated;

565 promoting between their countries the professional activity and co-operation of translators;

566 carrying out joint studies on ways of further promoting translations and their dissemination;

567 improving and expanding exchanges of books, bibliographies and catalogue cards between libraries;

568 — to envisage other appropriate measures which would permit, where necessary by mutual agreement among interested parties, the facilitation of access to their respective cultural achievements, in particular in the field of books;

569 — to contribute by appropriate means to the wider use of the mass media in order to improve mutual acquaintance with the cultural life of each;

570 — to seek to develop the necessary conditions for migrant workers and their families to preserve their links with their national culture, and also to adapt themselves to their new cultural environment;

571 — to encourage the competent bodies and enterprises to make a wider choice and effect wider distribution of full-length and documentary films from the other participating States, and to promote more frequent non-commercial showings, such as premières, film weeks and festivals, giving due consideration to films from countries whose cinematographic works are less well known;

572 — to promote, by appropriate means, the extension of opportunities for specialists from the other participating States to work with materials of a cultural character from film and audio-visual archives, within the framework of the existing rules for work on such archival materials;

573 — to encourage a joint study by interested bodies, where appropriate with the assistance of the competent international organizations, of the expediency and the conditions for the establishment of a repertory of their recorded television programmes of a cultural nature, as well as of the means of viewing them rapidly in order to facilitate their selection and possible acquisition.

574   *Contacts and Co-operation*

575   To contribute, by appropriate means, to the development of contacts and co-operation in the various fields of culture, especially among creative artists and people engaged in cultural activities, in particular by making efforts to:

576   — promote for persons active in the field of culture, travel and meetings including, where necessary, those carried out on the basis of agreements, contracts or other special arrangements and which are relevant to their cultural co-operation;

577   — encourage in this way contacts among creative and performing artists and artistic groups with a view to their working together, making known their works in other participating States or exchanging views on topics relevant to their common activity;

578   — encourage, where necessary through appropriate arrangements, exchanges of trainees and specialists and the granting of scholarships for basic and advanced training in various fields of culture such as the arts and architecture, museums and libraries, literary studies and translation, and contribute to the creation of favourable conditions of reception in their respective institutions;

579   — encourage the exchange of experience in the training of organizers of cultural activities as well as of teachers and specialists in fields such as theatre, opera, ballet, music and fine arts;

580   — continue to encourage the organization of international meetings among creative artists, especially young creative artists, on current questions of artistic and literary creation which are of interest for joint study;

581   — study other possibilities for developing exchanges and co-operation among persons active in the field of culture, with a view to a better mutual knowledge of the cultural life of the participating States.

582   *Fields and Forms of Co-operation*

583   To encourage the search for new fields and forms of cultural co-operation, to these ends contributing to the conclusion among interested parties, where necessary, of appropriate agreements and arrangements, and in this context to promote:

584   — joint studies regarding cultural policies, in particular in their social aspects, and as they relate to planning, town-planning, educational and environmental policies, and the cultural aspects of tourism;

585   — the exchange of knowledge in the realm of cultural diversity, with a view to contributing thus to a better understanding by interested parties of such diversity where it occurs;

586   — the exchange of information, and as may be appropriate, meetings of experts, the elaboration and the execution of research programmes and projects, as well as their joint evaluation, and the dissemination of the results, on the subjects indicated above;

587   —such forms of cultural co-operation and the development of such joint projects as:

588   international events in the fields of the plastic and graphic arts, cinema, theatre, ballet, music, folklore, etc.; book fairs and exhibitions, joint performances of operatic and dramatic works, as well as performances given by soloists, instrumental ensembles, orchestras, choirs and other artistic groups, including those composed of amateurs, paying due attention to the organization of international cultural youth events and the exchange of young artists;

589   the inclusion of works by writers and composers from the other participating States in the repertoires of soloists and artistic ensembles;

590   the preparation, translation and publication of articles, studies and monographs, as well as of low-cost books and of artistic and literary collections, suited to making better known respective cultural achievements, envisaging for this purpose meetings among experts and representatives of publishing houses;

591   the co-production and the exchange of films and of radio and television programmes, by promoting, in particular, meetings among producers, technicians and representatives of the public authorities with a view to working out favourable conditions for the execution of specific joint projects and by encouraging, in the field of co-production, the establishment of international filming teams;

592   the organization of competitions for architects and town-planners, bearing in mind the possible implementation of the best projects and the formation, where possible, of international teams;

593   the implementation of joint projects for conserving, restoring and showing to advantage works of art, historical and archaeological monuments and sites of cultural interest, with the help, in appropriate cases, of international organizations of a governmental or non-governmental character as well as of private institutions—competent and active in these fields—envisaging for this purpose:

594   periodic meetings of experts of the interested parties to elaborate the necessary proposals, while bearing in mind the need to consider these questions in a wider social and economic context;

595   the publication in appropriate periodicals of articles designed to make known and to compare, among the participating States, the most significant achievements and innovations;

596   a joint study with a view to the improvement and possible harmonization of the different systems used to inventory and catalogue the historical monuments and places of cultural interest in their countries;

597   the study of the possibilities for organizing international courses for the training of specialists in different disciplines relating to restoration.

598   *National minorities or regional cultures*   The participating States, recognizing the contribution that national minorities or regional cultures can make to co-operation among them in various fields of culture, intend, when such minorities or cultures exist within their territory, to facilitate this contribution, taking into account the legitimate interests of their members.

599   **4   Co-operation and Exchanges in the Field of Education**
600   The participating States,
601   Conscious that the development of relations of an international character in the fields of education and science contributes to a better mutual understanding and is to the advantage of all peoples as well as to the benefit of future generations,
602   Prepared to facilitate, between organizations, institutions and persons engaged in education and science, the further development of exchanges of knowledge and experience as well as of contacts, on the basis of special arrangements where these are necessary,
603   Desiring to strengthen the links among educational and scientific establishments and also to encourage their co-operation in sectors of common interest, particularly where the levels of knowledge and resources require efforts to be concerted internationally, and
604   Convinced that progress in these fields should be accompanied and supported by a wider knowledge of foreign languages,
605   Express to these ends their intention in particular:
606   *(a) Extension of Relations*
607   To expand and improve at the various levels co-operation and links in the fields of education and science, in particular by:
608   —concluding, where appropriate, bilateral or multilateral agreements providing for co-operation and exchanges among State institutions, non-governmental bodies and persons engaged in activities in education and science, bearing in mind the need both for flexibility and the fuller use of existing agreements and arrangements;
609   —promoting the conclusion of direct arrangements between universities and other institutions of higher education and research, in the framework of agreements between governments where appropriate;
610   —encouraging among persons engaged in education and science direct contacts and communications, including those based on special agreements or arrangements where these are appropriate.
611   *(b) Access and Exchanges*
612   To improve access, under mutually acceptable conditions, for students, teachers and scholars of the participating States to each other's educa-

tional, cultural and scientific institutions, and to intensify exchanges among these institutions in all areas of common interest, in particular by:

613   —increasing the exchange of information on facilities for study and courses open to foreign participants, as well as on the conditions under which they will be admitted and received;

614   —facilitating travel between the participating States by scholars, teachers and students for purposes of study, teaching and research as well as for improving knowledge of each other's educational, cultural and scientific achievements;

615   —encouraging the award of scholarships for study, teaching and research in their countries to scholars, teachers and students of other participating States;

616   —establishing, developing or encouraging programmes providing for the broader exchange of scholars, teachers and students, including the organization of symposia, seminars and collaborative projects, and the exchanges of educational and scholarly information such as university publications and materials from libraries;

617   —promoting the efficient implementation of such arrangements and programmes by providing scholars, teachers and students in good time with more detailed information about their placing in universities and institutes and the programmes envisaged for them; by granting them the opportunity to use relevant scholarly, scientific and open archival materials; and by facilitating their travel within the receiving State for the purpose of study or research as well as in the form of vacation tours on the basis of the usual procedures;

618   —promoting a more exact assessment of the problems of comparison and equivalence of academic degrees and diplomas by fostering the exchange of information on the organization, duration and content of studies, the comparison of methods of assessing levels of knowledge and academic qualifications, and, where feasible, arriving at the mutual recognition of academic degrees and diplomas either through governmental agreements, where necessary, or direct arrangements between universities and other institutions of higher learning and research;

619   —recommending, moreover, to the appropriate international organizations that they should intensify their efforts to reach a generally acceptable solution to the problems of comparison and equivalence between academic degrees and diplomas.

620   (c) Science

621   Within their competence to broaden and improve co-operation and exchanges in the field of science, in particular:

622   To increase, on a bilateral or multilateral basis, the exchange and

dissemination of scientific information and documentation by such means as:

623   —making this information more widely available to scientists and research workers of the other participating States through, for instance, participation in international information-sharing programmes or through other appropriate arrangements;

624   —broadening and facilitating the exchange of samples and other scientific materials used particularly for fundamental research in the fields of natural sciences and medicine;

625   —inviting scientific institutions and universities to keep each other more fully and regularly informed about their current and contemplated research work in fields of common interest.

626   To facilitate the extension of communications and direct contacts between universities, scientific institutions and associations as well as among scientists and research workers, including those based where necessary on special agreements or arrangements, by such means as:

627   —further developing exchanges of scientists and research workers and encouraging the organization of preparatory meetings or working groups on research topics of common interest;

628   —encouraging the creation of joint teams of scientists to pursue research projects under arrangements made by the scientific institutions of several countries;

629   —assisting the organization and successful functioning of international conferences and seminars and participation in them by their scientists and research workers;

630   —furthermore envisaging, in the near future, a "Scientific Forum" in the form of a meeting of leading personalities in science from the participating States to discuss interrelated problems of common interest concerning current and future developments in science, and to promote the expansion of contacts, communications and the exchange of information between scientific institutions and among scientists;

631   —foreseeing, at an early date, a meeting of experts representing the participating States and their national scientific institutions, in order to prepare such a "Scientific Forum" in consultation with appropriate international organizations, such as UNESCO and the ECE;

632   —considering in due course what further steps might be taken with respect to the "Scientific Forum."

633   To develop in the field of scientific research, on a bilateral or multilateral basis, the co-ordination of programmes carried out in the participating States and the organization of joint programmes, especially in the areas mentioned below, which may involve the combined efforts of scientists and in certain cases the use of costly or unique equipment. The list of subjects in these areas is illustrative; and specific projects would have to

be determined subsequently by the potential partners in the participating States, taking account of the contribution which could be made by appropriate international organizations and scientific institutions:

634   — exact and natural sciences, in particular fundamental research in such fields as mathematics, physics, theoretical physics, geophysics, chemistry, biology, ecology and astronomy;

635   — medicine, in particular basic research into cancer and cardiovascular diseases, studies on the diseases endemic in the developing countries, as well as medico-social research with special emphasis on occupational diseases, the rehabilitation of the handicapped and the care of mothers, children and the elderly;

636   — the humanities and social sciences, such as history, geography, philosophy, psychology, pedagogical research, linguistics, sociology, the legal, political and economic sciences; comparative studies on social, socio-economic and cultural phenomena which are of common interest to the participating States, especially the problems of human environment and urban development; and scientific studies on the methods of conserving and restoring monuments and works of art.

637   (d) Foreign Languages and Civilizations

638   To encourage the study of foreign languages and civilizations as an important means of expanding communication among peoples for their better acquaintance with the culture of each country, as well as for the strengthening of international co-operation; to this end to stimulate, within their competence, the further development and improvement of foreign language teaching and the diversification of choice of languages taught at various levels, paying due attention to less widely-spread or studied languages, and in particular:

639   — to intensify co-operation aimed at improving the teaching of foreign languages through exchanges of information and experience concerning the development and application of effective modern teaching methods and technical aids, adapted to the needs of different categories of students, including methods of accelerated teaching; and to consider the possibility of conducting, on a bilateral or multilateral basis, studies of new methods of foreign language teaching;

640   — to encourage co-operation between institutions concerned, on a bilateral or multilateral basis, aimed at exploiting more fully the resources of modern educational technology in language teaching, for example through comparative studies by their specialists and, where agreed, through exchanges or transfers of audio-visual materials, of materials used for preparing textbooks, as well as of information about new types of technical equipment used for teaching languages;

641   — to promote the exchange of information on the experience acquired in the training of language teachers and to intensify exchanges on a

bilateral basis of language teachers and students as well as to facilitate their participation in summer courses in languages and civilizations, wherever these are organized;

642   —to encourage co-operation among experts in the field of lexicography with the aim of defining the necessary terminological equivalents, particularly in the scientific and technical disciplines, in order to facilitate relations among scientific institutions and specialists;

643   —to promote the wider spread of foreign language study among the different types of secondary education establishments and greater possibilities of choice between an increased number of European languages; and in this context to consider, wherever appropriate, the possibilities for developing the recruitment and training of teachers as well as the organization of the student groups required;

644   —to favour, in higher education, a wider choice in the languages offered to language students and greater opportunities for other students to study various foreign languages; also to facilitate, where desirable, the organization of courses in languages and civilizations, on the basis of special arrangements as necesary, to be given by foreign lecturers, particularly from European countries having less widely-spread or studied languages;

645   —to promote, within the framework of adult education, the further development of specialized programmes, adapted to various needs and interests, for teaching foreign languages to their own inhabitants and the languages of host countries to interested adults from other countries; in this context to encourage interested institutions to co-operate, for example, in the elaboration of programmes for teaching by radio and television and by accelerated methods, and also, where desirable, in the definition of study objectives for such programmes, with a view to arriving at comparable levels of language proficiency;

646   —to encourage the association, where appropriate, of the teaching of foreign languages with the study of the corresponding civilizations and also to make further efforts to stimulate interest in the study of foreign languages, including relevant out-of-class activities.

647   (e) Teaching Methods

648   —To promote the exchange of experience, on a bilateral or multilateral basis, in teaching methods at all levels of education, including those used in permanent and adult education, as well as the exchange of teaching materials, in particular by:

649   —further developing various forms of contacts and co-operation in the different fields of pedagogical science, for example through comparative or joint studies carried out by interested institutions or through exchanges of information on the results of teaching experiments;

650   —intensifying exchanges of information on teaching methods used in various educational systems and on results of research into the processes by which pupils and students acquire knowledge, taking account of relevant experience in different types of specialized education;

651   —facilitating exchanges of experience concerning the organization and functioning of education intended for adults and recurrent education, the relationships between these and other forms and levels of education, as well as concerning the means of adapting education, including vocational and technical training, to the needs of economic and social development in their countries;

652   —encouraging exchanges of experience in the education of youth and adults in international understanding, with particular reference to those major problems of mankind whose solution calls for a common approach and wider international co-operation;

653   —encouraging exchanges of teaching materials—including school textbooks, having in mind the possibility of promoting mutual knowledge and facilitating the presentation of each country in such books—as well as exchanges of information on technical innovations in the field of education.

654   *National minorities or regional cultures*   The participating States, recognizing the contribution that national minorities or regional cultures can make to co-operation among them in various fields of education, intend, when such minorities or cultures exist within their territory, to facilitate this contribution, taking into account the legitimate interests of their members.

655   **Follow-up to the Conference**
656   The participating States,
657   Having considered and evaluated the progress made at the Conference on Security and Co-operation in Europe,
658   Considering further that, within the broader context of the world, the Conference is an important part of the process of improving security and developing co-operation in Europe and that its results will contribute significantly to this process,
659   Intending to implement the provisions of the Final Act of the Conference in order to give full effect to its results and thus to further the process of improving security and developing co-operation in Europe,
660   Convinced that, in order to achieve the aims sought by the Conference, they should make further unilateral, bilateral and multilateral efforts and continue, in the appropriate forms set forth below, the multilateral process initiated by the Conference,

661   1 Declare their resolve, in the period following the Conference, to pay due regard to and implement the provisions of the Final Act of the Conference:

662   (a) unilaterally, in all cases which lend themselves to such action;

663   (b) bilaterally, by negotiations with other participating States;

664   (c) multilaterally, by meetings of experts of the participating States, and also within the framework of existing international organizations, such as the United Nations Economic Commission for Europe and UNESCO, with regard to educational, scientific and cultural co-operation;

665   2 Declare furthermore their resolve to continue the multilateral process initiated by the Conference:

666   (a) by proceeding to a thorough exchange of views both on the implementation of the provisions of the Final Act and of the tasks defined by the Conference, as well as, in the context of the questions dealt with by the latter, on the deepening of their mutual relations, the improvement of security and the development of co-operation in Europe, and the development of the process of détente in the future;

667   (b) by organizing to these ends meetings among their representatives, beginning with a meeting at the level of representatives appointed by the Ministers of Foreign Affairs. This meeting will define the appropriate modalities for the holding of other meetings which could include further similar meetings and the possibility of a new Conference;

668   3 The first of the meetings indicated above will be held at Belgrade in 1977. A preparatory meeting to organize this meeting will be held at Belgrade on 15 June 1977. The preparatory meeting will decide on the date, duration, agenda and other modalities of the meeting of representatives appointed by the Ministers of Foreign Affairs;

669   4 The rules of procedure, the working methods and the scale of distribution for the expenses of the Conference will, *mutatis mutandis*, be applied to the meetings envisaged in paragraphs 1 (c), 2 and 3 above. All the above-mentioned meetings will be held in the participating States in rotation. The services of a technical secretariat will be provided by the host country.

670   The original of this Final Act, drawn up in English, French, German, Italian, Russian and Spanish, will be transmitted to the Government of the Republic of Finland, which will retain it in its archives. Each of the participating States will receive from the Government of the Republic of Finland a true copy of this Final Act.

671   The text of this Final Act will be published in each participating State, which will disseminate it and make it known as widely as possible.

672   The Government of the Republic of Finland is requested to transmit to the Secretary-General of the United Nations the text of this Final Act, which is not eligible for registration under Article 102 of the Charter of

the United Nations, with a view to its circulation to all the members of the Organization as an official document of the United Nations.

673   The Government of the Republic of Finland is also requested to transmit the text of this Final Act to the Director-General of UNESCO and to the Executive Secretary of the United Nations Economic Commission for Europe.

674   Wherefore, the undersigned High Representatives of the participating States, mindful of the high political significance which they attach to the results of the Conference, and declaring their determination to act in accordance with the provisions contained in the above texts, have subscribed their signatures below:

Text of letter from Government of Finland to the Secretary General of the United Nations, as recorded in Journal no. 80/bis for July 18, 1975, of the Coordinating Committee of the Conference on Security and Cooperation in Europe:

Sir, I have the honour to inform you that the High Representatives of the States participating in the Conference on Security and Co-operation in Europe have requested the Government of the Republic of Finland to transmit to you the text of the Final Act of the Conference signed at Helsinki on (1 August 1975).

I have also been asked to request you, Mr. Secretary General, to arrange for the circulation of this Final Act to Member States of the Organization as an official document of the United Nations, and to draw your attention to the fact that this Final Act is not eligible, in whole or in part, for registration with the Secretariat under Article 102 of the Charter of the United Nations, as would be the case were it a matter of a treaty or international agreement, under the aforesaid Article.

Accept, Sir, the assurance of my highest consideration.

Index

The Author

John J. Maresca is a career Foreign Service officer currently serving as Deputy Assistant Secretary of Defense for European and NATO Policy. Previously, he was deputy chief of mission at the U.S. embassy in Paris and director of the Office of Western European Affairs in the Department of State, and he has been a specialist in European affairs throughout his career. In 1970–73 he was the deputy director of the Office of the Secretary General of NATO under the late Manlio Brosio and Joseph Luns. During that period the alliance was preparing for the forthcoming European security conference by setting its conditions for participation and by internal coordination of negotiating positions. In the spring of 1973, Maresca joined the U.S. delegation to the Conference on Security and Cooperation in Europe (CSCE) in Helsinki, becoming the executive secretary and later deputy chief of the delegation. Following the Helsinki Summit in 1975, Maresca returned to the State Department to take charge of the office responsible for the CSCE (the Office of NATO Political Affairs), where he coordinated U.S. monitoring of the implementation of the Helsinki Final Act and preparations for the 1977 review meeting in Belgrade. He was also deputy chief of the U.S. delegation to the preparatory meeting in Belgrade, June–August 1977. Mr. Maresca is generally acknowledged to be the American most closely associated with the 1973–75 CSCE negotiations and their immediate aftermath.